JOURNEY OF THE UPANISADS TO THE WEST

Dr. PURNA CHANDRA MUKHOPADHYAY
M. A. (Double), Ph. D.

FIRMA KLM PRIVATE LIMITED
CALCUTTA * * 1987

Published by:
Firma KLM Private Limited
257B, B. B. Ganguly Street,
Calcutta-700 012
INDIA

First published : Calcutta, 1987

Price : 175·00

Printed by:
S. N. Jana
Marmabani Press
17/A, Yogipara Bye Lane,
Calcutta-700 006

Dedicated

to the memory of

Late Hiranmay Bandyopadhyay

whose immaculate and

illuminating philosophy of life,

let alone his erudition, has

inspired me not a little.

FOREWORD

Pusparag
1, Ballygunge Terrace,
Calcutta—19.
13. 11. 82

I have seen the manuscript of the book entitled "Journey of the Upaniṣads to the West" written by Dr. Purna Chandra Mukhopadhyay. In fact I had the occasion to go through it thoroughly as an examiner to evaluate it as a thesis submitted for the doctoral degree.

I am pleasantly surprised to find that the book has attained a level of excellence seldom met with by me in my long experience as an examiner of doctoral theses. The subject matter of the book is not only interesting, but difficult as well. In my opinion Dr. Mukhopadhyay has approached the subject with an open mind and adopted a logical treatment. Consequently he has been able to produce a compact book characterized by original thinking. I believe it will command a good sale when published, as it is likely to attract the attention of both academics and lay readers.

Hiranmay Bandyopadhyay
I. C. S. (Retd.) D. Litt.

PREFACE

My original dissertation entitled "Impact of the Upaniṣads on the nineteenth century western thought" appears with a modified caption. The book seeks to present the nature and extent of impact of the ancient Upaniṣads on some literary and philosophical systems of the west. In my introduction to the dissertation that follows I have outlined the pantheistic conception which constitutes the principal current of thought of the Upaniṣads and have referred to the eminent figures of the western world whose systems were directly or indirectly influenced by this unique conception.

Admittedly this impact of the Upaniṣads has been a continuous process and there is no gainsaying that the pristine Indian philosophical speculations as recorded in the Vedas and the Upaniṣads continue to captivate the thinkers and scholars even today. I have, however, endeavoured to pinpoint the traces of the pantheistic world-view of the Upaniṣads in the western systems covering a definite period for reasons mentioned in my survey. With all the dossiers available I have attempted to substantiate my view in an unbiased manner.

I convey my sincerest gratitude to the renowned scholar Dr. Govindagopal Mukhopadhyay, Professor and Head of the department of Sanskrit, Burdwan University for having extended his wise guidance in spite of all his academic preoccupations. There is no denying the fact that but for his kind assistance I could not have continued my research work on this subject. I must also express my deep sense of gratitude and indebtedness to the illustrious academic Late Hiranmay Bandyopadhyay for his inspiring guidance and active assistance. In fact it was he who for the first time ingrafted in me the desire to undertake a research work on this subject. It is a misfortune for me that he could not see the book in print which he so earnestly desired He had, however, favoured me by contributing a valuable 'foreword' before he passed away. I am also beholden to the authorities of Ramkrishna Mission Institute of Culture, Golpark for having assisted me in my work. I am particularly grateful to Swami Lokeswarananda, Secretary of the R. K. M. Institute for he took keen interest in my subject and invited me to deliver a series of lectures on it in his Institute in 1982. My obligations are also due to the authorities of Calcutta University for their commitment to grant a subsidy towards the cost of publication of this book.

Finally I must make no bones in recording my indebtedness to Firma KLM Private Ltd. for having undertaken the task of publication of this work. I remember with gratitude the benign deportment of Late K. L. Mukhopadhyay who kindly agreed to share the financial burden in publishing this work. My respectful compliments are due also to his able son Shree R. N. Mukhopadhyay who, in deference to his father's commitment, has whole-heartedly extended considerable financial assistance to facilitate publication of this volume. I offer my heart-felt thanks to Shri Surendranath Jana of Marmavani Press, Calcutta for the sterling service he has rendered in printing this book with meticulous care.

This treatise, I believe, will satisfy the curiosity of the students and teachers of literature and philosophy, also the western scholars interested in Indology. If they really find any interest in it I shall deem my labour adequately rewarded.

139/C/3, Ananda Palit Road,
Calcutta-14.
January, 1987.

P. C. Mukhopadhyay

CONTENTS

GENERAL INTRODUCTION

The Upaniṣadic concept of Brahman had left an immense impact on some metaphysical theories of the western scholars in the nineteenth century. Originally written in Sanskrit, the Upaniṣads with their profound philosophical thought remained inaccessible to the western thinkers for long. It was only when these immortal treatises had been translated into Latin by Anquetil Du Perron on the basis of Dara Shiko's Persian rendering of the same, that a tremendous sensation was created in the western world and a genuine urge was felt among the western thinkers to have a taste of the Upaniṣadic teaching.

In the ancient Upaniṣads which constitute the terminal part of the Vedic literature the question of ultimate Reality was enquired into with all earnestness and logical acumen. The knowledge of this Reality which the ancient sages attained after deep and prolonged contemplation has been recorded in the Upaniṣads. This is known as Brahmavidyā or Parāvidyā in which lies the quintessence of Indian philosophical thinking. Brahmavidyā does not, however, indicate mere intellectual grasp of the Supreme Reality. It is not simply 'knowing', but also 'being' Brahman. In other words, a living and concrete experience of Brahman is sought everywhere. The Upaniṣads abound in passages that corroborate this view. Shri Aurobinda has noted this point when he says : "Knowledge does not end with knowing, nor is it pursued and found for the sake of knowing alone. It has its full value only when it leads to some greater gain than itself, some gain of being. Simply to know the eternal and to remain in the pain, struggle and inferiority of our present way of being, would be a poor and lame advantage. ...... To be is the first verb which contains all the others ; knowledge, action, 'creation', enjoyment are only a fulfilment of being." Albert Schweitzer an eminent German thinker of the 20th century (born in 1875) subscribes to this view. In analysing the teachings of the Upaniṣads he says in his 'Indian Thought and its Development' – "Man does not attain to union with the Brahman by means of any achievement of his natural power of gaining knowledge, but solely by quitting the world of the senses in a state of ecstasy and thus learning the reality of Pure Being. The Brāhmanic doctrine is concerned with a truth that must not merely be known, but also experienced.

The whole edifice of Brahmavidyā rests on the two forms of the concept of Brahman Para and Apara, Unmanifest and Manifest. We have tried to analyse these two forms finally to show that they are but the two aspects of the same Brahman who is both immanent and transcendent. In fact immanence and transcendence are not in the Upaniṣads, as in many western theories, opposed and contradictory to each other. We have explained this point in Section 1. of this work.

The doctrine of pantheism—the basic teaching of the Upaniṣads clearly explains the unique conception of Brahman as one that encompasses the whole of existence. It is this concept of 'All—comprehensive Absolute' that was taken up in right earnest by Schelling and Schopenhauer in the nineteenth century western philosophy. In his analysis of the concept of 'World Soul' Schelling is found to have been deeply influenced by the Upaniṣadic concept of Brahman. Schopenhauer also develops the same idea in his famous work 'The World As Will And Idea'. After he had gone through Du Perron's Latin translation he observed : "In the whole world there is no study except that of the originals, so beneficial and so elevating as that of the 'Oupnekhat'. It has been the solace of my life, it will be the solace in my death". Although Schopenhauer is known as the father of western pessimism his system seems to have been powerfully impregnated with Upaniṣadic pantheism. How Schelling and Schopenhauer came to be acquainted with the Upaniṣadic teaching and how their philosophical systems were directly influenced by the pantheistic doctrine of the Upaniṣads have all been dealt with in Section 2. We have also touched upon the theosophy of Madame Blavatsky here to explore how far she is indebted to the Upaniṣads in her approach to the problem of Supreme Reality.

Glimpses of Upaniṣadic pantheism are also traceable in some works of the British and American poets of the nineteenth century. William Wordsworth, P. B. Shelley, Waldo Emerson and Walt Whitman are the principal figures which come within the purview of our discussion, In Section 3. we have tried to make a searching analysis of their works only to see how far they are imbued with the Upaniṣadic spirit and with how much success they reflect the pantheistic world-view. A brief survey of some contemporaneous French poets has also been included in our discussion with a view to examining their nature of acquaintance with and reverence for the Upaniṣadic teaching.

SECTION I

THE VEDAS AND THE UPANIṢADS

CHAPTER—I

THE VEDAS

The Vedas are looked upon as the earliest religious treatises of the Indo-Aryans and the fountain of India's culture and philosophical thinking. The spiritual attainments of the ancient sages are recorded here and the vedic knowledge has been transmitted since hoary antiquity by the preceptors to their disciples for generations. Because of this oral transmission the Vedas are otherwise known as Śruti, and it was after a long stretch of time that this knowledge was recorded in writing. The Vedas etymologically mean 'Knowledge' (the root 'vid' means 'to know') and this knowledge implies not only the knowledge of ordinary objects, but that of the ultimate reality as well, knowing which everything is known. In other words, the knowledge of the Vedas is two-fold viz., parāvidyā and aparāvidyā The knowledge of Brahman or parāvidyā is more logically and systematically developed in the Upaniṣads. The pantheistic doctrine which constitutes the kernel of the Upaniṣadic teaching owes its origin to the Vedas, Hence an analysis of the Vedas becomes indispensable for a proper understanding as to how in their attempt at unravelling the mystery of the world the ancient seers of the Vedic age resorted to the worship of many gods and how this polytheistic tendency was gradually converted into a monistic one in the Upaniṣads.

Four stages of Indian philosophical thought.

Arranged chronologically, four stages of philosophical thinking are discernible in India. The oldest type is represented by the hymns belonging to the 'Karmakāṇḍa' of the Vedas. At this stage the natural objects are deified and are invoked or worshipped in differnt sacrificial rites. The attitude of man towards gods and goddesses is strictly determined by the practical needs. The people try to propitiate the deities with a view to fulfilling their needs or desires. Śometimes they seek divine grace because of a sense of insecurity and helplessness at the natural perils or onslaughts perpetrated by the adversaries. Towards the end of the Vedas a leaning to knowledge is traceable, for even in the Ṛgveda the philosophical questions are raised. Thus an inquisitive spirit to know the ultimate reality finally leads to the emergence of the second stage i e., one of the Upaniṣads. The sages at this stage transgress the practical needs of worldly life and feel a strong intellectual urge to know the Supreme Spirit or Brahman which not only explains, but encompasses the whole of existence as well. The philosophy of this stage may, therefore, be called pantheistic. The third stage of thought virtually reflects the same intellectual urge although in a slightly different pattern. Six orthodox and two heterodox systems (the Jaina and the Buddhists) emerge at this stage. The doctrine of karma and rebirth seems to be an established theory to the protagonists of these schools. Here the thinkers are found to hold a firm belief that this world is full of evils and sufferings and the attainment of liberation is keenly felt to be the highest goal of life. The Buddhists and the Jainas in spite of being atheistic elucidate with particular reference to their doctrine of Karma, the ways and means for the attainment of liberation and avoidance of rebirth. Thus even the champions of these two heterodox together with those of six orthodox systems appear to be alive to the practical need in the sense that they want man to get rid of bondage and attain salvation. But the means adopted or prescribed here is chiefly knowledge. Finally at the fourth stage we come across the

Purāṇas where the standpoint of an intellectual seer is replaced by that of a devotee who approaches God with all sincerity and devotion of his heart. In the age of the six orthodox systems references to God are there, but the concept of a personal God has not been established there. The Nyāyasūtra of Gautama, for example, is chiefly preoccupied with the proofs of the existence of God. The Sāṁkhya does not acknowledge the existence of God. In the Yoga God is accepted as one of the realities. In the Pūrvamīmāṁsā the vedic Gods are given recognition. But in all these systems the personalistic conception of God is conspicuous by its absence and the theistic fervour of a devotee is not found here. It is in the age of the Purāṇas that theism blossoms with all its glory and grandeur, and a deep and spontaneous devotion to one personal God takes the place of intellectual approach to Him of the previous age.

Parāvidyā and Aparāvidyā.

Let us now direct our attention to the Vedas. The Vedic knowledge, as we have already indicated, is two-fold viz., Parāvidyā and Aparāvidyā. The Muṇḍaka Upaniṣad explains it clearly when it says that the enlightened seers prescribe the attainment of two-fold knowledge viz., parā and aparā. Aparāvidyā includes the Ṛgveda, the Yajurveda, the Sāmveda, the Atharvaveda, Śikṣā, Kalpa, Vyākaraṇa, Nirukta, Chanda and Jyotiṣ, while Parāvidyā is that by which Brahman is known.[1] The entire content of the Vedic literature is explained in this observation. It is expressly stated here that on the one side we should be acquainted with Brahmavidyā i.e., the knowledge of Brahman, the eternal and indestructible Being and this knowledge is

1. Vide :—Muṇḍaka Up :—1 1. 4. & 1. 1. 5.

recorded in the Upaniṣads. On the other side we should have knowledge of the four Vedas together with six other branches of study known as Vedāṅga. The study of Vedāṅga is helpful for the proper understanding of the Vedas. Thus Aparāvidyā by virtue of its practical utility makes one sufficiently strong and worthy of receiving Parāvidyā. No enlightened seer or Brahmavid cries down or belittles the need for food (Anna) and other daily necessities. A man with debility of mind and an emaciated physique can not turn out to be worthy of receiving the knowlede of Brahman.[2] It appears, therefore, that the Indian thinkers of the Vedic age give ample evidence of their profundity of thought. There is hardly any doubt that they have raised by far the most searching questions about life. When precisely these questions were raised and problems discussed—is a mater on which the scholars and critics widely differ. As far as we know, the oldest known religious literature is the series of hymns of the Ṛgveda written probably between 1500 & 1200B.C.[3] Maharshi Krishna Dwaipayan makes a

2. 'One who is without food (anna) is also deficient in intellect (Prajñā) and consequently has no strength, and thus can not have access to the knowledge of self. Knowledge of self paves the way for Parāvidyā.'
Vide :—Paritosh Thakur : 'SāmVeda Saṁhitā'—Introduction.

3. MaxMüller holds that the Vedas appear to have been written in 1200 B. C. According to Dr. Suniti Kumar Chatterjee the period is betwoen 1000 and 900 B.C. According to Haug it is 2400 B. C. Balgangadhar Tilak and Prof. Herman Jacobi hold, it is 4000 B.C. The famous British Indologist F. E. Pergiter and the historian Hem Chandra Roy Chowdhury draw almost the same conclusion regarding the period which is 10th century B. C. Stuart Piggot in his 'Prehistoric India' makes an historical analysis and infers that the period of composition of the hymns of the Ṛgveda must be between 1400 and 1500 B. C. He refers to the fact that the urban civilization of Harappa was established by 2000 B. C. and the Aryans after having entered into India collided with this civilization and destroyed the forts. This historieal event is well-marked in the

division of the Vedas into four classes[4] viz., the Ṛgveda, the Sāmveda, the Yajurveda and the Atharvaveda. This is why the name of this seer is Vedavyāsa. Each of the Vedas is generally said to have four parts viz., the Mantra Saṁhitā, the Brāhmaṇa, the Āraṇyaka and the Upaniṣad. It

---

description of the prowess of Indra in the Ṛgveda. The hymns of the Ṛgveda are, therefore, supposed to have been composed long after this collision. Winternitz holds that the Vedas in all probability appeared at the beginning of Indo-Aryan civilization. Dr. Radhakrishnan supports Piggot's view and assigns the Vedic hymns to the 15th century B. C., which in our view is difficult to challenge.

4. Some are in favour of limiting the number of the Vedas to three. According to this line of thought Atharvaveda is eliminated as it has no applicability in sacrificial rites. The Atharvaveda is no doubt of later origin and its subject matter is basically different from that of the earlier three Vedas. The earlier Vedas are naturally closely connected with each other, but are not so deeply related to the Atharvaveda. But it is not proper to ignore the importance of the Atharvaveda on these grounds. It is true that the two of the ancient Upaniṣads speak of 'Trayī Vidyā' (Chāndogya—1. 4. 2. & 1. 4. 3.; Bṛhadāraṇyaka—1. 5. 5.) and that the term 'Trayī' was well-known in the age of the Upaniṣads. But even these earliest Upaniṣads refer to the Atharvaveda (Chān.—7.1.2., Bṛh.—4. 5. 11.). Further, philosophical speculations are not completely avoided in this Veda. Hence it is not improper to consider the Atharvaveda to be a part and parcel of the Vedas.

Anirvāṇa enlightens us on this point. The Atharvasaṁhitā, in his opinion, is an appendix or supplementary to trayīvidyā. He has divided the Atharvaveda into three parts: (i) Book I to Book VII, (ii) Book VIII to Book XII, & (iii) Book XIII to Book XX, and has drawn our attention to the fact that although this Veda abounds in mantras relating to rites (ābhyudaik Karma) leading to the the welfare of family and society, it has also incorporated the Upaniṣadic thought. We get almost a poetic expression of Brahmavāda of the Upaniṣads in the second part of it (Bk VIII to Bk XII). ...On the whole the Vedic thought which is well-knit and compact in the 'Trayī Vidyā', is given an emotional rendering here in the Atharvaveda.

Vide :—'Veda mīmaṁsā', Vol. I, by Anirvāṇa; Ch 2; P p. 66-69.

is stated in the 'Āpastambha Śrauta Sūtra'—'mantra brāhmaṇayorvedanāmadheyam'. The famous commentator of the four Vedas Śāyanācārya has referred to it. The Vedas are broadly divided into two parts viz., Mantra and Brāhmaṇa. In fact the Vedic hymns of the mantra portion exhibit the spirit of worship and the devotional element implied here has been illustrated in the Brāhmaṇas with reference to the different ritualistic practices. According to the Vedic tradition the Āraṇyaka is the latter part of the Brāhmaṇa, and the Upaniṣads constitute the end of the Āraṇyaka. It is for this reason that Jaimini holds in his 'Mīmaṁsā Sūtra' that the Vedas have two divisions viz., Mantra and Brāhmaṇa. The entire Vedic literature comprising the four divisions is otherwise said to have two parts viz., Karmakāṇḍa and Jñānakāṇḍa. The matters relating to ceremonial rites are included in the Karmakāṇḍa.[5] Hence the Mantra and the Brāhmaṇa portion fall within the scope of Karmakāṇḍa, while mainly fhe Upaniṣads fall under Jñānakāṇḍa, since here the intellectual speculation on ultimate reality or Brahman forms the pivotal issue. In between these two stands the Araṇyaka where the discussion on karma or ritualistic practices as well as knowledge of reality are found. But it must be noted here that while each Veda has its Brāhmaṇa portion, it has not necessarily an Āraṇyaka attached to it.

5. The preponderance of religious rites and practices here sometimes serves as an impediment for some European scholars to follow the real import of the Vedic religion. Anirvāṇa refers to this point in hls 'Vedamimāṁsā' and says that these ceremonial practices have a particular significance in that they help an individual realize his own self.
Vide :—'Vedamīmaṁsā—Vol. I. Introduction, p p. 24-25.

Vedic gods : marks of pantheism.

It may appear from the foregoing discussion that the hymns of the Ṛgveda are nothing but the eulogistic songs sung in praise of different gods and goddesses. This estimation is not absolutely without foundation, since the spirit in most of the hymns is to pay respectful homage to the deities. As a matter of fact these hymns can be classified into three heads on the basis of the subject matter they deal with. First, as has been mentioned already, there are hymns composed for paying homage to one or more deities. Secondly, the hymns containing philosophical or speculative themes are there which are developed later in the Upaniṣads, and thirdly there are hymns on miscellaneous matters which are neither purely panegyric nor deeply philosophical in character.[6] The hymns containing deeply philosophical doctrines are mostly found in the 10th book of the Ṛgveda. This does not, however, mean that the earlier books do not reveal any philosophical thinking. An overhaul of the Vedic concept of god, therefore, is called for, so that we can ascertain how the polytheistic tendency culminates in a monistic view on the threshold of the Upaniṣads.

6. A few examples of the third type may be given here.
In the first book of the Ṛgveda (1/162) we find a description of 'Aśvamedha Yajña' where horse has been considered a deity. In another context in the same book (1/179) conversation between Agastya and Lopāmudrā throws light on 'Rati', the god of enjoyment. In the 10th book of the Ṛgveda the game on dice has been cried down (10/34). Again the conversation between Puraravā and Urvaśī (10/95) is just an allegory and not a hymn. There are again Sūktas dealing with commonplace themes, such as merits of freedom or gift (10/107, 10/117), marriage (10/85), description of forest (10/146) and such other descriptions of nature which exhibit the emotional outburst of the poet. These subjects are in no way connected with religion or philosophy of the Vedas.

When the question is raised as to what exactly is the number of the Vedic gods, we do not find any definite and unanimous answer. Rather we feel nonplussed at the quagmire of controversy on this point. The term 'deity' is used in different senses, sometimes in its widest denotation so as to include any knowable subject. The number of deities varies accordingly. What can be asserted without any fear of contradiction is that the Vedic sages have discovered enormous power in the different phenomena residing either in earth (bhūloka) or in sky (antarīkṣaloka) or in heaven (dyuloka), and considering them to be conscious, have ascribed deityhood to them. Thus the sages are found to invoke them in rituals and seek their grace. The hymns of the Ṛgveda are naturally meant to propitiate the deities. There is in such hymns neither any purely devotional attachment nor any intellectual approach to them. This has been indicated by Bloomfield when the observes: "The keynote and engrossing theme of Ṛgvedic thought is worship of the personified powers of nature."[7] The attitude of the votaries to the Vedic gods is initially that of the distressed or the endangered (ārta) and of the persons seeking fulfilment of personal wishes, (arthārthī)[8]. The natural objects thus having been personified are worshipped. The purpose here is to seek their grace and ensure safety and security in life which is threatened every moment, and also to fulfil some desires cherished by the people from time to time. Thus the polytheistic tendency[9] has been abundantly clear in

7. M. Bloomfield: 'The Religton of the Vedas'—p. 30.

8. In the Gītā we find a classification of the devotees into four heads, viz., ārta, arthārthī, bhakta or jñanī and jijñāsu. The worshippers of the early Vedic period belong to the first two groups. Cf. The Gītā, 7/16.

9. The existence of many gods has been referred to in different parts of the Ṛgveda. There are two identical hymns in the Ṛgveda (3. 9. 9. & 10. 52. 6) which speak of 3 3 3 9 deities worshipping Agni.

the earliest stage of the Vedic thought.

But the belief in plurality of gods could not satisfy the Vedic seers and very naturally an urge among them was subsequently found to give supremacy to one god.[10] It is

---

But even if all the deities referred to in the different hymns are taken into account, the number will not be so vast. Hence the deities mentioned in these two identical hymns should be understood to mean only those residing in heaven.
Vide :—'Ṛgveda Paricaya'—by Dr. Hiranmay Bandopadhyay ; Introduction to 'Ṛgveda Saṁhitā'—Atul Chandra Sen.

Accordding to Yāska, the author of Nirukta, the deities are classified into three groups on the basis of their habitation, e. g., the deities of earth (bhūloka), the deities of sky or air (antarīkṣaloka) and the deities of heaven (dyuloka). Further Yāska has explained the term 'devatā' (deity) in his own way and has thus declared that there are only three principal deities viz., 'Agni' belonging to earth, 'Vāyu' or 'Indra' to sky or air and 'Sūrya' to heaven. According to Yāska all other deities have been named on the basis of different positions and actions of these three principal gods. But this division of deities as explained by Yāska has not baen accepted by many scholars. Further sometimes it becomes difficult to ascertain the specific region to which the deities actually belong. There is, however, hardly any disagreement as to the classification of the principal deities on the basis of their abode which is as follows :—The region of earth (bhūloka) : Agni, Prithivī, Āpa and Soma. The aerial region (antarīkṣaloka) : Indra, Rudra and Paryanya. The region of heaven (dyuloka) : Sūrya, Savitā, Viṣṇu, Mitra, Varuṇa, Dyuti, Puṣā, Aśviyugal, Uṣā, Rātri, Yama and Bṛhaspati.

10. The opinion upheld by Anirvāṇ is worth considering here. He holds that the apparent contradiction between the belief in many gods and the belief in one god is something that the vedic mind was not aware of. Naturally the polytheistic and the monotheistic tendencies exist side by side and sometimes intermingle. A special leaning of some of the European scholars to 'one-god-theory', Anirvāṇ says, has led them to disparage the Vedic religion that demonstrates plurality of gods. Further, the western scholars lack miserably in sympathetic understanding which only could have helped them in appreciating the Vedic religion.
Anirvān has referred to the findings of anthropological researches

for this reason that whenever any deity is worshipped he is declared to have occupied the supreme position among gods and goddesses. Sometimes it is Agni, sometimes again it is Indra, while at other times it is Varuṇa. In the first book of the Ṛgveda, for example, we find a hymn where it is stated that Agni is head of the heaven, navel of earth, and the lord of earth and heaven alike (Ṛgvedasaṁhitā 1. 59. 2.). Again elsewhere it is stated that Agni is resolute in performing a vow (dhṛtavrata) and is comparable to Varuṇa (R. V. S.—2.1.4.). Almost in the same fashion Indra has been declared to have occupied the highest position (R.V.S.—1.63.1.) and is said to be the king of all deities (R.V.S.—1.174.1). MaxMüller holds, it is 'henotheism' and not polytheism which should be regarded as the keynote of the Vedic religion. The opinion of MaxMüller, however, is not accepted as valid by the eminent critic Prof. Macdonall whose view may by mentioned in this connection. According to him, 'the Vedic deities are not represented as independent of all the rest, since no religion brings its gods into more frequent and varied juxtaposition and combination, and that even the mightiest gods of the Vedas are made dependent on others. Thus Varuṇa and Sūrya are subordinate to Indra (R.V.S. 1. 101), and Varuṇa and Aśvins submit to the power of Viṣnu (R.V.S.—1. 156.). Even when a god is spoken of as a unique or chief (eka), as is natural enough in laudations, such statements lose their temporarily monotheistic force, through the modifications or corrections supplied by the context or even by the same verse. Henotheism is therefore an appearance rather than

and experiments of the present century which establish on the scientifically based facts that the natural tendency of the ancient mind was to believe in one god. The feeling of identity of the individual with the universal spirit is the keynote of the Vedanta and that is also the fundamental thesis of the Vedic religion. Vide :—'Vedamīmāṁsā', Vol. I, Introductian, p p. 20-24.

a reality, an appearance produced by the indefiniteness due to undeveloped anthropomorphism, by the lack of any Vedic god occupying the position of a Zeus as the constant head of the pantheon, by the natural tendency of the priest or singer in extolling a particular god to exaggerate his greatness and to ignore other gods, and by the growing belief in the unity of the gods each of whom might be regarded as a type of the divine'.[11] We can maintain however, the view that henotheism as it is declared by MaxMüller is only a step towards monotheistic belief. The Vedic sages are found to be increasingly conscious of only one supreme God. The claim of Varuṇa to hold the position of supreme God seems irresistible. All the qualities usually admissible in a monotheistic conception are ascribed to Varuṇa in different hymns of the Ṛgveda.[12] In fact 'monotheism is inevitable with any true conception of God. The supreme can only be one. We can not have two supreme and unlimited beings. Everywhere the question was asked whether a god was himself the creation of another. A created god is no god at all. With the growing insight into the working of the world and the nature of god-head the many gods tended to melt into one !'[13] Dr. S. Radhakrishnan has made the point clearer when he says : "The gradual idealisation of the concept of God as revealed in the cult of Varuṇa, the logic of religion which tended to make the gods flow into one another, the henotheism which has its face set in the direction of monotheism, the conception of Ṛta or the unity of nature and the systematising impulse of the human mind – all helped towards the displacement of a polytheistic anthropomorphism by a

11. Prof. Macdonall—'Vedic Mythology', P p. 16-17.

12. Vide :—The Ṛg Veda Saṁhitā : 1. 25. 20., 2. 28. 4., 6. 68. 9., 7. 87. 7., 8. 41. 9., 8. 42. 2.

13. Dr. S. Radhakrishnan : 'Indian Philosophy'—Vol. I. P – 90.

spiritual monotheism".[14] There has thus been a progressive realisation in the minds of the Vedic sages that God is one and he takes different forms and names only at different times. In a famous hymn this idea has been remarkably conveyed. It states that the scholars admit the existence of one Reality who is given different names such as, Indra, Mitra, Varuṇa, Agni, Garutmān, and again He is held to be Agni, Yama and Mātariśvā.[15] Another hymn tells us that one reality is imagined to be many and sacrificial rites are performed accordingly.[16] The fact that Agni, Varuṇa, Mitra, Savitā, Indra etc are the different names of one Supreme God has been adequately illustrated in different hymns of the Ṛgveda.[17] A very significant hymn of the eighth book of the Ṛgveda states that one Agni has been sacrificed in many ways and one Uṣa reveals everything. The implication is that one has become many. The statement bears a close resemblance to the thought developed

---

14. Ibid ; p. 91.
15. "Indraṃ mitraṁ varuṇamagnimāhu ratho' divyaḥ sa suparṇo' garutmān
    Ekaṁ sat viprā bahudhā
    vadanti agniṁ yamaṁ mātariśvā namahuḥ."
    Ṛgveda Saṁhitā, (1. 164. 46.)
    The same hymn is found also in the Atharvaveda, (A. V. S. 9.5.28.)
16. "Ekaṁ santaṁ bahudhā kalpayanti.
    ...Yamṛtvijo'bahudhā
    kalpayantaḥ, sacetaso yajñamimaṁ bahanti." (R. V. S. 8. 58. 1.)
17. 'Mūrdhā bhuvo bhavati naktam
    agnistataḥ sūryo' jāyate prātarudyan' (R. V. S. 10. 88—Agni and Sūrya being the same god)

    In the Atharvaveda saṁhitā we find :—
    "Varuṇa sāyaṁ agnirbhavati, sa mitro'
    bhavati prātarudyan, sa savitā bhūtvā
    antarikṣena yāti, sa Indra' bhūtvā
    Tapati madhyato divam."

in the Kaṭho'paniṣad.[18] Finally in the 10th book of the Ṛgveda the monotheistic tendency is forcefully illustrated in the Viśvakarmā Sūkta (R.V.S. 10. 82) and Prajāpati Sūkta (10. 121). Here God is conceived to be the creator and regulator of the universe. Viśvakarmā is described as the father of mankind. He is one who has created the heaven and earth, who resides alone and exists in different names. In the Prajāpati Sūkta the same god is referred to. When the question crops up :—to which God shall we offer our oblation ? (Kasmai devāya habiṣa vidhema ?), the answer is put forward with reference to the different qualities of God. He is declared to be the Supreme Lord of all beings. His command is obeyed by all other gods. He has produced the earth, the sky and water. He controls and guides all. Now all these descriptions go to account for the fact that the sages here seek to discover the existence of one personal God who is given different names from different standpoints. When the creatorship is emphasized He is called Viśvakarmā and when his controlling power or lordship is stressed He is known as Prajāpati.

In an attempt at discovering the fundamental reality behind the world of phenomena the Vedic thought adopts two different avenues. One line of thinking which finally seeks to establish monotheism, remains rather incomplete and inadequate in the Vedas. The seed of monotheism that is sown here finally germinates in the age of the Purāṇas when the notion of a personal God seems to be well-developed and the people approach God with fullest devotion of their heart. Another line of thought in the Vedas cul-

18. "Agniryathaiko' bhuvanaṁ praviṣto'
rūpaṁ rūpaṁ pratirūpo' vabhuva,
Ekastathā sarvabhūtāntarātmā
rupaṁ rupaṁ pratirūpo' vahiśca".
Kaṭha Up. 2. 2. 9.

minates in the Upaniṣads. Here the sages are intent upon unravelling the mystery of existence and positing one fundamental reality pervading the entire universe. Because of this tendency the monotheistic and monistic thoughts seem to be intermingled in some of the hymns of the Mantra Saṁhitā. We have indicated earlier that the Saṁhitā portion is ordinarily understood to include the eulogistic hymns and certain ritualistic practices and that the philosophical investigation is to be traced in the Upaniṣads only. But strictly speaking such a division of the Vedic literature into two watertight compartments is misleading, for there are numberless hymns in the Karmakāṇḍa where profound philosophical thought creeps in. Mahāmahopādhyay Yogendra Bagchi has brought home to us in his work[19] how philosophical thoughts are explained in the Mantra Saṁhitā. The second current of thought, therefore, which seems to be predominant and stronger than the first, is fully developed in the form of pantheism in the Upaniṣads. But it can not be ignored that this pantheistic note is well-marked towards the end of the Vedas. In the Ātmasūkta of the 10th book of the Ṛgveda (10. 125.) we get an idea of Brahmavāda which is made more prominent in the Puruṣa Sūkta (10. 90.). In the Ātma sūkta it is stated that this soul has very many abodes. He resides in innumerable beings. He pervades the ocean, the heaven and the

19. Vide :—'Veder Mantrabhāge Adhyātma Vidyā', by Yogendra Bagchi, p. 58-59. Referrlng to the hymns of the third book of the Ṛgveda Y. Bagchi says that those who think that there is no spiritual thinking in the Ṛksaṁhitā will be benefited by a study of those hymns. He further says that it is all-pervasiveness of God that is pointed out in the mantras of the Ṛgveda and it has been elaborated in the Upaniṣads. In his opinion, it is only because the Brahmavidya has been demonstrated in the Ṛk mantra that the same has been explained in the Upaniṣads. Had there been no reference to this in the Ṛk mantra, there would have been no menation of it in the Upaniṣads.

earth. The hymns of this sūkta naturally create an impression that the seers seek to discover here one Reality that pervades the entire universe. The deity referred to here is Ātma (Soul) which is highly significant, for this soul is identified with Brahman by the Upaniṣadic sages in the subsequent period. There is no gainsaying however, that this idea is not fully developed here. It is in the Puruṣa sūkta that the existence of an all comprehensive Reality is sought to be developed more systematically. Reality is imagined here to be a Puruṣa. All that is, all that will be, is Puruṣa.[20] The creation of the world is made possible by this Puruṣa. The sun, the moon, the air, the fire (Agni) and Indra are created from the eyes, the mind, the breath and the mouth of Puruṣa respectively. Further the three Vedas, the Brāhmins, the Rājanya, the Vaiśya and the Śūdra also emanate from him. In a word Puruṣa manifests himself in the universe and is considered an all-pervading Reality. Now here that which is considered to be an all- pervading Puruṣa is conceived as Brahman or Bhūmā in the Upaniṣads.

It is necessary to note in this connection that the effusions of awakening reflection of the Vedic sages reach their highest energy in the celebrated Nāsadīya sūkta (R. V. S. — 10, 129) where the monistic trend of thought is expressed with much poignancy. A. E. Gough remarks: "It is in this hymn that is first suggested the primitive type of Indian thought, the thesis of all the Upaniṣads viz., the emanation of the world and of all the forms of life that successively people it, out of the sole reality, the self that permeates and vitalises all things through the agency of the unreality that overspreads it, the self-feigned fiction, the cosmical illusion, Māyā".[21] Whatever be the merit of Gaugh's view, it is true that in answer to the interrogation-

---

20. 'Puruṣa evedaṁ sarvaṁ Yadbhūtaṁ yacca bhavyam. R.V.S. 10.90.2.
21. A.E. Gough :—'The Philosophy of the Upaniṣads'. Ch. I, p. 15.

'Whence are all these created' ?—the sages have penetrated deep into the problem and have attempted to reach a solution. They have declared that it was not entity, nor was it non-entity. There was neither the earth, nor the air. nor the wide-spread sky. Only the self-dependent sole reality was there. Then a will arose and that 'Will' is the power that produced everything, Thus a fundamental Upanisadic concept is found in the form of a seed. Here the reality (Ānīdavātaṁ svadhayā tadekam) is converted subsequently in the Upaniṣads when it is stated—'Sadeva Saumya Idamagra āsīt'. And that which is called a will or desire (Kāma) is expressed in the Upaniṣads thus: 'Sa aikṣata eko'ham bahu syām'.

Thus the Vedic thought can be said to have adopted two avenues—one following the path of monotheism and the other which is more bold and vigorous—that of pantheism. This pantheistic thought is found in the Upniṣads in its maturest form. We shall consider this at length in the next chapter.

CHAPTER—II

THE UPANIṢADS

Transition to the Upaniṣads

When we come to the age of the Upaniṣads we find certain marked changes in the thoughts of the ancient saints and seers. Here we move forward to a sphere of deep speculation on the question of supreme reality or Brahman. The sonorous verses of the Vedas with their imaginative tinge and emotional intensity are sacrificed here too much as a luxury. Some passages of the Ṛgveda, especially the the hymns to Varuṇa have a close analogy to the devotional psalms of the Bible both in point of language and ideas,—passages which are rarely to be met with in the literature of the Upaniṣads where we have more or less the coolness of intellectual argument exhibiting itself in a systematic search after the ultimate reality.[1] In tracing the development of the Upaniṣadic cosmogony Ranade says : "The settled recurrence of all happenings in nature must have filled the natural enquirer with an impulse to find out the real meaning of all these phenomena, and it is no wonder that as in Greek philosophy, so in the Upaniṣadic philosophy the primary search was after the prius of things. What is it that abides in the midst of changes ? What is it which, as the Upaniṣad puts it, may be called the 'Tajjalān' ? What is that from which all things spring, into which they are resolved and in which they live and have their being ?"[2] In one of the closing hymns of the

1. Vide :— Ranade : A Constructive survey of Upaniṣadic Philosophy; Ch. I. P-4.
2. Ibid ; P-73.

Ṛgveda (10. 151) it has been asserted that man winneth faith by 'Yearnings of the heart' and the same poem concludes with the words: 'O Faith, endow us with belief'. The Vedas are rich not merely in faith in the value of that which is seen, but also in the kind of enquiry which by endeavouring to penetrate behind that which is seen, leads to belief in a profounder sense.[3] In the Upaniṣads the 'Yearnings of heart' assume intellectual guise. As a matter of fact the sages here have recourse to 'inward scrutiny' instead of sweeping contemplation of the world with a view to establishing their knowledge of the ultimate source or ground of existence. They are said to have retired to the forests for the sake of secrecy where they were engaged in deep discussion. The element of exchange of views has been preserved in the word 'Upaniṣad' itself which is made up of 'Upa' (near) and 'Sad' (to sit). 'To sit at the feet of'—is still the phrase we use to convey the notion of receiving knowledge from a teacher of repute. The Upaniṣads are the confidential reports communicated to the disciples sub rosa. Hence Ranade aptly observes: "As we pass from the Vedas to the Upaniṣads, we pass from prayer to philosophy, from hymnology to reflection, from henotheistic polytheism to monotheistic mysticism."[4]

In sketching the transition from the Vedas to the Upaniṣads a few words on the Atharva Veda will not be out of place. This Saṁhitā, as we come to understand, appears at a considerably later period of the Vedic age. The general impression is that as a reader passes from the age of the Ṛgveda to that of the Atharvaveda, he passes from the universe of hymns to the universe of black art. In spite of occasional references to theosophic hymns dealing

3. Cf. E.W.F. Tomlin-'The Eastern Philosophers,-an Introduction'. P-164.

4. Ranade :— 'A Constructive Survey of Upaniṣadic Philosophy'. Ch-I, P-3.

with God or Brahman, the authors of the Atharvaveda are strongly directed more towards sorcery than to religion proper. Perhaps for this reason Ranade remarks: "The general impression which the Atharvaveda leaves upon our mind is that of the blood-sucking activity of the ghoulish demon which saps the fountain of both devotion and reason and leaves us in the arid waste of witcheries and incantations. The two are almost poles apart".[5] This view of Ranade contains an element of truth no doubt, but his observation seems to be hyperbolic, for we have indicated earlier that the value of the Atharvaveda can not be totally impugned. We can say, however, that when we pass from the Atharvaveda to the Upaniṣads, we pass in a sense, from the region of incantation to one of philosophical speculation.

We have already seen that in the Vedic age the hymns of the Saṁhitā are followed by the Brāhmanic ritualism. In the age of the Upaniṣads the general tone of the saints is more rational, for they declare that without the acquisition of spiritual knowledge mere performance of sacrificial rites is inane. Thus it appears that in the Upaniṣadic age an earnest intellectual quest for a universal instead of a particular world-ground led to a theory which postulates a world-ground that embraces all phenomena and which gradually seeks to identify everything with the world-ground. The preponderance of this spirit in the Upaniṣads has probably led many western thinkers to conclude that there is a mutual contradiction between the Jñānakāṇḍa and the Karmakāṇḍa of the Vedas. In other words, as these critics hold, the authors of the Upaniṣads lost faith in the efficacy of the Vedic sacrifices and resorted to the conception of one God or Brahman discarding the notion of many minor

5. Idid: P-15.

gods found dominant in the earlier Vedas.[6]

The critical observations of the western scholars, in our opinion, are misleading and do not stand the test of rational scrutiny. The Upaniṣads abound in passages which go a long way in proving the fact that the sages of this period have acknowledged the existence of minor gods and have confirmed the efficacy of Vedic sacrifices. In the Īśo'paniṣad we find the dying soul praying to god Agni to lead the soul by a pleasant path (Īśa. 18). In the Keno'paniṣad it is stated that Indra, Vāyu and Agni surpass other gods because they first perceived Brahman in close proximity (Kena—4. 2.). If the conception of minor gods is false, some minor gods can not then be said to surpass others. Again the same Upaniṣad considers the rituals to be the means of acquiring knowledge. 'Austerities, self-control and rituals are the foundations of true knowledge contained in the Upaniṣads. The Vedas are the limbs, truth is the body'. (Kena—4.8.). In the Katho'paniṣad Naciketā is found to have learnt first from Yama how to perform the Vedic sacrifices and there-

6. We may refer to a few opinions here in brief.

i) "While the Brāhmins were pursuing their barren sacrificial science, other circles were engaged upon those highest questions which were at last treated so admirably in the Upaniṣads".

—Dr. Winternitz ; History of Sanskrit Literature. P-237.

ii) "The Ātman doctrine is fundamentally opposed to the Vedic cults of the gods and the Brāhmanical system of the ritual".

—Deussen : 'Religion and philosophy of the upaniṣads'. P-21.

iii) "In these Upaniṣads the whole ritual or sacrificial system of the Vedas is not only ignored, but directly rejected as useless, nay as mischievous. The ancient gods of the Vedas are no longer recognized'.

—MaxMūller : 'Origin af Vedanta', P-16.

iv) "The whole religious doctrine of different gods and of the necessity of sacrificing to the gods is seen to be a stupendous fraud by the man who has acquired metaphysical knowledge of the monistic unity of the self and of the world in Brahman or Ātman".

—R. E. Hume : 'The Thirteen Principal Upaniṣads'. p-53.

after he receives the lessons in the knowledge of Brahman (Kaṭha—1. 1. 13.). When Naciketā enquires about the knowledge of Brahman, Yama says that 'gods' also desire to know Brahman. The Muṇḍaka Upaniṣad begins by saying that of all minor gods Brahmā first came into existence, (Muṇḍ. 1. 1. 1.). This Upaniṣad further categorically affirms the effectiveness of the Vedic sacrifices when it says—'All this is true – the rituals which were revealed to the sages and which were connected with the Vedic mantras. You should constantly perform these sacrifices with the desire for attaining the ultimate truth". (Muṇḍ—1, 2. 1.). In explaining a passage of the Taittirīya Upaniṣad viz., 'Dharmaṁ cara' – pursue the path of religion, Śaṁkara says that so long as one does not realize one's identity with Brahman, one should carefully perform the rites laid down in the Vedas. The two celebrated ancient Upaniṣads – the Chāndogya and the Bṛhadāraṇyaka enjoin on the performance of sacrificial rites. The Bṛhadārañyaka Upaniṣad holds, it is this Brahman whom the Brāhmins desire to know by the performance of sacrifices, charity and austerities. (Bṛh—4. 4. 22.). Likewise in the Chāndogya, sacrifices, study and charity are said to be constituting the first part of religious path.

It must, however, be admitted that the Upaniṣads do not always present a consistent view. In spite of the passages referred to above, there are statements denying the efficacy of sacrifices. But this apparent inconsistency does not establish any antagonism as is supposed, between the Upaniṣads and the sacrificial doctrine of the Bhāhmaṇas. The Upaniṣads on the contrary want to impress upon us that the path of knowledge is not opposed to the path of work. Further, we have indicated earlier that the authors of the Saṁhitā portion of the Vedas become increasingly alive to the conception of one supreme God and that their imagination is not strictly confined to the minor deities only. This, as we have seen, is admirably illustrated in the 'Puruṣa Sūkta' and the 'Nāsadīya Sūkta' of the Ṛgveda. There is thus no basis for the statement of the western scholars that there is a mutual contradiction between the Jñānakāṇḍa and the Karmakāṇḍa. The engrossing theme of the Upaniṣads as we shall explain in the sequel, can not be misunderstood in spite of the occasional digressions or contradictory observations. Hence there can not be any difficulty in tracing the progressive development of thought from the Vedas to the Upaniṣads. Hopkins makes a pregnant observation in this connection : "In the Vedic hymns man fears gods and imagines God. In the Brāhmaṇas man subdues the gods and fears God. In the Upaniṣads man ignores the gods and becomes God. Such in a word is the theosophic relation between the three periods represented by the first Vedic collection, the ritualistic Brāhmaṇas and the philosophical treatises called the Upaniṣads".[7]

The germ of pantheism, as we have already seen, has been particularly well-marked in the 10th book of the Ṛgveda. The comment of Richard Garbe is quite pertinent when he says : "Old hymns of the Ṛgveda which in other respects are still deeply rooted in the soil of polytheism, show already the inclination to comprehend multifarious phenomena as a unity, and may, therefore, be regarded as the first steps in the path which led the Indian people to pantheism".[8] Now our purpose is to show how pantheism has been developed as the kernel of the Upanisadic teaching. But the existence of an overwhelming number of the Upaniṣads makes it difficult and sometimes confusing too, in ascertaining what precisely the Upanisadic teaching is.

7. E. W. Hopkins : 'The Religion or India' Ch. X, Brāhmanic Pantheism-the Upaniṣads. P. 216.

8. Richard Garbe : 'The Philosophy of Ancient India', P 1.

The selection of the principal ancient Upaniṣads, therefore, becomes an indispensable prerequisite.

Selection of the ancient Upaniṣads

Referring to Śaṁkara's commentary on Brahma sūtra Deussen has in his 'The System of Vedānta', drawn our attention to the fact that the number of the Upaniṣads in Śaṁkara's age was fourteen. Again from the fact that Dara Shikoh translated fifty Upaniṣads into Persian language it is inferred that in his time the number of the Upaniṣads was fifty. In the Muktika Upaniṣad a reference has been made to one hundred and eight Upaniṣads. Vasudev Lakshmana Shastri has given a list of one hundred and twelve Upaniṣads in his edition published from Nirṇaya Sāgar Press of Bombay. Our task in the present context is to select the ancient Upaniṣads only, for it is on the basis of them that we have to discover their principal thought. It is necessary, however, to note that the Upaniṣads available so far are classified mainly into three heads viz., (i) those dealing with Brahman and explaining pantheism i.e., Brahmavādī Upaniṣads, (ii) those that are ascetic or rigoristic in character i.e., the Yogavādī and Sannyāsavādī Upaniṣads and (iii) those of the age of the Purāṇas dealing with devotional attachment to the mythological gods i e., Bhaktivādī Upaniṣads. The detailed analysis of these three types may appear to be redundant. A few words may, however, be added for convenience of treatment.

The first group (i.e., the Brahmavādī Upaniṣads) is solely concerned with the discussion on Brahman or Ātman which is known as Parāvidyā. The Yogavādī Upaniṣads aim at direct knowledge of the Supreme Reality and in order to accomplish this task they lay stress on the rigorous control of the senses. The Sannyāsavādī Upaniṣads go a step further and speak of complete renunciation. They insist upon complete abnegation of sensibility, total abjuration of all enjoyment, absolute detachment from woman and the like. These two types of the Upaniṣads, belonging virtually to the same group have a close ideological affinity. The former attaches importance to the direct knowledge of the Supreme Spirit while the latter to the salvation through renunciation, Then again those Upaniṣads which form a vast majority belong to the age of the Purāṇas. They emphasize the devotional aspect in their contemplation of God.

Now our first task would be to select the Brahmavādī Upaniṣads only which belong to the first age. This stupendous task becomes comparatively easy on the adoption of two-fold methods. The first task is to mark the growth of those treatises as the natural outcome of the Vedic literature and the second method is to note the gradual change in Indian philosophical thinking which will help us trace the antiquity of the Upaniṣads.

As to the first method, it is not difficult to ascertain that a large number of the Upaniṣads are somehow connected either with the Saṁhitā portion or with the Brāhmaṇa portion or with the Āraṇyaka portion. In those cases where no such direct connection is traceable, we find some tradition or other by virtue of which an Upaniṣad is connected with a particular Veda. Thus we find, the Īśo'paniṣad comes at the end of the Vājasaneya Saṁhitā of Śuklayajurveda. It is thus a part and parcel of the Saṁhitā. The Aitareya Upaniṣad is connected with the Aitareya Āraṇyak of the Ṛgveda. The Kauṣītaki Upaniṣad is the terminal part of Sāṁkhyāyan Āraṇyaka of the Ṛgveda. The Taittirīya Upaniṣad is connected with the Taittirīya Āraṇyaka of the Krişnayajurveda. The Bṛhadāraṇyaka Upaniṣad forms the part of Śatapatha Brāhmaṇa of the Śuklayajurveda. The Chāndogya Upaniṣad is a part of the Chāndogya Brāhmaṇa of the Sām Veda. The Keno'paniṣad is the terminal part of the Āraṇyak related to the Jaimini Brāhmaṇa of the

Sām Veda. The Kaṭho'paniṣad and the Śvetāśvatara Upaniṣad are, according to tradition, included in the Krisnayajur veda. Again the Muṇḍaka and the Māṇḍukya Upaniṣads are likewise included in the Atharvaveda, while the Praśno'paniṣad is a part of the Paippalāda branch of the Atharvaveda. The total number of the ancient Upaniṣads thus comes to twelve. Of these the last five (i.e., the Kaṭha, the Śvetāśvatara, the Muṇḍaka, the Māṇḍukya and the Praśno'paniṣad) are in no way connected with any Brāhmaṇa of the Vedas. Of these texts the Kaṭha and the Śvetāśvatara Upaniṣads appear to be of later origin since in both of them we find some influence of the Sāṁkhya and the Yoga philosophy[10] Again these two Upaniṣads together with the other two viz.. the Muṇḍaka and the Praśna Upaniṣads are written in verse. That is another reason for considering them to be of comparatively late origin, for one of the criteria of determining the antiquity of the Upaniṣads is the composition of the texts in prose. Besides, the twelve Upaniṣads as mentioned, can be said to be the principal ancient Upaniṣads, because the principal theme discussed in all of them is identical. All these texts reveal a zealous pursuance of the sages for Parāvidyā or the knowledge of Brahman that encompasses the whole of existence.

Now as regards the second method[11] of determining the

---

10. "Mahataḥ Paramavyaktamavyaktāt Puruṣaḥ Paraḥ,
Puruṣānna Paraṁ Kiñcit sā Kāṣṭhā sā parā gatiḥ"
—Kaṭha up. I. 3. 11.
"Nityo nityānaṁ cetanaścetanānāmeko bahūnaṁ yo' vidadhāti Kāmān, Tat Kāraṇaṁ Sāṁkhya yogādhigamyaṁ jñātvā devaṁ mucyate sarvapāśaiḥ".
—Śvetā. Up. 6. 13.

11. This is called 'the archeological method' by Dr. Hiranmay Bandyopadhyay. He says that we may apply the archeological method to ascertain which Upaniṣads actually belonged to the ancient Vedic age. When a human habitation is completely demolished and

antiquity of the aforesaid Upaniṣads we have to refer to the gradual change in Indian philosophical thought which we have already discussed in Chapter I. It will be adequate to mention here that the fundamental thought of the aforesaid Upaniṣads is virtually the logical development of what is faintly indicated in the Saṁhitā portion and more clearly elaborated in the Brāhmaṇa portion of the Vedas. In the third stage of Indian philosophical thought we come across six orthodox systems advocating right knowledge of reality as a means to attain liberation and avoid rebirth. The urge for the attainment of liberation and avoidance of rebirth is also found in the two heterodox systems viz., the Jaina and the Buddhists. The problem of rebirth has been established as a sound doctrine at this stage of thought. But ancient Upaniṣads, in spite of their occasional references to and interrogations on the problem of rebirth, do not give any decided opinion on the issue. The question of liberation does not very naturally arise in the minds of the sages. The sages of this age are found to have been deeply engrossed in the knowledge of Brahman not for liberation but for satiating their intellectual curiosity and deriving unearthly enjoy-

---

consequently its civilisation dies out, the things used or enjoyed by the people are buried in the ground. Civilizations of the different ages flourish and subsequently die out in the same way. Long after the archeologist excavates the ground and discovers things in different layers. Obviously the things found at the bottom are considered the oldest, while those on the surface, the latest. This investigation helps an archeologist explore the culture and civilization of different ages. Similar method may be adopted in determining the antiquity of the Upniṣads. On an analysis of the different stages of Indian philosophy and religion we may discover at which stage the Upaniṣads were written. We can thus arrive at an unerring conclusion regarding the period and number of the ancient Upaniṣads.

—Vide :— Dr. Hiraṇmay, Bandyopadhyay ; 'Upaniṣader Darśan', Ch. II.

ment. 'Bhūmaiva sukhaṁ, nālpe sukhamasti',--this having been their favourite slogan, they are prompted to shun all power and pelf and devote their energy and attention to parāvidyā. Hence the fundamental difference in spirit between the age of the Upaniṣads and that of the six orthodox systems is clearly discernible. Finally at the fourth stage of our religion we are acquainted with the Purāṇas where theism is established with all force and vivacity. God is here conceived as a person and is worshipped in different names and forms two of which viz., Viṣnu and Śiva seem to have been prominent. A steadfast devotion to God has been considered the only means to the fulfilment of all desires. Thus the ancient Upaniṣads can in no way be contemporaneous with the third and the fourth stage of Indian religious thought. It is only those twelve Upaniṣads mentioned earlier that can be considered truly ancient. The principal current of thought of these treatises closely resembles that of the later part of Vedic age. These are the real Brahmavādī Upaniṣads and our discussion will accordingly be confined to them only.

Principal currents of thought in the ancient Upaniṣads.

Now if we analyse closely the message of the ancient Upaniṣads we find three currents of thought inextricably bound up with each other. The first distinctive trait that draws our attention is the genuine urge for Parāvidyā. According to the definition given in the Muṇḍaka Upaniṣad, Parāvidyā is that which helps us know the Supreme Spirit (Akṣara).[12] This knowledge does not yield any practical results. It is the satisfaction of intellectual curiosity that is sought not only by the sages and erudite scholars of that

12. 'Atha parā Yayā tadakṣaramadhigamyate'.
—Muṇḍaka Up. 1. 1. 5.

age, but by the common people as well. Parāvidyā seems to have been preferable to them even to riches. This is why Maitreyī, the ardent aspirant for Brahmavidyā is found to have discarded wealth since wealth, she understands, can not help her reach Brahman.[13] The celebrated Yama Naciketā episode is also well-known to us. In spite of Yama's repeated persuasions to take to a life of pleasures Naciketā does not swerve from his keen interest in knowing the nature of self. He makes mincemeat of Yama's inveigling theories and declares firmly that man is never satisfied with wealth.[14]

The second principal current of thought that follows as a natural corollary to the first, is pantheism. According to this doctrine the entire world of things and beings is permeated bv the Supreme Spirit or Brahman. Unlike monotheism it does not posit God as the efficient cause of the world existing far apart from his creation. In monotheism God is considered a personal Being with whom a loving relation is sought to be established. But pantheism does not admit of any sharp cleavage between God and the world. It is through the path of knowledge and not through any devotional attachment that the Upaniṣadic sages have arrived at a conception of God that includes or encompasses all. This they call 'Brahman' or 'Ātman'. It is on the basis of the this doctrine of an all-comprehensive Brahman that a new ethical ideal is propagated in the Upaniṣads. This ideal is one of universal love and fraternity in which consists the 'good'. The Upaniṣads thus seek to resolve the conflict between the good (Śreya) and the pleasurable (Preya). This may be characterized as the third current of thought following necessarily from the second.

---

13. 'Yenāhaṁ nāmṛtā syāṁ Kimahaṁ tena Kuryāṁ ?'

—Bṛh. Up. 4. 5. 4.

14. 'Na vittena tarpaṇīyo' manuṣyaḥ'

—Kaṭha Up. 1. 1. 27.

Pantheism in the Upaniṣads

Now we shall consider the nature of Upaniṣadic pantheism which is established as the cardinal doctrine by the ancient sages in their assiduous search for the unitary world-ground. The necessity of a universal instead of a particular world-ground has led to a theory which postulates a world-ground that embraces all phenomena as parts of it. The theory thus speaks of the identification of everything with the world-ground. The sages come to believe that although Brahman is the creator and the world His creation, His mode of creation is different from that of the human beings. In the Upaniṣads the creator and the created universe are not considered separate and distinct from each other. Here the creator pervades the entire creation and regulates or sustains the created beings from within. It is in this sense that pantheism has been propagated in the Upaniṣads. To make the point clearly intelligible we shall refer to the fourfold causes sponsored by Aristotle and see how far they are applicable to Brahman.

Aristotle has defined and explained four different types of cause viz., material cause (Upādāna Kāraṇa) efficient cause (nimitta kāraṇa), formal cause (rūpa kārṇa) and final cause (uddeśya kāraṇa). These four causes are generally found to operate in the production of a man-made thing. When for example. an earthen vessel is made, clay is its material cause and the potter the efficient cause. The potter is also the formal cause in the sense that he gives the lump of clay a particular form or shape by the adept manoeuvering of his hand. The final cause is the purpose which the thing produced serves. In the Upaniṣads Brahman is related to the world in such a way as the application of causal theory becomes apparently meaningless. It is expressly stated in all the Upaniṣads that Brahman permeates the entire world. He holds everything within Himself and acts here unobserved. Everything owes its origin to Brahman, is sustained by Brahman and goes to Brahman when destroyed. We shall, however, try to explain how far the fourfold causes formulated by Aristotle can be applied to the Upaniṣadic concept of Brahman. In fact that Brahman is the material cause has been quite emphatically pronounced in the Upaniṣads so as to exhibit the deep relation between the creator and the created. A fine analogy has been used in the Chāndogya Upaniṣad to illustrate the point. Two characteristics are marked out in a man-made thing, —one is the matter and the other is the form. Clay is the matter of an earthen vessel and the pot is the particular form it takes. The fundamental or the primary reality here is the clay and what is secondarily real is the transformation of the same matter in different forms. These different forms are given the different names.[15] In the same way Brahman is the fundamental reality who manifests Himself in different forms and takes different names. This observation may lead one to suppose that the importance of Brahman as the formal cause has not been duly recognized. But there are passages in the Upaniṣads where the manifold forms of the universal spirit have not been undermined as secondary. In the Kaṭho'paniṣad, for instance, it is said that the same Brahman has taken different forms and is present in all objects acting as a connecting link among them.[16] It is this one spirit that permeates the world of multiplicity. An analogy is given to illustrate the point. Just as the same fire is recognized in different fiery objects, in like manner the same soul exists in different living beings. They are virtually the different manifestations

15. "Yathā ekena mṛtpindena Sarvaṁ mṛṇmayaṁ vijñātaṁ syādvācārambhaṇaṁ vikāro' nāmadheyaṁ mṛttiketyeva satyam".

—Chān. Up, 6. 1. 4.

16. "Eko' vaśī sarvabhūtāntarātmā ekaṁ rūpaṁ bahudhā yaḥ karoti".

—Kaṭha Up. 2. 2. 12.

of one spirit.[17] Again there are passages in the Upaniṣads explaining the nature of Brahman as the efficient cause of the world. In the human world an efficient cause, after having produced the effect, remains outside the effect. The cause and the effect (as in the case of an earthen vessel and potter) have a separate and independent existence. Here the regulation or control of the object produced is carried on by the efficient cause from outside. In the world of nature, however, the case is different. An atom, for example, is regulated by its inner powerful contents viz., proton, neutron and electron, Further, life that controls the body exists inside the body. In the same fashion it is stated in the Upaniṣads that Brahman acts as a controlling power in two ways First, under its control the entire universe is guided. The sun and the moon, heaven and earth, the moments, days and nights etc. are all pervaded and controlled by it.[18] Secondly it is asserted that Brahman exists in different jīvas and controls them unobserved. All the animals are its body and it is by residing within their heart and controlling them from within that it comes to be known as Antaryāmin. The body changes, but the controlling power of Brahman is unchangeable and eternal.[19] Next comes the final cause which constitutes the purpose aimed at. The ancient sages can be said to have discovered this cause too, since they

17. "Agniryathaiko' bhuvanaṁ praviṣto' rūpaṁ rūpaṁ pratirūpo' babhuva, ekastathā
Sarvabhūtāntarātmā rūpaṁ rūpaṁ pratirūpo' vahiśca".

—Kaṭha Up. 2. 2. 9.

18. "Etasya vākṣarasya praśāsane Gārgi Sūryācandramasau vidhṛtau tiṣṭhata etasya vākṣarasya praśāsane Gārgi dyāvāprthivyo' vidhṛte tiṣṭhata ...."

—Bṛh. Up. 3. 8. 9.

19. "Yaḥ sarveṣu bhūteṣu tiṣṭhan Sarvebhyo' bhūtebhyo' antaro' yaṁ sarvāṇi bhūtani na viduryasya sarvāṇi bhūtāni śarīraṁ yaḥ sarvāṇi bhūtānyantaro' yamayati eṣa tat ātmāntaryāmyamṛta iti"

—Bṛh. Up. 3. 7. 15.

hold that Brahman is 'Rasavān'. In revealing itself in multitudinous names and forms it feels a sort of joy which perhaps roughly corresponds to 'artistic joy'. It is difficult to find the exact English term of 'Rasa'. Some thinkers are in favour of using the term 'aesthetic emotion' implying thereby that Brahman feels a spontaneous joy in manifesting itself in the world. The enlightened seers come to know Brahman as 'Ānandam'.[20]

It will now be convenient for us to explain the pantheistic doctrine in detail in the light of the statements given in the different Upaniṣads. We have already seen that the principle of creation of Brahman as the creator is fundamentally different from that of the human beings. In the Upaniṣads the created world has been declared to be pervaded by the Supreme Creative Spirit who is given different names such as Brahman, Bhūmā, Ātman etc. This Spirit existing, as it does, within the created world controls and guides the flow of creation. The all-pervasive nature of Brahman has been forcefully demonstrated in almost all the ancient Upaniṣads. In the Īśo'paniṣad it is stated, 'whatever is perceived here in the world' is covered by God.[21] In the second chapter of the Kaṭho'paniṣad it is said that just as fire takes different forms, similarly one and the same Brahman adopts different forms. In the third chapter of the Śvetāśvatara Upaniṣad the same all-pervasiveness has been explained. 'His hands and feet, eyes, head, mouth and ears are present everywhere. Covering everything He exists.[22] This passage and the preceding one suggest the

20. "Tadvijñānena paripaśyanti dhīrā ānandarūpamamṛtaṁ yadvibhāti".
—Muṇḍ Up. 2. 2. 8.

21. "Īśāvāsyamidaṁ sarvaṁ yat kiñca jagatyāṁ jagat".
—Īśa Up. 1. 1.

22. "Sarvataḥ pāṇipādantat sarvato' kṣiśiro' mukham, sarvataḥ śrutimalloke sarvamāvṛtya tiṣṭhati". —Śvetā. Up. 3. 16.

profound influence of the Puruṣa Sūkta of the Ṛgveda.[23] In the Muṇḍaka Upaniṣad the same current of thought is signified when it declares, 'Brahman indeed is immortal. Brahman is before, behind, to right and to left' stretched forth below and above. Brahman indeed is the whole world —this widest extent.[24] The Brahmānandavallī of the Taittirīya Upaniṣad not only explains the manifestation of Brahman in the world of variety, but it also goes a step further when it holds that Brahman is transformed into objects of heterogenous and contradictory qualities. 'After having created this universe Brahman entered into it. It became both concrete (mūrta) and abstract (amūrta), conscious and unconscious, truth and falsity and 'true' and in fact it became all else'.[25] The universe, as we know it, is full of contradictions. Truth has as much a room as falsehood in the frame work of the worldly life. In fact truth and falsehood, good and bad, birth and death—all such contradictory traits constitute this world. Everything is true in this sense and Brahman becomes all these. That is why Brahman is known by the sages finally as 'true'. This is precisely the implication of the statement—'Satyaṁ cānṛtaṁ ca, satyamabhavat'. In the Chāndogya and the Bṛhadāraṇyakā Upaniṣad we get a detailed account of this line of thinking. The substantial thesis of pantheism has been admirably limned in the Chāndogya Upaniṣad when it states : "All this is Brahman : everything originates from it, is reabsorbed into it and lives in it".[26] In the opinion

23. 'Puruṣa evedaṁ sarvaṁ yadbhūtaṁ yacca bhavyam'
—Ibid, 3. 5. Cf. the Ṛgveda, 10. 90. 1.

24. "Brahmai vedamamṛtaṁ purastād Brahma paścād Brahma dakṣ inataścottareṇa, adhaścordhañca, prasṛtaṁ Brahmaivedaṁ, viśvamidaṁ variṣṭham". —Muṇḍ. Up. 2. 2. 12

25. "Tadanupraviśya, Sacca Tyaccā'bhavat,......Vijñānañcāvijñānañca, Satyañcānṛtañca, Satyamabhavat, Yadidaṁ kiñca, tat Satyamityācakṣate"........... —Taitti. Up. 2. 6. 4.

26. "Sarvaṁ khalvidaṁ Brahma tajjalāniti"—Chān. Up. 3. 14. 1.

of R. E. Hume this section of the Chāndogya Upaniṣad is the first clear statement of pantheism which had been latent in the previous conception of Brahman and of the relation of the world to it. Later that pantheism is made explicit and remains so through the rest of the Upaniṣads where the thought recurs that Brahman actually is everything".[27] In a different context the Chāndogya Upaniṣad brings home to us the relation between Brahman and the world. That Brahman exists unobserved in His creation is explained by Āruṇi to his son Śvetaketu in a pellucid manner. When Śvetaketu as per his father's advice poured some salt in a pot full of water he was asked by his father to find out the salt. Having failed to discover the salt Śvetaketu tasted the water on his father's instruction, from the different parts of the pot and found each time that the water was salty. By this Āruṇi wanted to prove that just as salt here had no separate existence from water, in the same way Brahman and the world are commingled and the world has no separate existence. The individual beings and the material world with its minutest particles are all true. Āruṇi says, 'the minutest particles which we all perceive are inhabited by Brahman. All that we behold outside is true and is Brahman. You are that too.'[28] This idea is more clearly explicated in the seventh chapter of this Upaniṣad, when Sanat Kumar imparts the teaching on Brahman to Nārada. He says : "Brahman is upwards and downwards, He is behind and to the front, to the south aud to the north and He is all this".[29] This current of thought has been

---

27. Vide :—R. E. Hume : 'The Thirteen Principal Upaniṣads'. Ch. IV, P-22.

28. "Sa ya eṣo'ṇimaitadātmyamidaṁ sarvam tat satyaṁ sa ātmā tattvamasi Śvetaketo...".—Chānd. Up. 6. 12. 3.

29. (i) "Sa evādhastāt sa upariṣṭāt, sa paścāt sa purastāt, sa dakṣinataḥ sa uttarataḥ sa evedaṁ sarvamiti". Ibid, 7. 25. 1.

further developed in the vast compass of the Bṛhadāraṇyaka Upaniṣad. 'As a spider might come out with his thread, as small sparks come forth from fire, even so from this soul come forth all vital energies, all worlds, all gods, all beings'.[30] That Brahman or Ātman is the real substrate of all beings has been impressed upon us in the second chapter of the Bṛhadāraṇyaka Upaniṣad. 'Just as all the spokes of the wheel of a chariot are placed in the centre and the circumference of the chariot, in the same way all beings, all gods, all worlds, all lives and all selves are located in this soul'.[31] Yājñavalka remarks here,—'this Brāhmaṇa, the Kṣ atriya all these different worlds, these different living creatures—all this is Ātman.[32] The second chapter of the Śvetāśvatara Upaniṣad is closed with a prayer to Brahman after having recognized its all-pervasive character.[33]

The excerpts quoted so far go a long way in ratifying the contention that Brahman as the cause does not exist apart from its effect-the world, On the contrary He resides in and pervades the entire universe. Naturally therefore, when it is interrogated : 'where is Brahman ?'—the answer put forward is—He is in His creation. Hence when the cause and the effect are not two absolutely distinct and separate entities,

---

(ii) Cf. "Dyāvāpṛthivyoridamantaraṁ hi vyāptaṁ tva'yaikena diśaśca sarvāḥ."—Thc Gītā, XI. 20.

30. "Sa yathā ūrṇanābhiḥ tantunā uccaret yathāgneḥ kṣudrā visphūlingā vyuccaranti evameva asmādātmanaḥsarve prāṇāḥ sarve lokāḥ sarve devāḥ sarvāṇi bhūtāni vyuccaranti..."—Bṛh Up. 2. 1. 20.

31. "Tad yathā rathanābhau ca rathanemau cārāḥ sarve samarpitā evamevā'sminnātmani sarvāṅi bhūtāni sarve devāḥ sarve lokāḥ sarve prāṇāḥ sarve ete ātmānaḥ samarpitāḥ."—Bṛh. Up. 2. 5. 15.

32. "Brahmedaṁ kṣatramime lokā ime devāi'māni bhūtānīdaṁ sarvaṁ yadayamātmā".—Ibid, 2. 4. 6.

33. "Yo' devo'gnou yo'psu yo' viśvaṁ bhuvanamāviveśa, ya osadhīṣu yo' vanaspatiṣu tasmai devāya namo namaḥ."

—Śvetā. Up. 2. 17.

any attempt at classifying the cause appears to be otiose. Nevertheless, from what has been said so far, it can fairly be said that the four-fold causes as formulated by Aristotle and as normally referred to in the human world, can be ascribed to Brahman who reveals Himself in the world of multiplicity and acts in and through His creation This is pantheism. When Dr. Radhakrishnan says, 'the Upaniṣads are not pantheistic in the bad sense of the term', what he means is that in the bad sense pantheism is a hollow monism that maintains the unity of the Absolute at the cost of the world of multiplicity. The Upaniṣads are not pantheistic in this sense. He rightly remarks :— "It is pantheism, if it is pantheism to say that God is the fundamental reality of our lives and we can not live without Him.........If the doctrine of the indwelling of the divine is enough justification for condemning a system as pantheism, the philosophy of the Upaniṣads is a pantheism. But pantheism in this sense is an essential feature of all true religion".[34]

Two concepts of Brahman: Mūrta (Cosmic) and Amūrta (Acosmic).

The expatiations of the Upaniṣads referred to in our previous discussion point unmistakably to the pantheistic doctrine that follows necessarily from the cosmic or Mūrta concept of Brahman. But another concept of Brahman is developed side by side in the Upaniṣads and this is known as Amūrta or acosmic concept. The former is changing, concrete and dynamic and is naturally amenable to our senses, while the latter is unmoving, abstract and static. In fact the discussion on these two concepts has been introduced as a means of reconciling the apparent inconsistencies and con-

34. Dr. S. Radhakrishnan : 'Indian Philosophy',—Vol. I. P-203.

tradictions involved in the varied definitions of the terms 'Ātman' and 'Brahman' as found in the texture of the Upaniṣads. Let us see how.

There are passages which define Ātman in the affirmative style[35] Again there are statements defining what Brahman or Ātman is not. The approach here is negative and the Reality is said to be not so, not so (neti neti). In the Yājñavalka-Gārgī episode of the Bṛhadāraṇyaka Upaniṣad (3.8.8.) Brahman is described negatively thus : "That is, which the wise call 'Imperishable' ; it is neither thick nor thin, neither short nor long, neither red like fire, nor fluid like water, neither shadowy nor dark, neither wind nor space, not touched, without taste or smell, without eye or ear, without speech, without understanding, without vital force, without breath, without mouth or size, without inside or outside, never consuming anything, nor consumed by any". Śuch statements as these blatantly contradict the positive affirmation mentioned elsewhere. It is on the basis of these statements that the famous western critic Keith observes : "Contradictions in adjecto are the normal characteristics of the Upaniṣads".[36] ...... "The hopeless inconsistencies of the view of Yājñavalka become painfully obvious".[37] But in our view what is 'painfully obvious' is the inability of Keith in grasping the real import of the Upaniṣadic teaching. It is perhaps the absence of avidity or sympathetic understanding in him that led him to advance this diatribe against the Upaniṣads, Inconsistencies in statements are certainly there in the Upaniṣads, but they are all apparent and not real. It is two concepts of Brahman-Saprapañca and niṣprapañca, apara and para, mūrta and amūrta, or cosmic and acosmic-that remove all

35. Bṛha. Up. 2. 4. 6. Chān. Up.—3. 14. 1.

36. A. B. Keith : Philosophy of the Vedas and the Upaniṣads, P-587.

37. Ibid : P-594.

inconsistencies, for they are but the two distinct forms of one, and the same Brahman. According to mūrta concept, Reality is sought to be identified with its manifestations. This is why the statements made in this connection are all affirmative. But the para or amūrta concept being not so related to the manifestations, the description of Brahman in such a case is naturally negative. The question still remains-are these two concepts of Brahman distinct or identical ? If they are really identical, what arguments are adduced in support of this view ? Before we come to this analysis, let us make a brief survey as to how these two concepts figure in the Upaniṣads.

The Bṛhadāraṇyaka Upaniṣad states: Brahman has two forms-the concrete and the abstract, the mortal and the immortal, the unmoving and the moving, the manifest and the unmanifest.[38] In the sensible world there is always a contact between two contrary entities viz., the knower and the known. Unless there is some such dualism there can be no scope for any perception or knowledge of 'the given'. When this dualism is admitted we can have access to Brahman as revealed in the world of sound, colour, touch, taste and smell. It is here that we get the idea of mūrta Brahman. When however., this dualism vanishes, the world of multiplicity disappears, and this leads to the conception of abstract monism according to which Brahman is static and unmoving, immortal and indestructible. This is amply illustrated in the Chāndogya Upaniṣad in the following words: 'when none perceives the other, none knows or hears the other, we get Bhūmā, but when one perceives the other, one hears or knows the other then that is limited (alpa). Bhūmā is indestructible, but the limited is subject

38. "Dve vāva brahmaṇo rūpe mūrtaṁ ca'ivāmūrtaṁ ca, martyaṁ cāmṛtaṁ ca sthitaṁ ca yacca sacca tyacca"—Bṛha. Up. 2. 3. 1.

to destruction'.[39] We sometimes find the juxtaposition of these two conceptions of Brahman in one and the same passage. In the Muṇḍaka Upaniṣad, for example, we have what is invisible, intangible, colourless, nameless, eyeless and earless, devoid of hands and feet—that is what is coeval with time and space, is all-pervading, subtle and changeless, which the wise know to be the source of all beings.[40] A fine description of the amūrta conception is found in the Kaṭhopanisad where it is remarked : 'Ātman is devoid of sound, touch, colour, taste and smell, is eternal and indestructible.[41] Thus instances can be multiplied to show that the mūrta and the amūrta conception of Brahman have been developed almost simultaneously in the Upaniṣads. It is also asserted in the same breath by the sages that the mūrta (Āparabrahman) and the amūrta (Parabrahman) are virtually the two different concepts of the same Brahman.[42] We find a clearer exposition of this idea in the Māṇḍukya Upaniṣad which deserves special mention. In analysing the nature of Brahman it has been said here that all this is Brahman ; Ātman is Brahman anb this Ātman admits of four-fold stages.[43] The first three stages describe the self as the enjoyer and the fourth stage refers to the amūrta ideal. The sense of dualism prevailing in the first three stages in the form of the enjoyer and the enjoyed is shown to have been enfeebled gradually. Let us see how.

39. "Yatra nānyat paśyati nānyat śṛṇoti nānyadvijānāti sa Bhumā'tha yatrānyat paśyati anyat śṛṇoti anyat vijānāti tadalpaṁ, yo' vai Bhūma tadamṛtamatha yadalpaṁ tanmartyaṁ..."—Chān. Up. 7.24.1.

40. "Yattadadreśyamagrāhyamagotramavarṇam acakṣuḥ śrotraṁ tadapāṇipādam, nityaṁ vibhuṁ sarvagataṁ susūkṣmaṁ tadavyayaṁ yadbhūtayoniṁ paripaśyanti dhīrāḥ.—Muṇḍ. Up. 1 1.6.

41. "Aśavdamasparśamarūpamavyayaṁ tathārasaṁ nityamagandhavacca Yat'...Kaṭha. Up. 1. 3. 15.

42. —Praśno'paniṣad, 5. 2. Here the sage Pippalād speaks to Satyakāma that the same Brahman is Para and Apara.

43. "Sarvaṁ hi etad Brahma, ayamātmā, Brahma So'yamātmā catuṣpāt." —Māṇḍukya Up. 2.

In the waking experience when an individual appears as an enjover and the entire world with all its sound, colour, touch, taste and smell as the object enjoyed, the sense of dualism is quite prominent. Hence the soul in waking experience is known as 'Bahiḥprajña i.e., conscious of the sensible world. In the dream experience that constitutes the second stage, the sense of dualism becomes comparatively feeble. Here the enjoyer is present, but the object enjoyed is only imaginary and not real. Hence the soul here is said to be 'Antaḥprajña'. The third stage is that of dreamless sleep (Suṣupti) where dualism almost vanishes atleast temporarily. So long as this state continues to exist there is no dualism whatsoever, but as soon as one is awake dualism appears again. The soul at this stage is known as 'Prajñānaghana' which asserts its own reality only, and in spite of its capacity to know, it can not have any knowledge. But even this stage is not campletely devoid of a sort of latent knowledge or feeling, since after being awake from profound dreamless sleep one remembers the peaceful state of sleep. The fourth stage, however, is radically different from the previous three stages, since in all the three stages discussed, dualism exists in some form or other, but in the fourth stage it vanishes altogether. Here Ātman exists as the only reality-one without a second. The world of multiplicity ceases to exist. This stage is one of unqualified monism.[44]

Creation : immanence and transcendence of Brahman.

In the foregoing analysis we have adumbrated that the mūrta and the amūrta concepts are explained in the Upani-

44. "Nāntaḥprajñaṁ na bahiḥ prajñaṁ no'bhayataḥ prajñaṁ na prajñānaghanaṁ na prajñaṁ nā'prajñaṁ.
Adṛśyamavyavahāryamagrāhyamalakṣaṇamacintyamavyāpadeśyamekatmapratyayasāraṁ prapañco'paśamaṁ sāntaṁ śivamadvaitṁ caturthaṁ manyante sa ātmā sa vijñeyaḥ".—Māṇḍukya Up.—7.

ṣads as having denoted the same Reality i.e., Brahman. Now we have to explain how actually the Upaniṣadic sages accomplish this task.

There is, in fact, no ambiguity in the Upaniṣads in pronouncing that Brahman or Ātman[45] is the root cause of the world. The term Brahman signifies its creative nature. But this gives rise to a dilemma. If creation is a fact—and since creation necessarily implies change, Brahman as the cause must undergo change. In that case His immutability is lost. Again if Brahman is Immutable, change must be denied of Him and creation then becomes a misnomer. The Upaniṣads, however, steer clear of this dilemma. Dr. G. Mukhopadhyay has enlightened us in the matter when he aptly maintains: "The Upaniṣads unfailingly point out the two broad features of Reality viz., 'Agni' and 'Ātman'. The whole structure of the Upaniṣadic wisdom rests on these two conceptions, and it is through the instrument of these two principles that the Upaniṣads solve all problems, however hard, with an ease that is striking and remarkable"[46] We may take a few examples. A telling proposition occurs in the Kaṭho'paniṣad viz., 'All these worldly objects emerge

---

45. The terms 'Brahman' and 'Ātman' widely differ in their original connotations. 'Brahman' seems at first to have meant 'Prayer', being derived from the root 'bṛha' meaning 'to grow' or 'to burst forth'. Brahman as prayer is what manifests itself in audible speech. From this should have been derived later the philosophic significance which it bears in the Upaniṣads viz, the primary cause of the universe – what bursts forth spontaneously in the form of nature as a whole and not as mere 'speech'. This derivation is given by MaxMüller in his 'Six Systems of Indian Philosophy' (P—52-55). As to 'Ātman' MaxMuller says: "In all probability Ātman originally meant 'breath' and then came to be applied to whatever constitutes the essential part of anything, more particularly of man i. e., his self or soul". (Ibid: P—70-72).

46. Dr. Govindagopal Mukhopadhyay :—'Studies in the Upaniṣads' Ch. I, P—48.

from Prāṇa'.[47] Equally pregnant with thought is the passage found in the Praśno' paniṣad—"All that is in earth and in heavens are under the control of Prāṇa.[48] Thus Agni or Prāṇa creates and sustains the entire existence. It is the conscious creative force as against Bergson's 'Elan Vital' which in spite of being a creative principle is blind and mechanical. The thought element and creativity or execution proceed from the same source. It is for this reason that in the Chāndogya Upaniṣad (1. 1. 8.) Prāṇa is said to be 'anujñā' or the command and 'Samardhaitā'—the executor of the flow of creation. Change or manifestation of Brahman is, therefore, accounted for with the help of the conception of 'Prāṇa.' Now if Brahman is changeful, how then can it be said to be 'Immutable' at the same time ? The question is answered and thereby the apparent contradiction resolved with the help of the concept of Ātman which is said to be transcendent.[49] Thus as 'Agni' or 'Prāṇa' Reality is immanent, as Ātman it is transcendent. It should be noted here that immanence and transcendence as explained in the Upaniṣads are totally different from the western view, for according to western scholars these two conceptions are considered diametrically opposed to each other. Immanence in their view means complete identification of God with His creation and when God is said to be transcendent He is supposed to be completely aloof from the world existing 'far from the madding crowd'. The theories of 'Pantheism' and 'deism' have been developed accordingly in the west. Between these two ex-

---

47. "Yadidaṁ kiñca jagat sarvaṁ prāṇe ejati niḥsṛtam".
— Kaṭha Up.—2.3.2.

48. "Prāṇasy'edaṁ vaśe sarvaṁ tridive yat pratiṣṭhitam".
—Praśna Up.—2.13.

49. In the 'Janaka-Yājñavalka' episode in the Bṛhadāraṇyaka Upaniṣad (4.3.16.) Ātman is defined thus : 'Asaṅgo'hi ayaṁ Puruṣaḥ',—meaning that it remains unaffected by the colourful changes wrought over it and retains its nature untarnished.

tremes stands the theory of 'Panentheism' according to which Reality is said to be immanent but partly transcendent. But in the Upaniṣads Brahman who is immanent has at the same time been declared transcendent without involving any contradiction. The Upaniṣadic conceptions of transcendence and immanence have been explained by Dr. G. Mukhopadhyay with adequate clarity and precision. In his opinion "Brahman of the Upaniṣads is not a unitary principle which is opposed to the multiplicity of creation".[50] He has referred to a very terse but significant statement of the Taittirīya Upaniṣad (2.6.3.) viz., 'tat sṛṣṭvā tadevānuprāviśat'—which means –'having created this all, it (i e., Brahman) has veritably entered into it'. To quote Dr. Mukhopadhyay—"The 'anupraveśa', the entering into creation, the very fact of immanence signifies its transcendence, because here the entering or 'anupraveśa' does not indicate the entering of one thing into another, but rather means that by the act of creation the Śupreme Reality has made itself acces sible to the intellect (buddhi). This access to the intellect is the true significance of 'anupraveśa'. But the intellect is the subtlest thing, being the very first and foremost principle in creation, and naturally that which can enter even into the subtlest thing must be subtler still. Hence Brahman surpasses even the intellect in subtleness and thus easily enters into it ; and being subtler than the intellect it is not touched or tainted by any of the blemishes of the intellect. By the very fact of its entering, it proves its transcending nature. Transcendence thus always signifies the uniqueness, the 'Vilakṣaṇatā', the distinctness of Brahman and never any exclusiveness or apartness".[51]

The exhortations of Yājñavalka in explaining the nature of Ātman in a negative way, should also be understood to

50. Dr. G. Mukhopadhyay : 'Studies in the Upansads'.—P. 51.
51. Ibid :—P 51-52.

mean the uniqueness of Ātman and not its exclusiveness as is normally understood. Thus 'neti neti' never denies the reality of existence, rather it denies the empirical characterization of Reality. To quote Dr. Mukhopadhyay again,—' If we keep this sense of denial in mind then it will be clear that the denial of attributes and qualifications to Brahman does not reduce it to a void, but on the contrary, to its inexhaustible fullness which remains absolutely undiminished even after the whole of creation streams out of it".[52] This is well indicated at the beginning of the Īśo' paniṣad.[53]

Uniqueness of the Upaniṣadic Pantheism.

We have seen so far that the ancient Upaniṣads attach due importance to both the concepts of Brahman—cosmic and acosmic, manifest and unmanifest, saprapañca and niṣprapañca finally to mean that both these co. epts signify one and the same Reality. Our purpose has been to demonstrate the pantheistic view (following from the cosmic concept) as the kernel of the Upaniṣadic teaching. But there are thinkers who strongly demur to this view. They adopt on the contrary, a non-dualistic standpoint and try to explain away the world. Before we can fully bring out the uniqueness of the Upaniṣadic pantheism we have to take cognizance of and also examine critically some such pejorative views.

On an analysis of the theories of creation as explained in the Upaniṣads, Deussen arrives at the conclusion that there is virtually no such thing as creation. In his view the spatio-temporal world is just an appearance or illusion and Brahman alone is real. To know Brahman we must reject the world of appearance. Dr. Radhakrishnan's rejoinder on

52 Ibid : P.—52.

53. "Pūrṇasya pūrṇamādāya
Pūrṇamevā'vaśiṣyate".—Īśo'paniṣad.

Deussen's verdict is worth considering here. He says : "What inclines Deussen to this view is his own belief that the essence of every true religion is the repudiation of the reality of the world. Having come to that conclusion on independent grounds, he is anxious to find support for his doctrine in the philosophic systems of ancient India. the Upaniṣads and Śaṁkara, ancient Greece, Permenides and Plato and modern Germany, Kant and Schopenhauer. In his eagerness to find support for his position he is not very careful about facts".[54] It is interesting to note that Deussen considers pantheism to be the 'prevailing doctrine' of the Upaniṣads, but in the same breath he seeks to maintain that the fundamental doctrine is the 'illusion hypothe̊is' (māyā vāda). In support of Deussen, Fraser also points out that the Upaniṣads advocate repeatedly the non-duality of the Ātman or Brahman as the sole reality. Illusionism, therefore, follows logically from such a concept. But both Deussen and Fraser are mistaken in assessing the purport of the Upaniṣads and consequently in nullifying the validity of the world of multiplicity. The Upaniṣads declare nowhere that the Infinite excludes the finite. In analysing the nature of Brahman the Upaniṣadic writers are careful enough to add that the world being rooted in Brahman has a share of reality. "From the doctrine of the sole reality of Brahman follows the relative reality of what is included in or based on it."[55] E. W. Hopkins agrees to this view, for he also holds that the ancient Upaniṣads do not declare the world as illusion. Hence the richness of the worldly life with all its variety can not, except by flouting logic, be reduced to an empty dream.

Following the cosmic conception of Brahman the Upaniṣads thus maintain that creation is a fact and that all

54. Dr. S. Radhakrishnan : 'Indian Philosophy ; Vol. I, P—189.

55. Ibid : P—190.

things flow from Him, are sustained by Him and are reabsorbed into Him. But the question may crop up—what is this creation for ? To put it otherwise,—why does Brahman feel the urge to abandon His state of pure unity and manifest Himself in this world of variety ? A luculent explanation is given by the Upaniṣadic writers themselves. The Supreme Reality is 'Rasavān'.[56] His nature is such that He wants to have a taste of joy, pure and unsullied. He enjoys the blissful existence only in being many on the basis of dualism. As a matter of fact there can be no real joy unless there are atleast two beings. In an unmixed state of unitary existence where communication of ideas, feelings or emotions is not possible, there is no scope for real joy. It is only when there is a dualism that one can communicate one's thoughts to the other.[57] Hence the sages imply that as Brahman could not remain content with His absolute unity, He manifested Himself in many concrete forms. The Chāndogya and the Bṛhadāraṇyaka Upaniṣads are precise on the point. "All this was one and non-dual at the beginning ; He could not by Himself derive joy and so He wanted the second.[58] He thus desired : 'I shall be many. I shall be produced or transmuted.[59] Thus emerged the two – the knower and the known, the perceiver and the perceived, the enjoyer and the enjoyed. In a word, the world of variety with all its sound, colour, touch, taste and smell came into being. This was necessary for the revelation of the joyous or blissful

56. "Raso'vai Saḥ. Rasaṁ hi evā'yaṁ labdhvānandī bhavati"
—Taittirīya Up.—2.7.2.

57. "Yatra hi dvaitamiva bhavati taditara itaraṁ jighrati taditara itaraṁ paśyati taditara itaraṁ śṛṇoti taditara itaraṁ manute taditara itaraṁ vijānāti..." – Bṛha. Up. 2.4.14.

58. "Sat eva...idamagra āsīdekamevā lvitīyam".—Chān. Up. 6.2.1.
"sa vai naiva reme. Tasmādekākī na ramate. Sa dvitīyamaichhat".
—Bṛha. Up. 1.4.3.

59. "So'kāmayata – Bahusyāṁprajāyeye'ti".—Taitti. Up. 2.6.3.

nature of Brahman. This line of thought has been poetized by Rabindranath with exceptional charm.[60] The seers of the Upaniṣads thus want to emphasize the fact that Brahman left His unapproachable solitude as it were and having left the ivory tower of pure unity transformed Himself into this world of multiplicity on the basis of a dualistic notion. Thus

60. The amūrta or acosmic conception of Brahman is given a fine poetic rendering by Rabindranath when he says :—

"The metaphysician (tattvajñānī) chants
rhythmically with his breath :
No, No, No—
Neither emerald. nor ruby, nor light, nor flower (rose)
Nor I, nor you.
On the other hand the One who is without limit,
is seriously engaged in creative
activity within man ;
'I' stands for that."

But the poet in the spirit of the Upaniṣads again, betrays in the next few lines of the same poem his leaning to the cosmic concept of Brahman based on a sense of dualism. So he says :—

"In the depth of that (Subjective) 'I'
Light made contact with darkness
And then emerged embodied forms,
and feelings awakened ;
By the touch of magic words
'No' became transformed into 'Yes',
In lines and colours,
in pleasure and pain".

—Rabindranath Tagore : 'Āmi' (Śyāmalī-Sañcayitā P—713).

Rabindranath thus seems to have a conviction that when the Supreme Spirit leaves His secluded and arid state of existence and pervades this world of multiplicity, He is revealed in a better and fuller way. This Brahman is known as 'Ānanda'. Hence the poet rhapsodizes on the 'mūrta' or cosmic conception and gives a luscious poetic expression of this idea in another poem thus :—

"The way the Supreme One eager for tasting joy,
Derives happiness by imposing duality on Himself,
And the unique shock of the impact between the two
Blossoms into colour. smell and music continuously".

– Rabindranath : 'Ramaṇī' (Sañcayitā P—449)

creation virtually affords Brahman an opportunity of exhibiting His luminosity and at the same time illuminating all objects of the jejune and work-a-day world. The world with all its living creatures as well as non-living objects looks sweet, graceful and resplendent. Hence the pervasion of this cosmic spirit in the universe overwhelms the sages of the Upaniṣads to such a degree as to make them discover and extol the immeasurable sweetness and beauty of the mundane existence. This world becomes sweet to all the creatures and vice versa.[61] The cosmic spirit which thus expresses Himself by encom-passing the entire existence is greeted by the sages as 'Ānandam'. The Muṇḍaka Upaniṣad states :— "The discerning see by their superior intuitive knowledge, the Ātman which shines with all bliss and immortality.[62]

Now it is true that the ordinary people are lacking in clairvoyance of the ancient sages and naturally they fail to get to the bottom of the Upaniṣadic message. According to these people and certain other dilettanti life is not all beer and skittles. Hence an apparently pertinent question raised by them is,—can there be any scope for genuine joy or 'ānanda' in the face of the fact that the worldly life is beset with so many ills and imperfections ? In the flow and flux of life we always come across birth and death, creation and destruction, pleasure and pain, love and hate, hope and despair. Can the Upaniṣadic message, therefore, give us any

---

61. "Iyaṁ pṛthivī sarveṣāṁ bhūtānāṁ madhu. Asyai pṛthivyai sarvāṇi bhūtāni madhu. Yaśca ayamasyāṁ pṛthivyāṁ tejomayo'—mṛtamayaḥ puruṣo' yaśca ayamadhyātmaṁ śārīrastejomayo'mṛtamayaḥ puruṣaḥ ayameva sa yaḥ ayamātmedaṁ aṁṛtamidaṁ Brahmedaṁ sarvam". —Bṛha. Up. 2.5.1.

The same Upaniṣad again declares :—"Madhu vātā ṛtāyate madhu kṣaranti sindhavaḥ, ...madhu naktamutaṣaso, madhumat pārthivaṁ rajaḥ. 6.3.6.

62. "Tadvijñānena paripaśyanti dhīrā ānandarūpamamṛtaṁ yadvibhāti". —Muṇḍaka Up. 2.2.8.

lasting impression and act as a solace to mankind ? All such interrogations and disputes are clinched by the Upaniṣadic sages themselves[63] according to whom a narrow outlook generated from 'avidyā' leads one to the abyss of despair. But if one resorts to parāvidyā and thus adopts a wider standpoint, one can feel the presence of one all-embracing spirit in the world of diversity. This helps us widen our outlook and catholicize our heart. We can feel that all the mutually exclusive and incongruous elements of mundane existence have their respective contributions and that none can be annulled without any prejudice to life as such. It does not appear difficult for us to understand that pain and suffering, death add destruction have as much importance as pleasure and comfort, life and creation. Parāvidyā helps us reach that stage when we can make the best of a bad bargain and are not adversely affected by the stings of sufferings or pangs of separation caused by death.[64] Thus all the heterogenous elements taken together constitute the world of pure joy—and we can share this joy or 'ānanda' only because in the midst of many we find 'One Supreme Spirit'[65] accepting all and rejecting none. This conception is indeed unique of its kind, and the joy we derive is priceless and immeasurable.

---

63. Cf. Dr. Hiranmoy Bandyopadhyay : 'Upaniṣader Darśan' P—85-86.
64. "Avidyayā mṛtyuṁ tīrtva vidyayā amṛtamaśnute"—Īśa Up.—11.
65. (i) "Manasai'vedamāptavyaṁ neha nānā'stī kiñcana,
Mṛtyoḥ sa mṛtyuṁ gachhati ya iha nāneva paśyati".
—Kaṭha Up. 2. 1. 11.

(ii) An identical sloka occurs in the Bṛhadāraṇyaka Upaniṣad (4. 4. 19).

(iii) "Yasmin sarvāṇi bhūtāṇi atmaivābhūd vijānataḥ,
Tatra ko' mohaḥ kaḥśoka ekatvamanupaśyataḥ.

(iv) "The uttermost distance I explore
with my mind and heart
in the boundless expanse
which Thou art,
I find no trace of sorrow,
death and separation".
—Rabindranath Tagore : Pūjā, Gītavitān, P-234.) No. 596)

SECTION 2

IMPACT ON THE NINETEENTH CENTURY WESTERN PHILOSOPHY

CHAPTER—III

Journey of the Upaniṣads to the West.

Our task in this section is to demonstrate how the Upaniṣadic thought had left an impact on the philosophical theories of the west in the nineteenth century. So long as the Upaniṣads were not translated into any European language, they remained as impervious as ever to the western scholars. It was Abraham Hyacin The Anquetil Duperron (1731-1805) to whom the credit of making the Upaniṣads accessible to the western world is due. Let us see how he undertook this pioneering venture.

Translation of the Upaniṣads.

The brilliance of the Upaniṣadic thought invited the attention of Dara Śhikoh, the eldest son of emperor Shajahan. A learned scholar and well-versed in Sanskrit language, Dara penetrated deep into the religious treatises of the Hindus and found that the Hindu thought was fundamentally the same as the Islamic thought. This he substantiated is his work 'Mazumā ue Vāharin' published in Persian language. When he was on tour to Kashmir he collected fifty two Upaniṣads and with the aid and effective guidance of the Kashmir Pundits he rendered these Upaniṣads into Persian in 1656.[1] The name of these collected works was—"Sirri

1. "He (Dara Shikoh) seems first to have heard of the Upaniṣads during his stay in Kashmir in 1640. He afterwards invited several Pundits from Benaras to Delhi who were to assist him in the work of translation. The translation was finished in 1656".

Vidc :—MaxMuller : 'The Sacred Books of the East', Vol—I. Introduction.

Akbar"—meaning mysterious knowledge. This work comprises four parts viz., (i) Introduction by Dara himself, (ii) the list of the translated Upaniṣads, iii) Persian rendering of the Upaniṣads and (iv) Word meanings – persian and Sanskrit. In the introduction Dara states that he undertook this task of propagating the message of the Upaniṣads for the spiritual uplift of himself as also of his near relations. This Persian rendering had a wide publicity.

Long after (in 1755) Anquetil Duperron, the French Scholar of repute came to India with a mission of being acquainted with the oriental thought, During his stay for about six years in India (1755-1761) he had collected about two hundred treatises including Persian and Sanskrit texts of the Vedic period. With the assistance of the Brahmin Pundits he got many Sanskrit texts translated into Persian language. It is during this period that he was acquainted with fifty Upaniṣads translated into Persian by Dara Shikoh. On his return to paris in 1762, Duperron's first venture was the publication of the 'Āvestā'—the persian religious treatise in original and also in French in 1771. But perhaps the greatest achievement of Duperron was the Latin translation of Dara Shiko's Persian rendering of the Upaniṣads ("Oupnek' hat......." 2 Vols). MaxMüller enlightens us on this point.[2]

2. "It is true that under Akbar's reign (1556-1586) similar translations had been prepared, but neither those, nor the translations of Dara Shikoh attracted the attention of European scholars till the year 1775. In that year Anquetil Duperron, the famous traveller and the discoverer of the 'Zend Āvestā' received one MS. of the Persian translation of the Upaniṣads sent to him by M. Gentil, the French resident at the court of Sujauddaula and brought to France by M. Bernier. After receiving another MS. Anquetil Duperron collated the two and translated the Persian translation into French and into Latin.

The Latin translation was published in 1801-1802".

Vide :—Maxmuller . 'The Sacred Books of the East',—Vol. I. ; Introduction.

By virtue of his keen and assiduous search for oriental knowledge, untiring tenacity and unparalleled patience and perseverence Duperron came out successful in his mission of propagating the message of the ancient Indian philosophy in the western countries. His Latin translation of the Upaniṣads obliterated the barrier caused by the Sanskrit language and made the Upaniṣadic teaching easily intelligible to the western scholars, for Latin was then not only one of the chief languages of the intellectuals, but was also widely known and cultivated in European countries. It is well-known to all that Raja Rammohan Roy translated a good number of the Upaniṣads into English in the early nineteenth century (1816-1819), and that these translations were widely appreciated in Europe. But there is no gainsaying that in the west the real impetus to study Sanskrit in general and the Upaniṣads in particular came much earlier from Duperron's Latin translation. It is also undeniable that prior to Duperron a few European scholars had undertaken the trouble in acquiring the knowledge of oriental literature and in disseminating the same in the west.[3] Before the

3. It must, however, be noted that with the foundation of 'Asiatic Society' in Calcutta in 1784 by William Jones, an attempt was made to learn and propagate the oriental culture. English traslations by William Jones of (i) Kalidāsa's 'Abhijñāna Śakuntalam' in 1789, (ii) Viṣnu śarmā's 'Pañcatantra' in 1791, (iii) Joydev's 'Geet-govinda' (published immediately after the death of Jones i.e., after 1794), (iv) 'Manusaṁhitā' (translated) jointly by Jones and Wilkins in 1794), and the English translation by Charles Wilkins of (i) The Bhagavadgītā (the first English version of the Gītā)—published in London in 1785 by the directors of East India Company on the recommendation of Waren Hastings, and of (ii) 'Hitopadeś' published in Bath in 1787—are some of the remarkable undertakings which make it clear that prior to Duperron's Latin translation of the Upaniṣads, the European Scholars had some opportunity of being acquainted with the vast treasures of Sanskrit literature.—Vide :—Gouranga Gopal Sengupta : 'Videśīya Bhārata Vidyā Pathik'.—P 12-35.

publication of the Latin translation Duperron is understood to have made a French translation of the Upaniṣads in 1775. But nothing is definitely known as to how far the French translation was circulated. The Latin rendering, however, was widely circulated and was greeted with ardour and enthusiasm, so much so, that many a thinker of the west had deeply imbibed the spirit of the Upaniṣadic philosophy. Schelling and Schopenhauer stand out as the two chief German philosophers of the nineteenth century who, we shall see presently, were profoundly influenced by the Upaniṣadic thought.

But the real impetus to know the Vedic literature in particular came from Duperron, and Wilkins and Jones are not understood to have done anything in this regard.

CHAPTER—IV

Friedrich Wilhelm Joseph (Von) Schelling (1775-1854)

Introduction : Schelling's acquaintance with the Upaniṣads.

In the history of western philosophical thought it is in the system of Schelling that a direct impact of the Upaniṣadic pantheism can be discovered for the first time. Anquetil Duperron's French translation of the Upaniṣads was published in 1775, the year of Schelling's birth. The major works of Schelling, we know, came to light at the fag end of tne 18th and the beginning of the 19th century. As to the circulation of the French translation nothing is definitely known and the Latin rendering was published in 1801-1802. Some of the principal works of Schelling had already been published by this time. The question may naturally arise as to how and when Schelling was influenced by the Upaniṣadic thought.

The first point in favour of the observation we have made is that Schelling had the opportunity of studying the French rendering of the Upaniṣads, and the inference that Schelling actually read those renderings contains a high degree of probability. Further Schelling had a deep admiration for the Upaniṣads—a fact which is corroborated by MaxMüller when he says : "That Schelling and his school should use rapturous language about the Upaniṣads might carry little weight with that large class of philosophers by whom everything beyond the clouds of their own horizon is labelled mysticism".[1] In recording his personal experience in 'The Sacred Books of the East' MaxMüller says that he had the privilege of coming in close contact with Schelling

1. MaxMuller : 'The Sacred Books of the East', Vol-I. Introduction.

at Berlin when Schelling was a teacher of the Berlin University and MaxMüller a student. To quote MaxMüller again : "My real love for Sanskrit literature was first kindled by the Upaniṣads. It was in the year 1844 when attending Schelling's lectures at Berlin that my attention was drawn to those ancient theosophic treatises and I still possess my collation of Sanskrit M/SS which had then arrived at Berlin, the Chambers Collection and my copies of commentaries and commentaries on commentaries which I made at that time. Some of my translations which I left with Schelling I have never been able to recover".[2] The intimate personal relation which MaxMüller had developed with Schelling bears out that Schelling had been entertaining for long a keen interest in and deep reverence for the profound teachings of the Upaniṣads. It is for this reason that he eagerly desired a wide circulation of the Upaniṣads and insisted on MaxMüller's translating those immortal treatises. This attitude of Schelling obviously brings out that he must have had some acquaintance with the Upaniṣads much earlier. We can, therefore, reasonably infer that his philosophy is influenced to a considerable degree by the Upaniṣadic teaching. His pantheism as we shall explain here, will go a long way in ratifying our impression.

Distinct phases of Schelling's thought.

What we must note at the beginning of our analysis is that in the history of modern western philosophy Schelling's reputation has considerably been on the wane and he has been given very little attention by the critics and historians presumably for the fact that there is no closely knit system which can properly be called Schelling's system of thought. The different phases of his philosophy are found to have recorded the different currents of thought and it is difficult

2. Ibid : Vol I. Introduction.

to trace any logical connection between the preceding thought and the succeeding one.[3] It is also difficult to ascertain the exact number of phases through which Schelling's thoughts seem to have passed. The programme for a system of philosophy as drawn up by Schelling in his youth (in 1796) helps us know the province of philosophy he wanted to cover.[4] This programme, apparently quite illuminating, amply illustrates a sort of discontinuity in his thought. Starting from all the Fichtean trappings of his early writings down to the posthumously published works such as 'Philosophie der Offenbarung' (Philosophy of Revelation) and 'Philosophie der Mythologie' (Philosophy of Mythology) certain distinct phases can be traced. But no such claim, if there be any, can be vindicated that each of these phases constitutes a self-enclosed system. Schelling's works as per his premeditated programme illustrate only the continuity of his philosophising, not the continuity of his thoughts or ideas. Hence his philosophy is just philosophising rather than a finished and coherent system.

In the first phase of his philosophical career Schelling is found to have developed his Philosophy of Nature[5] which

3. Probably it is for this reason that Schelling has been ignored by the modern critics. Will Durant has completely eliminated Schelling's philosophy from his 'Story of Philosophy'. Russell also leaves no room for any discussion on Schelling in his History of Philosophy.

4. Vide : Frederick Copleston : 'A History of Philosophy'—Vol-7. P-125.

5. In 1797 Schelling published 'Ideen Zu einer philosophie der Natur' (Ideas towards a philosophy of Natnre, in 1798 'Von der Weltseele' (On the World Soul), in 1799 'Easter Entwurf eines Systems der Naturphilosophie' (First sketch of a system of the philosophy of Nature), and 'Einleitung Zu dem Entwurf eines system der Naturphilosophie, oder über den Begriff der Speku lativen Physik' (An Introduction to the sketch of a system of the Philosophy of Nature, or on the concept of Speculative Physics.)

led him to the concept of a 'World Soul' which is very much akin to the concept of Brahman developed in the Upaniṣads. In his series of publications on the philosophy of Nature Schelling moves from the objective to subjective, from the lowest grades of Nature to the organic sphere. But his 'Transcendental Idealism[6] published immediately after this series shows the influence of Fichte's theory of Science ('Wissenschaftslehre') because here Schelling starts with the ego and proceeds to trace the process of its self-objectification. His transcendental idealism, however, culminates in a philosophy of art, for in 1802-03 he lectured on the philosophy of art at Jena and declared art as the key to the nature of reality. This fact alone is adequate to show the marked difference between his outlook and that of Fichte. The philosophical treatises that followed subsequently viz., 'Exposition of the true relation of Nature Philosophy to amended Fichtean views', 'Philosophy of Religion' etc. indicate a departure to a completely new direction of thought. At the early stage of his thought Schelling conceives God as an all-comprehensive Reality. But later he seems to have been influenced by Plato and accordingly holds that the Infinite is the only Reality and the world of finite beings is not real.[7] This evidently

---

6. 'System des transzendentalen Idealismus'—Published in 1800, was followed in 1801 by short piece 'On the true concept of the Philosophy of Nature' ('Über den wahren Begriff der Naturphilosophie').

7. We deem it necessary to touch upon the viewpoint of Plato in this connection.

In his 'Dialectic' or 'the theory of Ideas' Plato has dealt at length with the fundamental philosophical question viz., what the ultimate reality is. According to Plato it is the 'Ideas' which are universal, immutable, timeless, non-spatial and essence of things. In the hierarchy of Ideas there is one highest 'Idea' which is the absolutely real Being, the ultimate ground of itself and of other Ideas and of the entire universe. This idea, Plato says, is the 'Idea of the Good', which he equates with God in his 'Philebus'.

contradicts his earlier viewpoint on God and His relation to the finite world. As a matter of fact Schelling seems to be drifting to a different position under the influence of Jacob Böehme—a mystical thinker of the late 16th and early 17th century.[8] Schelling's earlier conviction of the intel-

The details of Plato's analysis on the deduction of different Ideas from the Supreme Idea of the Good need not be mentioned here. But what must be noted is that Plato was very much aware of the existence of the world of finite things. He also believed that an abstract monism (such as that of the Eleatics) can never explain the world of existence, for multiplicity can never be denied. Absolute Reality, in his view, must not be an abstract one, but a many in one. In his 'Physics' or 'the theory of existence' Plato takes up this problem and attempts (though not successfully) to explain how the world of sense and in general the entire existent universe arise from Ideas. The objects of the world of sense, as he tells us, are the copies or imitations of the Ideas. Now since the Ideas are the only reality or absolute Being, objects of sense are not-being except in so far as the Ideas are in them. Objects of sense are then half real and half unreal. Whatever reality they have, they owe to the Ideas. They, in other words, participate in Being and hence are partly real. But they are also partly unreal as they participate in not-being. By this Plato indicates that there is also a principle of not-being which is 'matter'—an unqualified, formless, featureless, chaotic mass. This point need not be dilated on here. Again as to the question—how the Ideas can give rise to things or copies of themselves or how the production of these copies is effected, Plato gives no convincing answer. He only resorts to myths and poetic descriptions (as is evident in his 'Timaeus') instead of any scientific explanation. These points, however, are left out here as unnecessary for us. All that we want to point out by our brief reference to Plato's thought, and on which almost all the critics agree, is that Schelling's idea of the Infinite and His relation to the world as it is found at the later stage of his philosophical thought, roughly corresponds to Plato's concept of the highest Idea as related to the sensible world.

8. Jacob Böehme, the founder of theosophical mysticism is considered by many the first German philosopher. Although he is not found to have constructed a systematic and coherent system of thought, his religious views, nevertheless, inspired many thinkers and

lectual perception of the Absolute and the construction of the whole of Nature as the manifestation of the Absolute is replaced by the thought that the origin of the world is

---

Schelling is one such thinker among the Post-Kantian German idealists.

Now a little explication about Böehme is necessary. Immediately after the Italian Renaissance another movement (in the field of religion) known as 'Reformation' originated from Germany with Martin Luther (1483-1546) as its initiator, This movement sharply reacted against the domination of Pope and the Church fathers. A sense had dawned upon the people that their salvation depended on their own efforts and not on Pope. Thus emerged the 'Protestant' religion, and with the changed outlook on religion philosophical thinking also began to change. It is at this transition period that we find the emergence of three principal figures viz., Geordano Bruno (1548—1600) in Italy, Jacob Böehme (1575—1624) in Germany and Montaigne (1553—1592) in France. (Vide : Tarak Chandra Roy : 'Pāścātya Darśaner Itihās—Vol. I).

According to Böehme, God considered in Himself is beyond all distinctions and differentiations—the original source of all things—a motionless Being. He is neither light, nor darkness, neither love, nor wrath, but is eternal One, an incomprehensible will which is neither evil nor good. When God is thus conceived as the primal ground, the problem at once crops up as to how the world of multiplicity arises. Böehme postulates that the 'primal objectless will' as God is conceived in Himself, must become differentiated, for God can not be conscious of Himself and express Himself without an object. Hence He creates the world in visible variety to reveal Himself. Thus the impulse of the divine will to self-revelation leads to the emergence of the world in its visible and tangible form which appears as external to God, but which is originally in God. This being the position, how can evil in the world be accounted for ? Troubled with this problem, Böehme tries to explain it as a necessary phase in the process of divine self-expression. One of the significant teachings of Böehme is that the world of reality is full of oppositions and contradictions. Just as there is no light without darkness, there can be no good without evil. In fact there is such an inherent dualism in everything that nothing in the world can be conceived without its opposite. Hence in order to know God as love, we have also to know His wrath. In his later writing Böehme tries to relate evil to wrath of God.

to be found in the falling away from God ('Abbrechen von Gott'). "From the absolute to the real there is no continuous transition ; the origin of the sensible world is thinkable only as a complete breaking away from Absoluteness by means of a leap".[9] This position is explained by Schelling in some detail to show that the 'essence' of the finite thing is 'infinite', but considered precisely and exclusively as a finite thing it is an image of an image (i. e., an image of the ideal essence which is itself a reflection of the Absolute) resembling the shadow accompanying the body. In other words, its existence as a distinct finite thing is an alienation from the Absolute, a negation of infinity. Finite things are not, however, simply nothing. They are, in the language of Plato, mixture of being and non-being. Particularity or finitude represents the negative element. Hence the emergence of the world of particular and finite things—i.e., 'Natura Naturata' is a fall from the Absolute. Deviating

---

Since all things come from God, He must be the primal ground of all oppositions and in Him must all the contrarieties remain concealed. The movement of history, he thinks, is towards the triumph of love and the triumph of good.

Böehme, however, does not remain consistent in his view. In his earlier writings (in 'Aurora' for example,—published in 1612) influenced by the Christian doctrines, he asserts that only what is good proceeds from God. But the good, as is represented by Christ, remains steadfast, and another good which falls away from goodness is represented by Satan (Lucifer). The end of history is supposed here to be rectification of this 'falling away' and redemption from sin. God reveals Himself to man as 'Pure love' and for that reason there is a need to posit a negative counterpart which is evil. Man in his spiritual journey overcomes all evils and oppositions and is finally redeemed by God who is not only the source or ground of all, but who also reveals Himself in all.

This line of thought inspired Schelling in dealing with the problem of the relation between God and the world in the later phase of his philosophical thought.

9. 'Works of Schelling' – Edited by Manfred Schröter – (1927-28) Vol. IV, P-28.

again, as he does, from his previous theory of the Absolute in relation to the world, Schelling passes on to another conception of God as an actually existing personal Being whom a truly religious man needs and through whose activity or grace man can overcome his state of alienation and be redeemed. This viewpoint is adopted and dealt with elaborately in his Philosophy of Mythology and Philosophy of Revelation.

It is, therefore, not surprising that Schelling faces invectives of the critics for not formulating a coherent system of thought. But it must be noted that Schelling advances his own arguments in support of his rapidly changing standpoints. When his Philosophy of Nature was published his own distinctive contribution to German idealism together with his divergence from Fichte was noted by all But when this work was followed by the publication of 'Transcendental Idealism' critics found the Fichtean leanings in it. But in Schelling's opinion his transcendental idealism is only a necessary complement to his Philosophy of Nature. Schelling's argument runs thus : 'In knowledge itself subject and object are united : They are one. But if we wish to explain this identity, we have first to think it away. And then we are faced with two possibilities. Either we can start with the objective and proceed towards the subjective, asking how unconscious Nature comes to be represented. Or we can start with the subjective and proceed towards the objective, asking how an object comes to exist for the subject. In the first case we develop the Philosophy of Nature, showing how Nature develops the conditions for its own self-reflection on the subjective level. In the second case we develop the system of transcendental idealism, showing how the ultimate immanent principle of consciousness produces the objective world as the condition of its attainment of self-consciousness. And the two lines of reflection are and must be complementary. ....It is

Schelling's conviction that the mutually complementary characters of the Philosophy of Nature and the system of transcendental idealism manifest the nature of the Absolute as identity of subject and object, of the ideal and the real'.[10]

Schelling tries to justify his position, particularly with reference to the contentions made in his later works, by drawing a distinction between a negative philosophy which deals with concepts and essences, and a positive philosophy which puts emphasis on existence. A true philosophy, he says, seeks to discover the ultimate principle or reality. But the negative philosophy discovers this reality as a supreme essence or absolute Idea. And from a supreme essence or Idea we can deduce only the other ideas. From a 'what' we can not deduce a 'that'. The negative philosophy thus fails to explain the existent world. Positive philosophy on the other hand does not simply deal with God as an 'Idea' as a 'what' or essence, but as a pure 'that' i.e., as pure act or Being in an existential sense. Here God is not understood to be an impersonal Idea, but a creative personal Being, the existing lord of the universe. But as it is impossible to construct any system of thought without concepts, Schelling does not overlook the value of negative philosophy. All that he wants to say is that there is a 'connection or the unity between the two'[11] It is for this reason that Schelling shifts from the idea of an impersonal Absolute to the conception of a personal God. He justifies his stand by holding the view that the existence of a personal God is based on an act of faith demanded by the will. In other words, a truly religious man definitely needs a personal Deity who should be actually existing, creative and redeeming Being. In Schelling's words—'the person seeks a person'[12] This personal God reveals Himself and accomplishes

10. F. Copleston : A History of Philosophy ;—Vol-7. P-144.

11. Works of Schelling—Edited by Manfred Schröter—Vol. V. P-746.

12. Ibid—P-748.

man's redemption. He is not conceived just as a Kantian postulate for synthesizing virtue and happiness. "The longing for the real God and for redemption through Him is, as you see, nothing else but the expression of the need of religion. ....At the end of negative philosophy I have only possible and not actual religion, religion only within the limits of bare reason. It is with the transition to positive philosophy that we first enter the sphere of religion".[13]

It may occur to our mind why Schelling concentrated so much on the study of mythology and revelation and did not abandon his earlier contentions, or why again he did not reshuffle his philosophical thought in the light of the distinction made between positive and negative philosophy. Possibly Schelling, at the later stage of his philosophical thinking, was very much keen on demonstrating the nature of actual religion and its needs and on relating the history of religious consciousness to the history of divine self-revelation to man. He never intended to annul his earlier metaphysical speculations. He is found to have reiterated his conviction all through that philosophy as a whole must be a combination of positive and negative philosophy. It is true, as Copleston observes, that 'if we look at Schelling's philosophical pilgrimage as a whole, there is obviously a great difference between its point of departure and point of arrival'.[14] Since Schelling fails to give us a closely-knit system he does not escape the scathing diatribes of his critics who maintain that his early pantheistic view is replaced in his works on mythology and revelation by a sort of speculative theism. But if we consider Schelling's thought with an initial sympathy with his mentality, it may not be difficult for us to discover that to raise contradiction in

13. Ibid—P-750.

14. F. Copleston : A History of Philosophy, Vol. 7, P-175.

thought was not his aim. When he deals with a problem and reaches a conclusion, fresh problems arise for him which again demand the adoption of a new standpoint. But nevertheless, he has tried to synthesize the apparently conflicting points of view and to show that they were really complementary. Of all his earlier writing his Philosophy of Nature has a special importance in that the doctrine of pantheism is demonstrated here with adequate clarity for the first time in the history of western thought and it is here that he seems to have been profoundly influenced by the Upaniṣadic thought. What is therefore chiefly relevant for our purpose is to pause and consider the principal current of thought indicated in his Philosophy of Nature.

The possibility and metaphysical grounds of a Philosophy of Nature.

From the common sense point of view man looks upon 'Nature' as an objective reality. A rift is thus sought to be maintained between what is subjective and what is objective. Generally speaking the distinction between the objective external world of Nature and the subjective inner life of ideas i.e., between 'Nature' and 'Spirit' is considered to be the result of reflection of man. The opposition between Nature and Spirit thus becomes conspicuous and man is set apart or alienated as it were from Nature altogether. Schelling's idealistic outlook overcomes this rift and restores the original unity between Nature and Spirit. Schelling explicitly states that a philosopher must exhibit that Nature is 'visible spirit' and Spirit 'invisible Nature'. In his view Nature is ideal through and through in the sense that it is an immediate manifestation of the Absolute.—a unified Self-organising, dynamic and teleological system which moves and develops as it were, to the emergence of consciousness and to Nature's knowledge of itself in and through human spirit. Now this picture of Nature, Schelling holds, helps us remove the supposed antagonism between Nature and Spirit, the real and the ideal. Schelling is of opinion that both Spinoza and Leibnitz are found to have had an inkling of this truth that the ideal and the real are ultimately one, although their modes of explanation of the relation between the ideal and the real are somewhat different and also faulty. Spinoza has explained the correspondence between them by means of parallel modifications of thought and extension of one infinite substance, while Leibnitz has recourse to the theory of 'Pre-established harmony'. Schelling thinks that Spinoza finally leaves the modes unexplained and Leibnitz only makes an inexplicable postulate of pre-established harmony. But in spite of their faulty explanation they have vaguely suggested the ultimate unity of the real and the ideal, of Nature and Spirit which a philosopher must exhibit. Schelling has conviction that the intelligibility of Nature is pre-supposed in all scientific enquiries. In all scientific investigations Nature is forced to respond whenever any question is put to it. This clearly indicates that Nature conforms to the demand of reason and thereby makes itself intelligible and in this sense it is ideal.

Now the question may be raised as to what exactly is the justification of the view of Nature as outlined by Schelling. The ultimate justification is for him a metaphysical theory about the Absolute. To quote Schelling :—"The first step towards philosophy and the indispensable condition for even arriving at it is to understand that the Absolute in the ideal order is also the Absolute in the real order."[15] The Absolute, in other words, is the pure identity of subjectivity and objectivity and this identity is reflected in the mutual interpenetration of Nature and Nature's knowledge of itself in and through man. Schelling's obser-

15. Works of Schelling—Manfred Schröter Vol. I. P-708.

vations sometimes appear to be confusing and misleading for he holds that nature as a system of particular things i.e., 'Natura Naturata', considered as the symbol or appearance of Absolute in the ideal order (i.e., of 'Natura Naturans'—to use Spinoza's term), is said to be outside the Absolute. It is not unlikely for the critics to infer from this proposition that Schelling makes a distinction between the unchanging Absolute in itself and the world of particular things. But this is not the actual explanation Schelling intends to advance. It must be taken note of, as we shall consider later, that the Absolute, in Schelling's view is an all-comprehensive Reality. For the present we may content ourselves with the general picture of the Absolute as the eternal essence or Idea objectifying itself in Nature and finally knowing itself as the identity of the real and the ideal, of Nature and Spirit. The supratemporal life of the Absolute as pure essence is manifested in the temporal order of this world that stands to the Absolute in itself as consequent to the antecedent. Schelling thus advances a metaphysical justification of the possibility of a philosophy of Nature whose purpose is to develop a systematic ideal construction of Nature by removing the supposed cleavage between the subjective and the objective. Nature which ordinarily appears as lifeless must be shown to have life at all its levels. The Philosophy of Nature must, therefore, demonstrate how Nature by virtue of its independent power and potentialities exhibits itself as a living organic unity. Nature, in fact, is nothing but the 'Extinguished Spirit' and the manifestation of the Absolute Ego'. We shall now see how Schelling proceeds to conclude this way and with what results.

Analysis of Philosophy of Nature.

In analysing Nature Schelling has dealt with three different concepts viz., (i) Organic Nature, (ii) Inorganic

Nature and (iii) Reciprocity between the organic and inorganic Nature.

In the organic sphere Nature is creative. There is slow but ceaseless activity in the bosom of Nature. Now this activity lying at the basis of Nature expands itself in the phenomenal world and is infinite and unlimited, for Nature is, as supposed by Schelling, the self-objectification of the Infinite Absolute. Had there been no opposition to this eternal act, Nature would then have created everything at a time and everything would have been infinite. That is to say, this finite world of experience would not have been created. Hence it can be reasonably inferred that the act of creation or the urge of the organic nature to create is thwarted by some opposing force, which force is also within the Nature itself. Schelling does not make any categorical observation as to what this opposing force is. But in all probability he wants to say, it is matter or material force as is demonstrated later in the philosophy of Bergson. Organic Nature thus appears to involve two opposing forces, one of which helps and the other hinders the act of creation. This opposition is found to exist in all organic objects as a result of which only like beings are produced and no organic being is capable of creating any object basically different from it. The aim of Nature is not to produce infinite variety of individual and particular objects; it proceeds onwards in its ceaseless creative urge only for the preservation of organism as a class. The particular individual being is ignored as it were having been regarded only as a means to an end. In its creative activity Nature exhibits the adaptation of means to an end. The particular individual organic being is even destroyed as it is deemed necessary for the preservation of a class or race which Nature finally aims at. Organic Nature has three fundamental qualities viz., reproductivity, irritability and sensibility dominating the plants, lower animals and men in varying degrees. There are obviously distinguishable levels within the organic sphere itself. The living organisms whose sensibility plays a dominant role (e.g , in man) belong to the higher level. Again those who display a comparatively strong mark of irritability belong to the second group, and on the lower levels reproductivity is particularly conspicuous whereas sensibility and irritability are com paratively undeveloped and it is clearly manifested in the vegetable kingdom.

As opposed to the organic sphere there is 'Inorganic Nature' which is devoid of creative power. This sphere is just a conglomeration of different material phenomena. Distinct from one another, they are only spatially located side by side. The power which holds them together is gravitation existing apart from them. The inorganic sphere bears some resemblance to the organic one in spite of the the basic difference between the two, for some amount of activity is traceable even in the inorganic level. The reproductive activity of the organism, for instance, is found in the form of chemical action of different matters (e.g , combustion). In the same way what is irritability and sensibility in the organic sphere is comparable to electricity and magnetism respectively in the inorganic sphere.

It appears from above, as Śchelling expressly states, that there is an interaction or reciprocity between the organic and the inorganic level. Without the existence of the inorganic level organic Nature can not function. In orher words, it is by depending on the material or the inorganic sphere that organic Nature reveals itself. To make his position clear Śchelling refers to the faulty standpoint of the materialists according to whom there is a sharp opposition between the mechanical laws of the inorganic and the laws of the organic life. The materialist tends to reduce the higher level to the lower and seeks to explain the organic life in terms of mechanical causality without introducing the concept of finality.

In Śchelling's view a philosopher is primarily concerned with exhibiting the fundamental and necessary teleological pattern in Nature, and to do this it is necessary to show that the explanation of the lower is always to be found in the higher. It is true that from the temporal point of view the inorganic is prior to the organic, but from the philosophical point of view the latter is logically prior to the former. In other words, the lower level exists as a foundation for the higher level and the latter subsumes the former in itself. Hence there is no point in denying or suspending the laws of mechanics in the organic sphere. Rather these laws serve as the necessary setting in the realization of the ends of Nature in the production of organism. Viewed thus, 'the opposition between mechanism and the organic sphere disappears'.[16] Apart from this argument, as Śchelling proceeds to contend, the point of opposition between mechanism and the organic sphere is more easily overcome if Nature as a whole is looked upon as an organic unity. On the lowest level which Śchelling calls the first potency (Potenz) of Nature, there is an elementary operation of the forces of attraction and repulsion and their synthesis in matter is mass. At the higher level i.e. , in the second potency of Nature the same forces are found in the phenomena of magnetism, electricity and chemical processes. At a still higher level i.e., in the third potency of Nature again the same forces are found to have actualized their potentialities in the phenomena of sensibility, irritability and reproduction. This is the level of organism. Śchelling thus holds that Nature can not at any level be regarded as lifeless. Copleston rightly interprets when he says : "It is a living organic unity which actualizes its potentialities at ascending levels until it expresses itself in the organism".[17] Just as in the organic Nature there is adequate evi-

---

16. Ibid : Vol. I. P-416.

17. F. Copleston : A History of Philosophy. Vol. 7. P-140

dence of teleological action in the same way in the inorganic Nature also there is a 'dynamic order' of power. It is on this ground that Schelling infers that both the organic and the inorganic level originate from one source. A third reality is thus posited who is supposed to hold and regulate these two levels together. Throughout his construction of Nature, as we have seen, Schelling employs the idea of polarity of forces. But to quote Schelling,—"these two conflicting forces lead to the idea of an organizing principle which makes the world a system".[18] To this organizing principle is given the time-hallowed name of 'World-Soul'. This World-Soul preserves the existence of the organic and the inorganic Nature and thus holds the entire universe within itself and makes the interaction of the two levels possible. In other words, both the organic and the inorganic levels are the manifestations of one World Soul who stands related to the former just as a whole is related to its parts. That the organic and the inorganic world are so intimately related is due to the fact that the same force or power is manifested in both. Organic sphere, as we have indicated, is only a higher level than the inorganic. Magnetism, electricity and chemical action dominating the inorganic are also found in the organic level in the form of sensibility, irritability and reproduction. Hence it is maintained that the force which regulates human thought also regulates Nature as a whole. In other words, the entire Nature covering the organic and the inorganic level is permeated by one unifying Supreme Soul. This concept of World-Soul is considered by Schelling to be a postulate or "an hypothesis of the highgr physics for explaining the universal organism".[19] In itself the World-Soul is not a conscious intelligence. It is just a creative and organizing principle manifesting itself in Nature and attaining consciousness

18. 'Works Schelling'—Manfred Schröter. Vol. I, P-449.

19. Ibid : Vol. I, P-413.

in and through the human ego. It is the universal spirit or reason the conception of which is broadened by Schelling so as to include the unconscious, instinctive, purposive force manifesting itself in inorganic Nature as well as in the self-conscious mind of man. It is thus pure activity or self-determining creative energy which is common to both unconscious nature and self-conscious mind. It is the absolute ground or source of all things. Schelling opines, it is the absolute will or ego—the one all-pervading world-spirit in which everything dwells in potency and from which everything actual proceeds. Thus thought and being, or the ideal and the real are virtually identical in their root. Schelling believes that unless we postulate the World-Soul, we can not look upon Nature as a unified, self-developing super-organism.

Schelling's construction of Nature, as we have indicated, is sometimes objected to by saying that it appears to be somewhat fanciful and arbitrary to the scientific mind. But even if we overlook the details of Schelling's theoretical construction of Nature, that is, the allegedly fanciful speculations about magnetism, electricity, chemical process and the like, there is no gainsaying that in its general outlines his philosophy of Nature has an abiding value in so far as Nature is here presented as an immediate and objective manifestation of the Absolute and as a teleological system. Nature is here ideal through and through, not in the sense that it is the creation of the human ego, but because it expresses the eternal 'Idea' and because it is oriented towards self-reflection in and through human mind.

As an ardent sponsor of idealistic philosophy Schelling attempts to explain the world of experience in terms of mind. But in so doing he clearly opposes his predecessor Fichte's conception of Nature according to which Nature is the product of the Absolute Ego and as such it only serves as an impediment or incentive to our will. Reality, according to Schelling, is at bottom a living self-determining process, almost akin to the human spirit. If that is so, Nature can not be conceived as a mere external impediment to the will or as a dead mechanical order. We can understand Nature because it is not lifeless and because there is law, reason and purpose in it. There can be neither dead static substance, nor complete flux in Nature. With Fichte Schelling rejects the old notion of the unchangeable static substance and accepts instead the dynamic idea, the conception of a universal life, of a creative and purposive principle of evolution which proceeds from unconsciousness to consciousness and whose ultimate goal is reached in the self-conscious reason of man. Nature and mind, or being and thought are not the two parallel aspects of the Absolute as Spinoza thought. They are only the different stages in the evolutionary history of the Absolute. Just as in our own selves we rise from the unconscious or sub-conscious stage to clear self-conscious ness and yet remain one and the same self, so the universal Ego or the World Soul rises from the darkness of unconsciousness to the light of consciousness. In other words, as the principle of organisation and creative force it passes from the so-called dead and unconscious products of nature exhibiting unripe intelligence to the self consciousness in man. The graduated scale of the organised objects both in the organic and in the inorganic nature clearly accounts for the fact that the different forces or products of nature are fundamentally the same, for they are all held together by one creative spirit. Hence granting that Schelllng in his philosophy of Nature has at times used many figures of speech or fanciful language instead of advancing adequately convincing arguments, the value of his Nature-Philosophy can not, only on this ground, be ignored. Above all else, his acceptance of a teleological viewpoint as against one-sided mechanism, his emphasis on the dynamic and evolutionary conception of reality together with his craving for unity in multiplicity are the distinctive marks of his philosophy of Nature.

From what has been said above it becomes clear that Schelling has established a pantheistic world-view or a composite monism. Thilly very aptly observes : "Schelling's philosophy in its most developed stage is a form of pantheism in which the universe is conceived as a living evolving system, an organism in which every part has its place and subserves the whole. Subject and object, form and matter, the ideal and the real are one together and inseparable. The one is in many and the many are in one. Just as in an organism we can not tear the part from the whole, nor understand the whole without its parts, so reality is an organic whole of interrelated parts".[20] Schelling brings home to us that this reality which as an unconscious blind impulse forms and moves an individual body, becomes conscious of itself later only when it is expressed in conscious minds. While retaining its existence at the unconscious level the same reality reveals itself in numberless individual selves and becomes pure self-consciousness. Individual beings are real in so far as they are rooted in the universal Ego and they are not real as independent isolated individuals.

Impact of ihe Upaniṣads on Schelling.

Now it will be convenient for us to trace the impact of the Upaniṣads on Schelling's thought. In the first section of our work we have made a detailed analysis of the concept of Brahman as found in fhe Upaniṣads. We have seen that the ancient Upaniṣads adequately explain and establish the doctrine of composite monism or pantheism. The all-pervading Reality which is given different names there such as, 'Brahman' 'Ātman', 'Bhūmā' etc.., is known to have exercised its unifying power among the heterogenous phenomena of the world of experience. The Upaniṣadic sages have expres-

20. Vide : Thilly : History of Philosophy ; P-470.

sed their earnestness to know this Supeme Spirit. Instead of establishing any devotional attachment to God or the Absolute they have only recourse to a deep intellectual faculty or intuition [21] as the means to know Brahman who pervades the entire universe by holding everything together. Schelling likewise, as we have seen, develops the conception of an impersonal and all-pervading World-Soul emphasizing its unifying and organising power. The quintessence of the Upaniṣadic pantheism is, as we have already found, admirably illustrated in the Chāndogya Upaniṣad[22] where it is stated that all this is Brahman ; everything orginates from it, is reabsorbed into it and lives in it. Schelling's concept of 'World-Soul' is an exact counterpart of this view.

In the Upaniṣads we have seen that the idealistic thought has been voluntaristic as well as teleological. It is voluntaristic in the sense that Brahman expresses His will to be many and thus manifests Himself in the world of multiplicity.[23] It is again teleological in the sense that Brahman creates every thing from within Himself with a view to tasting 'ānanda' or aesthetic joy.[24] Schelling in his exposition reflects very much the Upaniṣadic spirit when he advocates that the World-Soul is a pure activity or self determining creative energy pervading the inorganic as well as the organic nature culminating in human organism and attaining selfconsciousness in and through human ego. Schelling is particularly conscious of the task of a philosopher which consists in tracing the fundamental and necessary teleological pattern in Nature. His Nature-philosophy, as a matter of fact, has given adequate

21. "Tat saviturvareṇyaṁ bhargo' devasya dhīmahi—"Bṛhadāraṇyaka Up.—6. 3. 6.
22. ' Sarvaṁ khalvidaṁ Brahma tajjalāniti"—Chāndogya ; 3. 14. 1.
23. Vide :—The Taittirīya Up.—2. 6. ; Aitareya—2. 1. ; Chāndogya—2.3.
24. 'Raso' vai saḥ, rasaṁhi evā'yaṁ labdyvānandī bhavati'. —Taittirīya – 2. 7. 2.

evidence of teleology. Nature at all levels has been conceived to be a living organic unity. Its objective is the production of organism as such and not any specific individual unit of it. Keeping the lower inorganic level with its mechanical laws as the necessary setting or background, this unifying force proceeds in ascending levels in the production of organism finally attaining self-consciousness in and through the human ego. There is, however, a marked difference between Schelling's concept of world-Soul and the Upaniṣadic concept of Brahman in that according to Schelling this universal spirit is in itself unconscious and it attains consciousness later as we have already seen. In the Upaniṣads the creativity and consciousness are indissolubly mixed up in the concept of Brahman and it has been well explained through the concept of Prāṇa.[25]

If we penetrate into the later writings of Schelling we find that he looks upon God as a personal Being. But nevertheless the influence of the Upaniṣadic thought is not completely obliterated there, because there also the pantheistic view is retained although in a slightly modified form. Inspired by the writings of Jacob Böehme, as we have indicated earlier, Schelling has, in his later dissertations, introduced the notion of a cosmic fall and has tried to grapple with the problem of the relation between the finite individuals and Infinite Absolute. Individual beings are said to be alienated from the Absolute. The particular finite things as finite constitute the 'Natura Naturata' and it is supposed ro have a relative independence or subsistence. This is strictly speaking the stand-point of a fallen creature. But their true centre is Infinite Absolute and they are one in essence with Him and can rise above their egoistic point of view to the true centre from which they are alienated. In determining the relation between the human spirit and this Absolute Sche-

25. Vide :—Kaṭho'paniṣad—2. 3. 2. Praśno'paniṣad—2. 13.

lling applies the notion of personality to it which is, he thinks, in itself impersonal. He, in fact, adopts this viewpoint with a view to explaining the problem of evil and the problem of freedom of will. We need not dilate on this point here. What we want to emphasize is that although Schelling here puts stress upon the personal concept of God he does not fundamentally diverge from his original pantheistic stand resorted to earlier. His pantheism at this stage is not advocated in the sense that the entire visible world or 'Natura Naturata' is identical with God, nor in the sense that the finite things are non-existent and that there is only the simple undifferentiated unity of God-head. His view is pantheistic in the sense that God is the ground or antecedent and the world is the consequent. As a consequent the world is dependent on God and not identical with Him in the sense that there is no distinction between them. Thus the world is a consequence of the first principle or God and it is a real consequence. The Divine Being manifests Himself and this manifestation is real. Hence God is self-revealing and self-manifesting, and all things and beings are anchored in God although distinguishable from Him.

As to the knowledge of the all-comprehensive Reality again, we find Schelling closely approaching the Upanisadic viewpoint. Like the Upaniṣads Schelling also holds that some sort of intuition is necessary for the apprehension of the World-Soul. We can, therefore, make here a brief survey of the Upaniṣadic approach to Reality and this, we think, will enable us to determine to what extent Schelling is influenced by it.

The vast texture of the Upaniṣads is replete with confabulations on the knowledge of Brahman.[26] In fact on the

26. A few illustrations may be given in this connection ;—
The Chāndogya Upaniṣad records the conversation between (i) Āruni and his son Śvetaketu and between (ii) Nārada and his preceptor Sanat Kumar.

question as to how Brahman is known we do not find any unanimity among the Upaniṣadic writers. The different views reflected there may be categorized thus :—

(1) First, there are some who seem to rule out the possibility of knowing Brahman. To a sciolist this view may appear to be agnostic roughly corresponding to the western view of agnosticism. But it must be noted that the spirit of the Upaniṣadic sages is never agnostic. In other words, the ancient seers never convey the sense of unknowability of Brahman. All that they mean is that Brahman is not known from a limited stand-point (Khaṇḍa dṛṣti). It is precisely this spirit that has been given elaborate exposition in different texts. In Keno'paniṣaḍ, for example, Brahman is said to be beyond all comprehension ('abāng mānasagocara'). 'Eyes can not see Him, speech can not comprehend Him, mind can not grasp Him. So He (Brahman) can not be known. He is neither known nor unknown.[27] The Kaṭho'paniṣad sounds the same spirit when it is said : "All that can be said is that-He is and nothing more can be ascertained.[28]

(2) Another opinion regarding the knowledge of Brahman which sometimes appears to be prominent is that Brahman can not be known but for the divine grace. It is observed that only those who attain moral perfection can reach Him.[29] In the Kaṭho'paniṣad it is clearly stated that

---

In the Bṛhadāraṇyaka Upaniṣad we find the eonversation between (i) Yājñavalka and his wife Maitreyī (2nd and 4th Chapter). Again we find that under the patronage of the King Janaka a debate on the knowledge of Brahman is arranged with Yājñavalka and Gārgī as the principal participants (Ch. III).

27. "Na tatra cakṣurgachhati, na bāg gacchati na mano' na Vidmo na vijānīmo yathā etat anuśiṣyāt anyadeva tad viditādatho aviditā-dadhi".—Kena Up.—1. 3.

28. "Naiva vācā na manasā prāptuṁ śakyo' na cakṣuṣā. Astīti vruvato'nyatra kathaṁ tadupalabhyate".—Kaṭha—2, 3. 12.

29. "Tamakratuḥ paśyati vītaśoko' dhātu prasādānmahimānamātmanaḥ"—Kaṭha ; 1. 2. 20.

none can claim to know Brahman through discussion and debate or through the exercise of piquant intellect or on hearing much about shastric injunctions. The person whom He greets by His own grace reaches Him.[30]

(3) The path of knowledge or intellectual understanding, howerver, is not impugned at all. Rather the same Upaniṣad which speaks of divine grace also refers to the power of intellect in the apprehension of the Absolute. In the Kaṭho'paniṣad, therefore. we find that emphasis is laid on the intellect as the most effective instrument for the knowledge of Brahman.[31] This idea is echoed in other Upaniṣads also.

(4) Finally intellect and a sort of intuition combined together constitute another method facilitating the realization of Brahman. This view is effectively presented in the Kaṭha and Śvetāśvatara Upaniṣad. The Kaṭha Upaniṣad upholds that Brahman is not amenable to the sense of sight. The Śvetāśvatara Upaniṣad declares that Brahman has created the world and He resides always in the hearts of men, while both these treatises hold that a seer realizes Him through intuition together with reason and thus becomes Amṛta.[32]

30. "Nā'yamātmā pravacanena labhyo' na medhayā na bahunā śrutena, yamevaiṣa vṛṇute labhyastasyaiṣa ātmā vivṛṇute tanuṁ svām".
—Kaṭha—1. 2. 23. Cf. Muṇḍaka 3. 2. 3.

31. "Eṣa sarveṣu bhūteṣu gurdo'tmā na prakāśate, dṛśyate tvagrayā budhyā sūkṣmayā sūkṣma darśibhiḥ.
—Kaṭha—1. 3. 12. Cf. Muṇḍaka—3. 1. 8.

32. "Na saṁdṛśe tiṣṭhati rūpamasya na cakṣuṣā
paśyati kaścanainam.
Hṛdā manīṣā manasā'bhiklipto ye etad—
viduramṛtāste bhavanti".—Kaṭha—2. 3. 9.

(ii) "Eṣa devo' viśvakarmā mahātmā
sadā janānāṁ hṛdaye sanniviṣṭaḥ
Hṛdā manīṣā manasā'bhiklipto
ye etadviduramṛtāste bhavanti.
—Śvetāśvatara—4.17.

By the term 'intuition' the Upaniṣadic seers mean 'direct vision, (aparokṣānubhūti) or immediate insight into the heart of Reality. The term 'aparokṣa' is used for the non-sensuous immediate knowledge evidently to make it distinct from sensuous knowledge of object (Pratyakṣa) that is literally presented to the sense. Now this insight or vision is a special prerogative only of those seekers of truth whose heart is made serene and purged of all defilements and impurities of life by moral training and prolonged contemplation. Intuitive knowledge thus virtually indicates a state of mind where there is a complete fusion with the Supreme Reality. Whoever knows 'I am Brahman', becomes this all.[33] He who knows that Supreme Reality or Brahman becomes that Brahman.[34]

Now this intuitive apprehension is fundamentally different from conceptual knowledge. In other words intuition is not discursive understanding which operates in our epistemological enquiry. In any knowledge situation there is a duality not only between the subject and the object, but also between the 'knowledge' of the thing and the 'being' or reality of the thing. In the sphere of intuition there is no such distinction. In the words of Dr. Radhakrishnan, —'What is immediately apprehended is different from what is conceptually constructed. The self immediately known in experience is known as a 'that' and not a 'what'. We have in this immediate apprehension a knowledge of acquaintance with being and not knowledge about its essence or nature. ...... There is no 'real' but only 'logical' distinction between subject and object in the immediate intuitive awareness of self as as real being".[35] When however, the Upaniṣads speak of intuition as the surest guide to the knowledge of Brahman, they mean by it 'intellectual' intuition and thus the supposed

33. Vide :—The Bṛhadāraṇyaka Up—I. 4.
34. Vide :—The Muṇḍaka Up.—3. 2. 9.
35. Dr. S. Radhakrishnan : **An Idealistic View of Life ; Ch. IV, P—110.**

antagonism between intellect and intuition is sought to be obliterated by the Indian sages. The expressions 'hṛdā', 'manīṣā' and 'manasā' used simultaneously make it demonstrably clear that there is no opposition between intellect and intuition. Here 'manīṣā' stands for the intellect which is different from discursive understanding in that it signifies an unerring mental faculty which controls, guides and regulates the mind. The point is further explicated by 'manasā' which stands for ratiocination which is operative only when the mind is no longer ruffled by the sensuous desires, passions and inclinations. Thus when the mind with its faculty of intellect is completely free from all that is dross, and becomes pure and serene there arises 'bodhi' or 'Vijñāna' (indicated by the word 'hṛdā') which is intuition proper. This helps one realize Brahman. Hence the passage goes : 'Tat vijñānena paripaśyanti dhīrā Ānandarūpamamṛtaṁ yadvibhāti'.

From what has been said above it becomes clear that in spite of the apparently conflicting views presented by the Upaniṣads on the knowledge of Brahman there is a main stream of thought that advocates a composite process of ratiocination and contemplation (manana and nididhyāsana). The idea of divine grace does not appear to have been developed in the ancient Upaniṣads. It only gave rise to a devotional attitude (bhaktivāda) wellmarked in the worship of God in rhe later period. That the reasoning faculty was given much importance in the Upaniṣadic age is quite understandable. But it is equally true that 'contemplation' was recognized as another important factor inextricably linked up with reasoning. It has been repeatedly observed that there is no multiplicity here, and the Absolute as one unifying Reality has to be realized by reasoning and contemplation.[36] This idea is expressed poignantly in the different laconic say-

36. 'Manasai'vedamāptavyaṁ neha nānā'sti kiñcana'—Kaṭha Up—2.1.11.

ings of the Upaniṣads. Evidently all such statements involve an intuitive element in them.

In Schelling's philosophy the Word-Soul is taken up as a postulate or an hypothesis for explaining the universal organism. But the question precisely here is: how can we be sure of this system? What, in other words, is the guarantee that action or life or will is the principle of things that passes through the stages of evolution? It is true that Schelling's answer to this question is not always the same. But nevertheless at every stage of his philosophy he is found to adopt as the ideal for man, the knowledge of the Absolute through some kind of intuition. Schelling is of opinion that intellectual intuition is the unique endowment of a philosopher. Many western thinkers go along with Schelling on this point.[37] In explaining his position Schelling maintains that

37. A brief reference to some western views on the efficacy of intuition and the actual role of reason in grasping the reality may be given in this connection.

Bradley and Bergson are of opinion that whatever be the object of knowledge—physical or non-physical intellect does not take us to the heart of it. For Bradley, thought is discursive and relational and any intellectual analysis is naturally a falsification of the real in so far as it breaks up the unity into a system of separate terms and relations. This apart, the whole life of feeling and emotion, 'the delights and pains of the flesh, the agonies and raptures of the soul' remain outside of thought. Hence Bradley recommends a higher mode of apprehension than discursive reason and maintains that the unified structure of reality is revealed more in feeling than in thought,—in what he calls the higher unity in which 'thought, feeling and volition are blended into a whole'. It is the creative effort of the whole man as distinct from mere intellectual effort that can comprehend the nature of reality. (Vide: F. H. Bradley: 'Appearance and Reality'—P 70-71 & P 160). Bergson opines that logic with its immobile and dead concepts can not know reality in its fullness; for reality, according to him, is 'Duration'—a movement, a concrete continuity, a life-flow. It is a 'continuous progress of the past which gnaws into the future'. It is something that pulsates through our very being. We are, in

the living, moving element in nature, the inner meaning of reality can be grasped not by the scientific understanding with its spatial, temporal and causal categories, but through intuition. In the final stage of his philosophical thinking, however, we find him resorting to a sort of religious mysticism, conceiving the world as a 'fall' from God-a personal Being, and the goal of man as a return to God. Here the human soul strips off its self-hood and becomes absorbed in the Adsolute through a mystical intuition. Hence the knowledge of the Absolute in any case is attained through some kind of intuition. Intellectual intuition which Schelling very much insists upon can not, in his view, be imparted by any instruction. Only a negative approach to the Absolute can facilitate the intuitive act of which the soul is capable through its fundamental unity with the Divine Reality. Schelling here clearly follows the Upaniṣadic approach to Reality.

---

fact, the conscious expressions of the life-flow from which the whole universe has been derived. To seize this reality in the fullest sense, Bergson holds, we have recourse not to intellect, but to intuition which means 'entering into' it. Intuition is the means whereby we plunge into the stream of flux or 'Becoming' and apprehend it from inside.

What we note in most of such opinions of the west and the east is that though intuition lies beyond intellect, it is not generally supposed to be contrary to it. Almost all the thinkers mean to say that intuition stands to intellect in the same relation as intellect stands to sense. Reflective knowledge is a preparation for the integral experience which we have in intuition. Śaṁkara observes in his commentary on Brahmasūtra (iii—4—15) that the fruit of knowledge is manifest to intuition. Plato also agrees on this point when he holds that his 'Dialectic' is a progressive rational enquiry which helps the mind to a direct vision of reality. He says that the vision of 'The Good' is possible only for those who are prepared for it by intellectual discipline and hard thinking. Bergson seems to have been profited by this teaching of Plato, and we find that although he professes an opposition between intellect and intuition, he acknowledges the value of intellect very much because he repeatedly urges that intellect prepares the ground for intuition.

(Vide : Henry Bergson :—'An Introduction to Metaphysics',—P-77.

CHAPTER—V

Critical examination of some pantheistic views prior to Schelling's

In our foregoing analysis we have pointed out that the system of Schelling echoes the Upaniṣadic spirit and it is Schelling who for the first time in the history of western thought enunciates the pantheistic doctrine after the Upaniṣads. Now this view may not be accepted on the nod by many a critic, for it may be argued that traces of pantheism are discovered in some of the philosophical systems prior to that of Schelling. In order, therefore, to substantiate our position it is necessary for us to explain and examine the so-called pantheistic theories. The systems of Geordano Bruno, Nicolas Malebranche and Benedict Spinoza come within the purview of our discussion.

Geordano Bruno (1548 – 1600).

An undaunted thinker of the 16th century, Bruno appears to have sharply departed from the dogmatic outlook of the schoolmen of the middle ages. According to the Scholastic theologians God, located at a particular point of space, was supposed to have created the heaven and earth some six thousand years before. Both the Catholics and the Protestants had a belief that heaven and earth had definite limits in space, that the hell was situated beneath the earth, and the angels descending from the heaven and the devils ascending from the hell were all supposed to be intervening in human affairs. The earth was supposed to be stationary around which the sun and the planets moved. These popular scientific and theological beliefs were opposed tooth and nail by Copernicus according to whom all the planets in our Solar System including the earth move about the sun. It is Bruno who for the first time accepts the astronomical findings of Copernicus with seriousness and formulates various scientific and philosophical principles as consequences of his extension of the Copernican view. Accepting the heliocentric system unreservedly Bruno holds that space has no limits and there is no insuperable barrier separating our world from the extra-mundane region supposed to be reserved for pure spirits, angels and the Supreme Being. Heaven is the infinite universe. The fixed stars are virtually so many suns surrounded by the planets. The earth does not enjoy any central or privileged position in the heavens. It is just a planet revolving round the sun in the infinite universe which is a system of Solar Systems.

Now for Bruno this new view of the world demands a new conception of God. God, in his view, can by no means be believed to have taken His seat upon a throne at a definite point in space outside of the heaven and the earth which He is supposed to have created some six thousand years before. Since the universe is infinite and since there can not be two infinites, God and the universe are, according to Bruno, identical. The universe does not admit of any beginning or end, but the world has a beginning and an end. Hence Bruno makes a distinction between the universe and the world particularly with a view to escaping the charge of atheism.[1]

1. "God, the Infinite Being or the Universe, is the principle or the eternal cause of the world : 'natura naturans' (nature as a source), the world is the totality of his effects or phenomena : 'natura naturata' (nature as effect). It would, he (Bruno) thinks, be atheism to identity God with the world, for the world is merely the sum of individual beings and a sum is not a being, but a mere phrase. But to identify God with the universe is not to deny him ; on the contrary it is to magnify him ; it is to extend the idea of the Supreme Being far

Now the question before us is,-how does Bruno actually develop his conception of God-universe ? He does not, in fact, give us any definite and consistent view on the point probably because he is found to have wavered between different interpretations. First, he is found to hold the view that just as light emanates from the sun without affecting or diminishing the power of the sun, in the same way the world is an emanation from God on whom it is dependent. To explicate his position Bruno opines that God is both the efficient cause and the inward essential principle of the world. As an efficient cause God is supposed to be distinct from what He creates. The relation between God and the world in this case does not appear to be intimate. Hence as an efficient cause, Bruno says. we know very little of God. But of God as the inward immanent principle we can have a clearer idea of Him and His relation to the world. In this sense God is the underlying reality, the infinite substance of the world. As an immanent principle God is thought of as an inner artificer who shapes and forms the materials from within Himself. Because He is indivisible and immutable, God is present in His entirety at all places and in all things in the universe. Because of His omnipresence everything in nature is alive. Nothing can be totally destroyed, for death is but a transformation of life. When we say that a thing dies we mean that a new thing is produced. The dissolution of a combination means the formation of a new one. As the underlying reality of everything God-universe

---

beyond the limits assigned to him by those who conceive him as a being 'by the side' of other beings i.e., as a finite being. Hence Bruno loved to call himself 'Philotheos' or lover of the divine in order to distinguish clearly between his conception and atheism. "Vide : History of philosophy by A. Weber and R. B. Perry ; P-229. This precaution, however, proved to be abortive, because the inquisitors of Bruno misunderstood him and he had to face grim consequences by being burnt at the stake in Rome in 1600.

appears to be both spiritual and material.[2] But matter is explained by Bruno as something spiritual or immaterial or inextended in its essence that does not derive its being from any positive principle outside of itself. On the contrary it is the real source of all forms containing them all in germ and producing them in succession. Thus what Bruno wants to establish is that this God-universe, by unfolding Himself produces a countless number of genera, species, individuals and infinite variety of cosmical laws and relations which constitute the life of the universe and the phenomenal world without subjecting Himself to any law or entering into any relations. It appears, therefore, that by insisting on the principle of unity and identifying God with the universe as a whole, Bruno tries to give a monistic or pantheistic colouring of his thought, But the chief difficulty that is common to all monistic systems arises here also. The question remains how can we prove that all things are at bottom one ? How again from their essential unity does the multiplicity arise ? To put it otherwise : how can we reduce the many to the one and how can the many be derived from the one ?

Troubled with this question Bruno upholds a theory of pluralism which clearly indicates a deviation from his original stand, Having affirmed the ultimate reality of God he maintains in the same breath that the world consists of an infinite number of eternal and ultimate individual units which he calls 'monads'. Each monad has its distinctive or unique character and none can be resolved into any other. Each is both material and spiritual at the same time. In Bruno's view human soul is an eternal monad. Each particular atom is a monad and again the stars and planets are also monads. God is considered by him a monad of monads.

The only merit of Bruno may be said to consist in his

2. "Bruno sometimes calls the Infinite the Universe or God matter". Vide : Weber & Perry : History of Philosophy, P-230.

contention that we can not think of God as located at a particular point in space. A man who believes in God can think of Him as present every where (transcending space in some way). God reveals Himself to a man more intimately in the inner experiences of man than in outward events. This, in brief, is probably his only contribution to philosophy. But he does not make any satisfactory attempt at reconciling pantheism with pluralism. It is quite evident that his views of God in relation to the world is full of contradictions and inconsistencies, God can not be at the same time (i) an inexhaustible source from which a universe separate from Him proceeds, (ii) a universal substance of which everything consists and (iii) a monad from which all the others are distinct and yet within which they are all included and on which they all depend.[3] If God is finally regarded as a monad of monads, Bruno then must be said to have a stronger tendency towards pluralism controlled and regulated by God than towards pantheism proper. His philosophical system, therefore, has a leaning more to theism than to pantheism.

Nicholas Malebranche (1638 – 1715).

After Bruno we come across a pantheistic tendency in the thoughts of Nicholas Malebranche, the reputed Catholic priest of France. His immediate predecessor Geulinex with his theory of occasionalism tried to solve the problem of mind-body relation initiated by Descartes. But he failed miserably since his views on God virtually relegated Him (God) to a Deus-ex-machina', for God was supposed to be a transcendent reality occasionally intervening to make the interaction between mind and body possible. Malebranche following Geulinex tries to set up a more consistent view of God. But our question precisely is how far he has been successful in

3. Vide : W. K. Wright : A History of Modern Philosophy : P-33.

giving us a truly consistent pantheistic world-view. The following analysis will make it clear.

One of the fundamental problems raised by the Cartesians viz., the dualism of thought and extension provides the starting point for Malebranche's doctrine. Accepting the Cartesian dichotomy between thought and extension he says that one can not directly act on the other. Although he speaks of the dependence of mind on body and of the close relation between them, his substantial thesis is that mind and body are entirely opposed to each other and there is a correspondence but no interaction between them. In other words, he has in his mind Psycho Physical parallelism rather then interactionism. In our common experience it appears that our arm moves because we 'will' to move it. We are thus the natural cause of the movement of our arm. But natural causes are not the 'true causes'; they are just the 'occasional causes' which act only by the power and efficacy of God's will. It is evident, as Malebranche holds, that there is no necessary connection between our 'will to move our arm, and 'the arm's movement'. A true cause is that between which and its effect mind perceives a necessary connection. To be a true cause again is to be a creative agent and no human being can create God thus as a true cause moves my arm on the occasion of my willing that the arm should be moved. It is thus by distinguishing between the natural or occasional cause and the true cause that Malebranche tries to bring in the concept of God. When in ordinary experience we find a particular event e g., 'A' being followed by anothgr event 'B', we regard 'A' as the cause of 'B'. But Malebranche would say that on metaphysical reflection 'A' is only the occasion of God's activity in producing 'B'.

The definition of substance as given by Descartes logically precludes any interaction between body and mind, Malebranche's theory, although untenable, appears to have atleast an advantage in avoiding the difficulties of Descartes' speculation on mind-body problem. It must be conceded, however, that Malebranche's conception of God as a Being constantly involved in producing all effects in the world or as engaged in producing sounds, tastes, smells and motions in the physical world is hardly satisfactory,

Malebranche's idea of God as related to the world is clearly revealed in his analysis of the knowledge situation. We have already seen that Malebranche acknowledges the opposition between mind and matter, the one being composed of nothing but ideas and the other of extended events. In fact mind can not even claim to know the body. All that mind is capable of, is to receive ideas. When we think of bodies what we are thinking of is 'intelligible extension' rather than 'physical extension'. So when mind and matter are totally different from each other, how can the mind have the knowledge of the external world ? Malebranche is of opinion that the knowledge which we have of the external world is always in the form of ideas. Now since mind or pure understanding is passive, it only receives ideas and can not produce them. The question naturally arises as to how or from what source it receives them. How, in other words, do the ideas of things distinct from ourselves come to our minds ? There is no possibility of receiving these ideas from the external world of material objects. Had it been possible, the ideas or impressions received from innumerable objects would have contorted or destroyed one another. These ideas again can not be produced by human mind for their production by man would imply his power of creation which he does not actually possess. Nor again can it be supposed that God has implanted in the mind from the beginning a complete stock of innate ideas. Hence the only reasonable explanation, as Malebranche holds, is that the human mind must receive the ideas neither from any human soul nor from external matter, but from a third source which is God. We see all things in

God. To quote Malebranche : 'God has in Himself the ideas of all the things which He has created ; for otherwise He could not have produced them'.[4] Hence all our ideas are in the efficacious substance of the divinity. The material world and the world of spirits or minds, although distinct from each other, are the ideas in the mind of God. God is thus supposed to be the repository of all ideas of all possible objects. Hence God being conceived as a Supreme Reason embracing the ideas of all posssible objects, the material world remains 'terra incognita'.

Now in view of what has been said so far it is almost clear that Malebranche's Philosophy does not reflect the pantheistic spirit. Pantheism proper as we have indicated in our previous analysis, involves the idea of an all-pervading Supreme Reality who embraces all and annuls none. In other words, the distinctive mark of pantheism is that it recognizes the reality of the different parts of the outer world and considers them to be the manifestation of one all-pervading unifying principle, This is what has been established in the philosophy of the Upaniṣads with all clarity and precision. There is no doubt that Malebranche has attempted to reach this conclusion, but he has failed to advance convincing arguments. His analysis serves to indicate a leaning more to the dualism of a theist than to pantheism. In fact he brings in the concept of God only to explain the possibility of knowledge of the external world. In his later writings he develops the concept of God in the spirit of a Christian philosopher and is intent on interpreting the world and human experience in the light of his catholic faith. T, C, Roy is absolutely correct when he observes : "Malebranche carried the Cartesian view to the threshold of pantheism,

4. Malebranche : 'De la recherche de la Verité ; (The Search for the Truth)—3. 2. 6.

but his catholic bias stood in the way of establishing pantheism proper.[5]

Benedict Spinoza (1632—1677).

A contemporary of Malebranche, Benedict Spinoza is considered to be a philosopher of outstanding merit, because he appears to have propounded almost a revolutionary theory of God or Substance to the utter surprise and bewilderment of the Jewish and Christian thinkers of his time. The general impression on him is that he is a pantheist, for his doctrine of substance helps one reach some such conclusion. Our purpose here is to examine his fundamental tenets finally to see whether or not he can truly be regarded as a pantheist.

Exposition of Spinozistic View.

The central teaching of Spinoza is that there is only one, infinite, divine substance which is identified with 'Nature,- 'Deus Sive Natura'. One of the striking features of his philosophical analysis is the geometrical form of presentation. Just as in geometry the conclusions follow necessarily from the axioms and definitions, in like manner the conclusions of Spinoza's philosophy are arrived at from certain fundamental definitions. Axiomatic truths are self-evident and absolutely certain and they are discerned by intuition. In Spinoza's opinion the idea of God is absolutely certain from which all other ideas follow. With full confidence in 'necessary know ledge' demonstrated in geometry, Spinoza has recourse to geometrical method and seeks to explain everything with the help of 'ground and-consequence' formula. God or Substance is said to be the ultimate ground from which everything necessarily follows. The question of any purpose or aim and

5. Vide : 'Pāścātya Darśaner Itihās' by Tarak Chandra Roy ; Vol. 2 ; P-40.

free choice is thus ruled out, Spinoza, according to many critics, develops the logical implications of the philosophy of Descartes in a monistic direction, As a matter of historical fact, however, he has not based his thoughts purely on Descartes and there is reason for thinking that before he devoted his attention to Cartesianism some Jewish mystical writers of the late middle ages had exercised some formative influence on his thought. Futher, he was also considerably influenced by another pantheistically inclined thinker viz. Geordano Bruno. Let us see first how far Spinoza develops his concept of Substance in a logically consistent way from the definition of it given by Descartes.

In defining substance Descartes held that it is an existent thing which requires nothing but itself in order to exist. He could not, however, stick to this definition, since besides God he also accepted body and mind as two other fundamental substances in explaining the world process, although God, for him was supposed to be more fundamental than the other two. In defining Substance Spinoza holds : "By Substance I mean that which is (exists) in itself and is conceived through itself, in other words, that of which a conception can be formed independently of any other conception".[6] What Spinoza means by this definition is that Substance is 'causa sui', infinite, eternal, absolutely free and indeterminate. Now this Substance is equated by him with God and Nature. The conception of God here is different from the Christian conception in as much as God, for Spinoza, is not an external or transcendent cause of the world in the sense in which a father is the cause of his son or the sun is the cause of sunshine. God is the immanent cause of the world in the sense in which an apple is the cause of its red colour or milk is the cause of its whiteness. Spinoza, therefore,

6. Vide : Spinoza's 'Ethics' ; Part 1 Defiition III.
The full meaning of this definition emerges in propositions II, III & VI.

appears to hold that God does not create the world. Nothing virtually exists independent of God and nothing is produced by or emanates from God. Rather all that exist in the phenomenal world follow necessarily from the nature of God in the way in which the characteristics of a triangle follow necessarily from the nature of the triangle. To Spinoza God is not only the ground of everything, but He is also considered the totality of being. Thus God, Nature and Substance mean the same reality. He has tried to explain his position in his theory of attributes and modes. Let us see how.

"By attribute", says Spinoza, "I understand that which the intellect perceives as constituting the essence of Substance".[7] Of the infinite attributes of God only two viz., 'extension' and 'thought' are known to us. Differing from his predecessor Descartes, Spinoza says that these two attributes are the two ways of understanding one Substance. They are the parallel manifestations of God or Nature. Although they belong to the same Substance they are independent of each other and no conscious thought can de explained with the help of matter (as is done by the materialists), nor can matter be explained with the help of conscious thought (as the idealists do). But because the two are the manifestations of the same reality, a physical change is always accompanied by a corresponding mental change and vice versa. Spinoza thus seeks to solve the problem of Cartesian dualism by the theory of psycho-physical parallelism as against Descartes' interactionism.

Now in explaining the world of finite beings Spinoza makes a thorough analysis of 'modes'. Finite minds are, in his view, the modes of God under the attribute of thought, and finite bodies are the modes of God under the attribute of extension. "By modes", says Spinoza, "I understand the modifications (affections) of a Substance or that which is

7. Ibid : Part I, Definition IV.

in something else through which it may be conceived".[8] He means to say naturally that nothing finite is possessed of self-subsistent individuality. Corresponding to two attributes, there are two different modes, 'Motion' and 'rest' are the modifications of 'extension', and 'understanding' and 'will' are the modifications of 'thought'. Here Spinoza makes a distinction between infinite and finite modes. Motion, for example, is infinite and eternal, but the corporeal forms which it constitutes or through which it is manifested are subject to origination and decay. In the same way intellect and will are eternal and infinite, but each particular intellect has a limited duration' What Spinoza intends to assert is that each of the infinite modes constitutes an infinite series of finite modes. These finite modes are contingent, relative and merely possible, while Substance or God is the absolute, eternal and necessary cause of itself, In view of the opposition between immutable Substance and mutable modes a question invariably crops up: How much reality do the modes possess in the system of Spinoza? A mode is not conceivable without a Substance that is modified, Now the Substance, as Spinoza has defined it, is not modifiable; hence the movement or change.-in a word the entire relative world with all its particular and individual beings, bodies and souls seems to have no existence. But Spinoza is not supposed to have aimed at this conclusion. He is fully alive to the changing phenomena of the existent world. Unmindful of the principle of contradiction, but supported by experience, Spinoza tries to smooth over the difficulty by affirming both the immutability and perpetual change of being. In order therefore, to do justice both to reason and facts of experience he makes a distinction between infinite and eternal mode and finite or temporal mode of God. Thus according to Spinoza's version it appears that from the modifications

8. Ibid: Definition V.

of two infinite attributes viz., thought and extension, the sensible world of multiplicity comprising conscious beings and extended objects arises. To put it otherwise, the different particular bodies and minds or material and conscious phenomena constitute the changing perceptible world. The being that controls or actively determines this external manifestation of the world is God which is the fundamental reality. Hence in Spinoza's view God is operative in nature and the principles or laws regulating the external nature are determined by the nature of God. This point is sought to be made clear with the help of an analogy. "From the infinite nature of God all things.........follow by the same necessity and in the same way as it follows from the nature of a triangle from eternity to eternity, that its three angles are equal to two right angles".[9]

Critical evaluation of Spinozistic approach.

The above exposition of Spinoza's viewpoint encourages many critics in holding the view that Spinoza is an ardent exponent of pantheism. According to these commentators the unmistakable mark of pantheism is noted in the identification of God with Nature. This 'Nature' is viewed either as an infinite Substance (Natura Naturans) without any reference to its modifications or as a system of modes (Natura Naturata). The first way of considering Nature is logically prior to the second. When 'Nature is considered in the second way i, e., as 'Natura Naturata' Spinoza is found to explain that a particular mode is caused by some other particular mode and this again by some other mode or modes and so on. There is thus an endless chain of particular causes. Spinoza is careful to add that this series does not admit of the intervention of any transcendent God for the creation of particu-

9. Ibid : 1/17.

lar modes. Further the series of finite causes and effects is logically and ontologically dependent on 'Natura Naturans' or Nature viewed as self-determined, self-dependent, unique Substance. Nature or God expresses itself in modifications and in this sense it is the immanent cause of all its modifications or modes. This analysis has evidently led the critics to hold that Spinoza is undoubtedly a pantheist and his pantheism takes the form of saying that God is an infinite being including within itself all beings or all reality, and that since God is an infinite Substance, finite beings must be the modes of this Substance. Thus if one stresses the metaphysical aspect one's attention is likely to be directed to the fact that 'Natura Naturans' and 'Natura Naturata' are ontologically co-extensive or identical, and the former is only logically prior to the latter.

But several questions crop up here which, we think, can not be answered satisfactorily from the Spinozistic standpoint. Our first question is,—does the definition of substance, as given by Spinoza, indicate in any way that it 'must' have modes ? The answer must be in the negative. As a metaphysician Spinoza is found to have started his system with the concept of Substance or God. But he also appears from the beginning to have been aware of the existence of the finite world of multiplicity. It is quite possible, therefore, that in "developing his deductive system he knew in advance his point of arrival and it seems probable that his knowledge that there are finite beings encouraged him to believe that he had achieved a logical deduction of 'Natura Naturata".[10] But then the question remains : how far has Spinoza been succ essful in deducing the 'Natura Naturata' from his concept of of Substance ? Substance is said to be the ultimate and supreme cause of the finite world of experience. But this substance, in Spinoza's view, is one, undivided and partless.

---

10. F. Copleston : A History of Philosophy ; Vol. 4, P-232.

How then these innumerable finite modes constituting the 'Natura Naturata' appear from such a concept of Substance remains in deed a riddle.[11] How, in other words, the individual, particular and finite modes are evolved from the one Infinite Being has not been adequately accounted for by Spinoza. In the Upaniṣads we have seen that the one desired to be many and this 'desire' serves as the genuine cause that produces the multiplicity.[12] But Spinoza's God does not evince any such causal efficacy as 'desire'. Again the relation between Substance and the modes is one between the infinite and the finite. The infinite and the finite are the correlative terms and the existence of one logically implies the existence of the other. But Spinoza's arguments do not proceed this way either. Spinoza observes that the two infinite attributes viz., extension and thought give rise to finite modes. But how this actually takes place has not been convincingly explained by him. He is aware that an infitite being can only give rise to what is infinite and not what is finite. Thus Spinoza, being fully aware of the existence of the phenomenal world and at the same time of his inability of explaining this world as the modification of substance or the attributes, resorts to another train of thought. He says that the finite object is infinite in 'essence' and its 'existence', is finite. Thus the 'infinite essence' and the 'finite existence' combined together give rise to finite modes. But to the fundamental question as to how the 'infinite essence' and the 'finite existence' are harmonized together so as to give rise to finite modes, Spinoza has given no answer. In the first part of his 'Ethics' Spinoza has declared God or Substance as infinite and this God again is 'Nature' outside of which nothing ex-

---

11. Cf. Tarak Chandra Roy :—Pāścātya Darśaner Itihās, Vol. 2. Ch. IV, P-71.
12. 'So'kāmayata—eko'ham bahusyāṁ prajāyeye'ti—The Taittirīya Upaniṣad -2.6.
Also Vide : The Aitareya (2.1) and the Chāndogya (6 2.[illegible])

ists. His observations in this section give an impression of Nature as an all-comprehensive reality signifying that both what is actually existing and what is possible for anything to exist, are all included within this infinite. If this be the real implication, what then, is the difference between 'Natura Naturans' and 'Natura Naturata' ? Spinoza opines that 'Natura Naturans' is the creative power of Nature. But if nothing can exist except that which is already in Nature, this creative force of Nature becomes meaningless. There are critics according to whom the term 'creation' has virtually no room in Spinoza's system. From the definition or essence of a triangle its characteristics (viz., that its three angles are equal to two right angles etc.) are not produced as effect but only follow necessarily and what is suppressed is made clear to the intellect. In the same way the creativity of Nature, it is argued, implies that the objects which come out of Nature by way of logical necessity, remain unmanifested within Nature and become manifested to the intellect. There is thus no new creation. But this way of arguing obviously obliterates the basic difference between 'Natura Naturata' and 'Natura Naturans' which Spinoza is keen on maintaining. The external nature is considered by Spinoza to be separate and distinct from God. He makes an explicit reference to Nature in its two-fold aspects. The first i.e , 'Natura Naturans' which closely resembles Bergson's 'Elan Vital' is identified with God. But the material, or sensible i.e., 'Natura Naturata' is set apart from God. He says that as an active force or cause he does not consider God to be separate or different from Nature. It is in this connection that he declares God as the immanent and not the extraneous cause of all things. But he is not agreeable to accept the proposition that the created material world is identical with God. To quote his words : "It is, however, a complete mistake on the part of those who say that my purpose......... is to show that God and Nature under which last term they understand a certain mass of corporeal matter, are one and the same ; I had no such intention".[13]

No Upaniṣadic pantheism discovered.

In view of what has baen analysed so far, it becomes clear to us that as in the cases of Bruno and Malebranche, so also in the Spinozistic system, the essential marks of pantheism are not consistently developed. Pantheism proper, as we have found in the Upaniṣads, involves the conception of a Reality that must comprehend the multiplicity in a unity. The 'one' will reveal itself in 'many' and the 'many' must be within the one. This feature is conspicuous by its absence in Spinoza. The reason probably is two-fold. First, a sharp line of demarcation is drawn between 'matter' and 'mind' in such a way as to make an interaction between them inadmissible. All that Spinoza says in justifying his position is that extension and thought being the attributes of the same Substance, any physical change is accompanied by a corresponding mental change and vice versa. In order thus to maintain consistency in the mutual relation of mind and matter he takes the help of a third concept i.e., God or Substance. Here Spinoza's argument hardly appears to be more convincing than Leibnitz's theoryof 'Pre-established harmony'. His psycho-physical parallelism can not thus solve the problem. Secondly, he admits the presence of God as the creative force in Nature, but the created or manifested Nature which he calls 'Natura Naturata' is considered completely alien to God. This is no doubt quite repugnant to the pantheistic spirit.[14] Spinoza's endeavour to give a pantheistic explanation may have been quite earnest, but his success is little. We see, therefore, that the systems of Bruno, Male-

13. Vide : Spinoza's Epistle'—31.
14. Cf. Dr. Hiranmoy Bandopadhyay : 'Viśvajijñāsā'—P 193-94 & P—292-93.

branche and Spinoza can not be called pantheistic in the sense in which the philosophy of the Upaniṣads is,

It will, therefore, be no arrogation for us to assert that it is Schelling who for the first time propagates pantheism successfully in his Philosophy of Nature and in so doing he follows the message of the oriental savants as depicted in the ancient Upaniṣads.

CHAPTER VI

Arthur Schopenhauer (1788-1860)

Introduction.

The philosophical system that now comes within the purview of our discussion is that of Arthur Schopenhauer who occupies a distinctive position in the history of the nineteenth century western philosophy. What chiefly preoccupies him is the question of evil in the world, A pessimist by temperament, he keenly felt the trouble of existence and found in the world what he felt in himself—a futile drive towards the acquisition of ever new objects of desire which yield no lasting satisfaction. This regnant tendency of his thought determines to a high degree the general complexion of his philosophy. In fact his philosophy is considered by some to be 'in its outcome, a doctrine of redemption from sin',[1] We shall consider at the end of this chapter the factors that led him to take to pessimism. But it must be noted at the outset that in spite of his pre-occupation with pessimism, he does not remain nonchalant to the theoretical problems of phIlosophy. As a matter of fact on the theory of knowledge and the nature of reality and also on the real import of the beautiful and the good, Schopenhauer offers his solutions which are striking and original. His famous treatise-'Die Welt als Wille und Vorstellung' ('The world as will and Idea') which appeared in 1819, gives us a fresh and stimulating insight into the nature of the world and human life. Long before this he had the occasion to

1. Vide : T. Whittaker : 'Schopenhauer' ; P-2.

peruse the Latin translation of the Upaniṣads made by Anquetil Duperron. That this study had left an ineffaceable impression on his mind is amply proved by his rapturous appreciation worded thus : "And oh : how thoroughly is the mind here washed clean of early engrafted Jewish superstitions ! In the whole world there is no study except that of the originals, so beneficial and so elevating as that of the 'oupnekhat'. It has been the solace of my life, it will be the solace in my death".[2] Pointing out the value of the Upaniṣads as the products of the highest wisdom, Schopenhauer says : "If he (the reader) is a partaker of the benefit conferred by the Vedas, the access to which, opened to us through the Upaniṣads, is in my eyes the greatest advantage which still young century (i.e., 1818-the beginning of the nineteenth century) enjoys over the previous ones, because I believe the influence of the Sanskrit literature will penetrate not less deeply than did the revival of the Greek literature in the fifteenth century : if I say, the reader has also already received and assimilated the sacred, primitive Indian wisdom, then he is best of all prepared to hear what I have to say to him".[3] It is not enough to say that Schopenhauer had only a deep respect for the Upaniṣadic message. What counts most is that the thoughts incorporated in his principal philosophical writing—'The World as will and Idea' bear adequate testimony to the fact that he was profoundly influenced by the Upaniṣadic thought. Our impression is shared by MaxMüller who records his observations, in his 'The Sacred Books of the East'.[4]

2. A Schopenhauer : 'Parerga Und Paralipomena',—Third Edition, Ch. II ; P-426.
3. Preface to the first edition, of 'Die Welt als Wille Und Vorstellung. Engligh Translation—by R. B. Haldane and J. Kemp.
4. "This translation (Anquetil Duperron's 'Oupneknat'), though it attracted considerable interest among scholars, was written in so utterly unintelligible n style that it required a lynx-like perspicacity

Schopenhauer explains the universe through his concepts of 'Will' and 'Idea'. 'Will', according to him, is the inner core or substratum and 'idea' is the outer crust. He equates 'Will' with a 'force' which desires to maintain through the species the flow of life. It uses the individual as the instrument for this purpose and in the process inflicts misery on it. The 'idea' is the experience an individual goes through and is the only basis on which the reality of the outside world depends. The material world has no essence independent of mental perception.

These essential features of Schopenhauer's philosophy bear striking resemblance to some thoughts formulated in the Upaniṣads and the Advaita Vedānta. There is evidence (which we shall refer to in our analysis) that Schopenhauer himself is conscious of this. In order, therefore, to trace the extent of the Upaniṣadic impact on him, it is necessary for us to explain and examine his fundamental thesis on the world as idea and the world as will in some detail.

The World as idea.

Let us first take up his concept of the world as idea as formulated in the first book of 'Die Welt als Wille Und Vorstellung'. Schopenhauer starts with the proposition 'The world is my idea or presentation. The German word 'Vorstellung' conveys the generalized meaning of the Lockean 'idea', now frequently expressed by the more technical term

---

of an intrepid philosopher such as Schopenhauer to discover a thread through such a labyrinth, Schopenhauer. however, not only found and followed such a thread, but he had the courage to proclaim to an incredulous age the vast treasure of thought which were lying buried beneath the fearful jargon......Schopenhauer not only read this translation carefully, but he makes no secret of it, that his own philosophy is powerfully impregnated by the fundamental doctrines of the Upaniṣads".

—Maxmuller : The 'Sacred Books of the East'. Vol. I. Introduction.

'presentation' or 'representation'. By Schopenhauer the word 'Idea' (with an initial capital letter 'I' in contrast with 'idea' just mentioned) has been used exclusively in the sense of the Platonic 'Idea' which plays an important part in his philosophy.[5] Now this truth viz., 'that the world is my idea' is something a man is fully conscious of, although it holds good for all beings who live and know. The world that lies before us, exists only as an idea in relation to the mind. In other words, the whole world is only an object in relation to a subject, the perception of a perceiver – in a word 'idea'.[6] Appreciating Berkeley's contribution to philosophy, Schopenhauer says that Berkeley was right in denying the 'I-know-not-what-substratum' or the material substance of Locke serving as the cause of the ideas we perceive. We have no reason to believe that any thing exists apart from the ideas and the mind that knows them. The phenomenal world is thus purely mental in its constitution. Schopenhauer here is a thorough-going subjective idealist or mentalist.[7] But he is careful to observe that this view viz., 'that the world is an idea'-is only one-sided and not the whole truth. He says that although nobody can free himself from such a conception, it is also to be noted that the other side of the truth which is more serious and impressive, is that a man can emphatically say, 'the world is my will—a view developed in the second book of his principal work. It is no doubt true to say that Schopenhauer is an idealist in the sense in which we call Berkeley's theory of external world 'idealism'. But his difference from Berkeley is also clearly marked when we come to consider his concept of 'will'. This difference

5. Cf. T. Whittaker ; 'Schopenhauer' ; P-15.
6. "All that in any way belongs or can belong to the world is inevitably thus conditioned through the subject and exists only for the subject. The World is idea,—'The world as Will and Idea'.—Schopenhauer. Translated into English R. B. Haldane and J. Kemp. Book-1, P—3-4
7. C. Wright : 'A History of Modern Philosophy' P-360.

proceeds from his following of Kant. Kantianism as accepted by Schopenhauer consists in the recognition of apriori forms by which the subject constructs for itself an objective world of appearances. While allowing that Berkeley was more consistent than Kant in the general formulation of idealism, he thinks that Berkeley was altogether inadequate in working out the principle. Kant's systematic construction is however reduced in effect to a very little by Schopenhauer. In fact his is a quite simplified apriorism. Of the twelve categories of the understanding Schopenhauer accepts only causality side by side with space and time which are in Kant's view forms of intuition. Thus these three forms, according to Schopenhauer, make up the understanding of men and animals. All intuitions are thus intellectual. It is not true to say in the Kantian spirit that the intuitions first come under the spatio-temporal background and wait for the understanding to organise them, but in animals as in men they are put in order at once under the three froms that suffice to explain the knowledge we have of the phenomenal world. To 'Reason' as distinguished from Understanding Schopenhauer does not assign any exalted function as is attributed to it by Kant, for according to Schopenhauer 'Reason' should be restricted to mean a faculty of abstract concepts. This reason and not understanding is that which distinguishes men from animals. It discovers and invents nothing, but only puts in a generalized form what the understanding has discovered in intuition. Hence following Berkeley and kant, Schopenhauer proceeds to consider that aspect of the world which is knowable and finds that all presented objects including even our own bodies are merely ideas. 'Will' by itself, as we shall see in our subsequent analysis, constitutes the other aspect of the world. To quote Schopenhauer —

"As the world is in one aspect entirely 'idea', so in another it is entirely 'will'. A reality which is neither of these two, but an object in itself (into which the thing-in-itself has unfortunately dwindled in the hands of Kant) is the phantom of a dream".[8]

In an attempt at establishing his idealistic position Schopenhauer makes a detailed analysis of his theory of knowledge. He holds, all that exists in the external world, exists only for the subject who knows all things, but is known by none. Everybody finds himself to be subject only in so far as he knows, not in so far as he is an object of knowledge. But his body is an object or rather an immediate object and may be called an idea, since like all other objects of perception the body is conditioned by the universal forms of knowledge (in kant's language, 'apriori forms of intuition) i.e., space and time. The subject on the contrary does not come under these forms for the simple reason that he is always the knower and never the known. The world as idea in Schopenhauer's view has two fundamental, necessary and inseparable halves. The one half is the objective world of multi plicity appearing through space and time and the other half is the subject which is not in space and time since it is present entire and undivided in every percipient being. These two halves are inseparable even for thought, for each of the two has meaning or existence only through and for the other and each appears with the other and vanishes with it. Following Kant Schopenhauer affirms that it is with the help of apriori forms the mind imposes on the sensations, that the sensations are organised into objects of perception. That space, time and causality lie apriori in our consciousness is a fact on which Schopenhauer fully agrees with Kant, but he goes beyond Kant in maintaining that the 'principle of sufficient reason' is the general expression for all these forms of the object of which we are apriori conscious. Hence all that we know purely apriori is only the content of that prin-

8. Schopenhauer's 'The World as Will and Idea'—Translated by Haldane & Kemp. Book I., P 5.

ciple and what follows from it. Kant, according to Schopenhauer, drew up only a somewhat miscellaneous list of apriori forms including space and time and the twelve categories of the understanding. He did not adequately explain the relationship between them, nor did he trace their common origin back to a single principle. Fichte made an attempt at finding such a principle in his concept of the Ego. But Schopenhauer thinks that Fichte was not successful in his attempt. Schopenhauer believes that he has been successful in tracing this common principle which is the 'principle of sufficient reason' with its four fold root vfz,,, (i) cause and effect explaining that every change implies a cause, making natural science possible ; (ii) ground and consequent, the grounds on which the logical judgements are based and inferences drawn ; (iii) space and time making mathematics possible and (iv) motive and action, every action being the outcome of an assignable motive making apparently social sciences possible. Thus according to Schopenhauer every event that occurs in human experience and every object that appears in the external world are subject to the laws of sufficient reason and are determined according to the universal and apriori laws. Human conduct is as subject to law as external events. Like Kant Schopenhauer also seems to be a thorough determinist in the domain of human experience subject to the principles of space, time and causality.

Two-fold ideas : ideas of perception and abstract ideas.

Schopenhauer makes a distinction between ideas of perception and abstract ideas. Abstract ideas signify only one class viz., concepts which are the possession of man alone and the faculty which forms these concepts is reason. The ideas of perception on the other hand comprehend the whole of the visible world or the sumtotal of experience with rhe conditions of its possibility. The relation between the ideas of perception and those of reflection or abstract ideas is analysed by Schopenhauer with the help of an analogy : "As from the direct light of the sun to the borrowed light of the moon, we pass from the immediate idea of perception which stands by itself and is its own warrant, to reflection, to the abstract, discursive concepts of the reason, which obtain their whole content from knowledge of perception and in relation to it".[9] So long as we continue to perceive, everything is clear and certain, and doubts and errors hardly arise here. What springs purely from perception and remains true to it, can not be false since it does not present an opinion but the thing as such. But with abstract knowledge, with reason, doubt and error appear in the theoretical, care and sorrow in the practical. In the idea of perception however, illusion may sometimes take the place of the real, but in the sphere of abstract thought error may reign for a thousand years. Nevertheless when ideas are considered with reference to the subject we get, as Schopenhauer holds, a distinctive faculty of man i. e., reflection which distinguishes consciousness of man from that of the lower animals and by virtue of which human behaviour also becomes very much different from that of the irrational brutes. Hence we pass from immediate ideas of perception to reflection i.e., to the abstract or discursive concepts or ideas of reason in which lie the special prerogative of man over other lower creatures. In the language of Schopenhauer "the brute feels and perceives ; man in addition to this 'thinks' and 'knows' ; both 'will'".[10] Thus concepts, according to him, form a distinct class of ideas existing in the mind of man only and entirely different from the ideas of perception which are always considered with reference to time, space and matter. In spite of the concepts being fundamentally different from the ideas of

---

9. Ibid ; P-45

10. Ibid ; P-47.

perception there is a necessary relation between them. Reason, which is said to be the faculty of forming concepts, is feminine in nature ; it can only give after it has received. Of itself it has nothing but the empty forms of its operation. Concepts in general can only exist after the experience of the ideas of perception and as their entire nature consists in their relation to these, it is clear that they (i.e., concepts) presuppose them (i e., perceptual ideas). The concepts may, therefore, be called ideas of ideas. Thus the entire world of reflection must ultimately rest on the world of perception as its ground of knowledge. Knowledge in the form of sense-perception is valid only of the particular case and as it can not, therefore, extend beyond what is immediately present, reason must come in, in order to substitute abstract concepts for ideas of perception and take them as the guide of action. On the value and importance of rational or abstract knowledge which can be communicated and permanently retained Schopenhauer says : "Any one may have a direct perceptive knowledge through the understanding alone, of the causal connection, of the change and motions of natural bodies, and he may find entire satisfaction in it", but he can not communicate this khowledge to others until it has been made permanent for thought in concepts.[11]

Criticism of materialism.

It has already been indicated that the objective world or the world of idea is regarded by Schopenhauer as the outer crust of the real world whose inmost kernel or essence is 'Will'. But the exponents of materialism get hold of the wrong end of the stick when they take this outer world for the real world and explain the origin of everything including

11. Ibid ; P-72.

the self and the will from 'matter'. Schopenhauer naturally launches his invectives against materialism which regards matter and with it time and space as existing absolutely, ignoring thereby the relation to the subject in which alone all this really exists. Materialism seeks to discover the primary and most simple state of matter and then tries to develop all the others from it. If we suppose this to have been done the last link in the chain would be animal sensibility i.e., knowledge which would consequently appear as a mere modification of a state of matter produced by causality. Thus the knowledge which is reached so laboriously is presupposed as the indispensable condition of its very starting point,—mere matter. When we imagine that we think matter, we really think only the subject that perceives matter. Hence Schopenhauer points out that the fundamental absurdity of materialism consists in the fact that it starts from the 'objective' and takes as the ultimate ground of explanation something 'objective', whether it is matter in the abstract simply as it is 'thought' or after it is empirically given as a substance. Schopenhauer is quite dicided on the principle that there is no object without a subject, and this renders all materialism for ever impossible.[12]

---

12. This idea is illustrated by Schopenhauer in detail. Some important passages may be quoted here :—"Suns and Planets without an eye to see them, and an understanding that knows them, may indeed be spoken of in words, but for the idea, these words are absolutely meaningless".

* * *

"The existence of the whole world remains ever dependent upon the first eye that opened, even if it were that of an insect. For such an eye is a necessary condition of the possibility of knowledge, and the whole world exists only in and for knowledge, and without it, is not even thinkable. The world is entirely an idea and as such demands the knowing subject as the supporter of its existence."

* * *

Fichte's viewpoint trounced.

The examination of materialism leads Schopenhauer to declare forcefully that there is clearly a reciprocal and inseparable relation between the subject and the object and at the same time an inevitable antithesis between them. This knowledge, as we shall consider later, leads him to discover the 'will' as thing-in-itself which steers clear of this antithesis. Now as opposed to materialism just examined, there is the system of J. G. Fichte which Schopenhauer proceeds to examine with equal severity, for Fichte, in his opinion, goes to the other extreme by starting from the subject—'Ego', and attempting to derive object from it con amore.

Considering Fichte to be one among the 'false philosophers', Schopenhauer holds that Fichte failed to penetrate deep into Kant's 'Critique of Pure Reason' and grasp the exact import of Kant's doctrine of thing-in-itself. In Schopenhauer's view an honest attempt on the part of Fichte to follow Kant could have made him realize that the principal teaching of Kant is that the principle of sufficient reason is valid only in the sphere of phenomena. Hence the inner nature of the world or the thing-in-itself can not be found by the guidance of this principle. Further the principle of sufficient reason does not concern the subject, but is only the form of objects which are therefore not things-in-themselves. The subject must exist along with the object, and the object along with the subject, so

---

"Thus we see on the one hand the existence of the whole world necessarily dependent upon the first conscious being, however undeveloped it may be ; on the other hand, this conscious being just as necessarily entirely dependent upon a long chain of causes and effects which have preceded it and in which it itself appears as a small link".

Ibid ; P—38-39.

that the subject and the object can not stand in a relation of reason and consequent. But, for Fichte, the 'Ego' stands for the ground of the world and the 'non-ego' for the object which is just its consequent, its creation. To be more specific, it is under the guidance of the principle of sufficient reason of existence in space, that Fichte's ego produces and fabricates the non-ego from itself. It is thus, in Schopenhauer's view, the tardy expression of the converse of old materialism. Just as materialism overlooked the fact that with the simplest object it assumed the subject also, so also Fichte overlooked the fact that with the subject (Ego) he assumed the object also, for no subject is thinkable without an object. So Fichte's system begins by assuming what it proposes to deduce—the necessary correlative of its starting point. Thus by opposing materialism and Fichte's system Schopenhauer tries to make his position clear. To quote him: "The method of our own system is toto genere distinct from these two opposite misconceptions, for we start neither from the object, nor from the subject, but from the 'idea' as the first fact of consciousness. Its first essential, fundamental form is the antithesis of subject and object".[13]

Critical analysis of the outer world.

In order to corroborate his proposition that the outward world is merely an idea in relation to self Schopenhauer insists upon a critical enquiry into the constitution of the outer world with reference to time, space and matter. All that takes place in the outer world goes on in time. But time is nothing but succession. As to space, it is nothing but the possibility of the reciprocal determination of parts of one another in their respective positions. Again matter on reflection, is found to be nothing but causation. The true meaning of matter consists in its action. Only as active

13. Ibid ; P-44.

phenomenon does it fill space and time. The consequence of action of any material object upon any other is known only by the difference in the way it acts now from the way it acted before. Cause and effect thus constitute the whole nature of matter. Certainty in mathematics shows that space and time are the forms which mind gives apriori to all the contents of perception which constitute the outer world. Time and space can be mentally presented apart from matter, while matter can not be so presented apart from time and space. Space and time are not only each for itself, presupposed by matter, but a union of the two (i.e., of space and time) constitutes the essence of matter, for this as we have indicated, consists in action i.e., causation. In fact according to Schopenhauer causation means that at the same point of space one thing is followed by another at a different instant in time. Thus causality unites space and time, depends upon them and could not occur without them. What is determined by the law of causality is, therefore, not merely a succession of things in time, but this succession with reference to a definite space, and not merely existence of things in a particular place, but in this place at a different point of time. Change or variation which takes place according to the law of causality, implies always a determined part of space and a determined part of time together and in union. Thus causality unites space with time. The unalterable characteristics of matter which we know apriori such as impenetrability, indestructibility, mobility etc.—all imply occupation of space and persistence in time. Hence causality and with it matter are merely ideas presupposing the prior presence of the opposition between objects that are known and the subject that knows them. Schopenhauer explains this thought repeatedly in many different passages in his work.[14]

14. "The understanding unites space and time in the idea of matter, that

Impact of the Advaita Vedānta and the Upaniṣads.

The analysis made so far makes it clear that Schopenhauer wants to establish one of his fundamental propositions that the material world has no essence independent of the perceiving mind. This idea of Schopenhauer is supported by the contention of the Advaita Vedānta as interpreted by Sir William Jones. The opinion of Jones presumably refers to the Vedāntic concept that the material world is an appearance induced by faulty perception.[15]

The same idea is developed by Schopenhauer in a different way when he specifically refers to the concept of 'māyā' as developed in the Advaita Vedānta in order to substantiate that the phenomenal world has only an apparent reality and that this outer world is an idea. Schopenhauer makes a candid confession that this doctrine viz., that the objective world has a merely relative existence, is quite old.

is causal action. As the world as idea exists only through the understanding, so also is exists only for the understanding."

—Ibid ; P-14.

★ ★ ★

"The demand for an existence of the object outside the idea of the subject.........has absolutely no meaning, and is a contradiction."

—Ibid ; P-17.

15. "How early again this truth was recognized by the wise men of India, appearing indeed as the fundamental tenet of the Vedānta Philosophy ascribed to Vyāsa, is pointed out by Sir William Jones in the last of his essays—'On the philosophy of the Asiatics', (Asiatic Researches, Vol. IV, P—164) where he says : "The fundamental tenet of the Vedanta school consisted not in denying the existence of matter, that is, of solidity. impenetrability and extended figure (to deny which would be lunacy), but in correcting the popular notion of it, and in contending that it has no essence independent of mental perception ; that existence and perceptibility are convertible terms." These words adequately express the compatibility of empirical reality and transcendental ideality".

—Ibid ; P-4.

It is in this connection that we find him referring to the māyā concept of the Advaita Vedānta.[16] which he does not accept as valid.

We shall now close our analysis of this part by referring to an important point of similarity between Schopenhauer and the Upaniṣads. Schopenhauer, as we have found, rejects the doctrine of māyā as explained by the Advaita Vedānta and in the light of the interpretation given by William Jones recognizes the relative reality of the outer world. It is here that Schopenhauer comes very close to the Upaniṣadic thought (perhaps without his being aware of it), for in the spirit of the Upaniṣads he holds that the phenomenal world is real and not an illusion. In explaining the concept of the all-comprehensive Brahman the Upaniṣads have only touched upon and not fully developed the illusion-hypothesis (māyā vāda). On the contrary these texts, as we have explained (in section I of this work), have asserted that the world being rooted in Brahman has a share of reality. Brahman could not remain content with its absolute unity and in order to have a taste of joy (ānanda) it wanted to be many. (So'kāmyata'bahusyāṁ prajāyee'ti') It is only when there is a dualism that the communication of thoughts is

---

16, "The substance of this doctrine is old ; it appears in Heraclitus when he laments the eternal flux of things ; in Plato when he degrades the object to that which is ever becoming ; in Spinoza as the doctrine of the mere accidents of the one Substance which is and endures. Kant opposes what is thus known as the mere phenomenon to the thing-in itself. Lastly the ancient wisdom of the Indian philosophers declares—'it is Māyā, the veil of deception, which blinds the eyes of mortals, and makes them behold a world of which they can not say either that it is or that it is not : for it is like a dream ; it is like the sunshine on the sand which the traveller takes from after for water, or the stray piece of rope he mistakes for a snake'.

(These similes are repeated in innumerable passages of the Vedas and the Purāṇas)"—Ibid ; P-9.

made possible.[17] Hence the Upaniṣadic sages contend that Brahman created the world of multiplicity out of itself and manifested itself into many concrete forms on the basis of dualism. Now this Brahman is the sole reality and the world of variety including the living individuals has no independent existence apart from Brahman. Thus the phenomenal world is given a relative reality and is not annulled outright as illusory. In the same way Schopenhauer maintains that the phenomenal world is not ultimately real, for ultimate reality according to him is 'Will' and the entire world is an objective manifestation of this 'Will'. The concept of 'Will', however, is not an exact counterpart of the Upaniṣadic concept of Brahman. Nevertheless we can hardly deny that in ascribing relative existence to the outer world Schopenhauer appears to be voicing the spirit of the Upaniṣads.

Transition from the view of the world as idea to that of the world as will.

After having explained the theory of the world as idea, Schopenhauer in the second book of his 'Die Welt als wille und Vorstellung' proceeds to establish his doctrine of 'Will' as objectified in nature. It is in this section that we discover how Schopenhauer's thought is 'powerfully impregnated' by the fundamental teaching of the Upaniṣads.

Schopenhauer first clearly outlines the limitations of scientific enquiries. Scientific explanations are strictly confined to the presentations ordered in space and time. This is as true of the sciences of causation (the Etiological Sciences) as it is of mathematical science. The province of

17. "Yatra hi dvaitamiva bhavati taditara itaraṁ jighrati taditara itaraṁ paśyati taditara itaraṁ śṛṇoti......"
The Bṛhadāraṇyaka Upaniṣad.
2. 4. 14.

natural science is divided by Schopenhauer. broadly into two parts viz., Morphology and Etiology.[18] The first treats of the permanent forms and structures of things and the second indicates the order of the changes occuring in them according to some laws. Natural sciences can tell us absolutely nothing about the inner nature of the phenomena which they classify and the regular order of occurrences which they describe When we consider the investigation made by mathematical science we find that it treats of animals, plants and inorganic objects as they fill space and time, that is, as they are quantities. It can not tell us what they really are.

The sciences thus can disclose nothing about the real nature of anything. So long as we are in the domain of sciences the ultimate reality beyond the world of presentation remains inaccessible. Schopenhauer says,—'the most complete etiological explanation of the whole of nature can never be more than an enumeration of forces which can not be explained, and a reliable statement of the rule according to which phenomena appear in time and space, succeed and make way for each other. But the inner nature of the forces which thus appear, remains unexplained by such an explanation which must confine itself to phenomena and their arrangement, because the law which it follows does not extend further'.[19] Here Schopenhauer is found to follow Kant in holding the view that the world of human experi-

18. "Etiology proper comprehends all those branches of natural science in which the chief concern is the knowledge of cause and effect. The sciences teach how, according to an invariable rule, one condition of matter is necessarily followed by a certain other condition; how one change necessarily conditions and brings about a certain other change; this sort of teaching is called 'explanation'. The principal sciences in this department are Mechanics, Physics, Chemistry and Physiology".
—Vide : English rendering of 'Die Walt als Wille und Vorstellung' —by Haldane & Kemp ; Book II, P-125.

19. Ibid ; P-127.

ence explained by the science and subject to the laws of space, time and causality is not ultimate reality. Kant calls it a world of phenomena or appearances. and so does Schopenhauer. Kant, however, thought it impossible to say anything definite about the thing-in-itself. No categories of the understanding can, in his opinion, be applied to it, and hence a scientific knowledge of the thing-in itself is impossible. Kant only speculated about it with the help of moral postulates and aesthetic analogies. Schopenhauer claims to have advanced beyond Kant in discovering the real nature of the thing-in-itself. In asserting the existence of the world as 'my idea' he does not deny the reality of the world. He clearly distinguishes between (i) the world as it is in itself and (ii) the phenomenal world which is 'my perception', 'my idea' or 'my intellectual organisation'. "As a reality", as Weber and Perry clearly explain the point, "it exists independently of me, but as an object of sensibility and the understanding, or in a word as a phenomenon, it depends on the 'subject' which perceives it : it is a wholly relative thing created by the ego and the apriori conditions of thought".[20] Hence it is palpable that although Schopenhauer follows Kant to a considerable degree, he seems to go beyond Kant when he holds that the thing-in-itself is 'Will' which he claims to have discovered through 'immediate intuition'. It will be clear from our subsequent analysis that this 'Will' is conceived by Schopenhauer in its broadest sense so as to include not only the consciously reasoned volition, but also the unconscious inward drives, impluses and desires together with the entire conative side of nature, and then we find that we are all primarily the creatures of 'Will'. But for the genuine desire, man would never have taken the trouble of perceiving anything or thinking about anything or of acting with reference to it.

---

20. Weber and Perry : History of Philosophy : P-447.

Man discovers that all his thoughts and actions are virtually prompted by 'Will'. So this truth we all discover by direct intuition or introspection and not through the medium of ideas.[21] We can infer a similar will in other persons because of their resemblance to ours. According to Schopenhauer the fundamental essence of us is 'Will', while thought is only a derived phenomenon—an accident of 'Will'. Thought or consciousness is considered the essence of mind by the rationalistic philosophers which. Schopenhauer thinks, is an initial mistake and hence should be set aside. Consciousness, in his view, is the mere surface of our mind of which, as of the earth, we do not know the inside but only the crust. It may be a fact that sometimes under the conscious intellect there is the conscious or unconscious will, a striving, persistent vital force, a spontaneous activity, a will of imperious desire, or that the intellect sometimes leads the will, but only as a guide leads the master. Schopenhauer, therefore, clings to his conviction that intellect is in the service of the individual will and it is only designed to know things so far as they afford motives for will, but not to fathom them or to comprehend their true being. Will Durant explains this viewpoint of Schopenhauer when he says that 'Will' is the only perma-

21. Regarding the 'knowledge of will' Schopenhauer makes an important observation later in connection with his remark on bodily action as an act of will objectified. He says: "The knowledge which I have of my will, though it is immediate, can not be separated from that which I have of my body. I know my will not as a whole, not as a unity, not completely according to its nature, but I know it only in its particular acts, and therefore in time, which is the form of the phenomenal aspect of my body, as of every object. Therefore the body is a condition of the knowledge of my will. Thus I can not really imagine this will apart from my body".
—Schopenhauer: 'The World as Will and Idea—Eng. tran. by Haldane & Kemp; Book II, P-132.

nent and unchangeable element of the mind. It is will which obviously through continuity of purpose gives unity to consciousness and holds together all its ideas and thoughts accompanying them like a continuous harmony.[22] On the basis of empirical evidence Schopenhauer emphatically declares that what is the essence in us is also the essence of all other phenomena in nature. Just as we are aware of ourselves inwardly as 'Wills', so also the entire universe considered in its essence is 'Will' which is ultimately real[23] and the external aspect is the objectification or phenomenal manifestation of it.

Objectification of Will : its all - pervasive nature.

Schopenhauer now proceeds to demonstrate with meticulous care and precision the process of objectification of 'Will'. He holds that the starting point for the metaphysical knowledge we seek is given to us in our own body. The animal body is the immediate object of the subject. We perceive our own bodies as ideas among all other ideas, as objects among objects, subject to the same scientific laws as other objects; but at the same time we experience our inward wills. Whittaker rightly explains the point when he says : "In virtue of his own body the investigator is not a pure knowing subject standing apart from that

22. Vide : Will Durant : 'The Story of Philosophy', P—339-40.

23. Schopenhauer repeatedly asserts in his work that this ultimate reality which is 'Will' is groundless and hence inexplicable through causation. In other words causal explanation of science can not give ultimate account of anything. To quote him : "Only the appearance, the becoming visible in this place, at this time is brought about by the cause and is so far dependent on it, but not the whole of phenomenon, nor its inner nature",
—The World as Will and Idea ; Tran. by Haldane & Kemp ; P—179.

24. T. Whittaker : 'Sehopenhauer'—P-30.

which he knows. In the case of the particular system of presentations constituting his organism he knows what these presentations signify, and that is his 'will' in a certain modification".[24] "This 'will' alone gives him the key to his own existence, reveals to him the significance, shows him the inner mechanism of his being, of his action, of his movement".[25] In fact the subject appears as individual through its identity with the body, and this body is given in two different ways. On the one side it is given as an object among objects and subjected to their laws, on the other side as the 'will' immediately known to every one. The act of will and the movement of the body are not two different states related as cause and effect They are one and the same act given in different manners; the will immediately to the subject, the movement in sensible intuition for the understanding. Hence the action of the body is nothing but the act of the will objectified, i.e., passed into perception. Schopenhauer believes that this is true not only of those bodily actions that follow upon motives, but also of those involuntary movements which follow upon mere stimuli. Hence he holds that the whole body is nothing but objectified will i.c., will become idea. To quote Schopenhauer: "In a certain sense we may also say that 'will' is the knowledge apriori of the body, and the body is the knowledge aposteriori of the will. It is only in reflection that to will and to act are different; in reality they are one. Every true, genuine, immediate act of wlll is also, at once and immediately, a visible act of body.[26]

In the first book of "The World as Will and Idea", Schopenhauer is driven to the conclusion that the human body like all objects of this world of perception, is merely an idea

25. Schopenhauer: 'The World as Will and Idea'—Eng. Tran. by Haldane and Kemp; Book II—P-129.

26. Ibid; P-130.

of the subject who knows it. But in the second book when he enquires into the essence of the objects, he finds that our body, apart from being an idea, appears in consciousness in quite a different way and this is denoted by the word 'Will'. In other words, as we have seen, our body is the product and instrument of will.[27] Now this double knowledge of the nature and activity of our own body furnishes the clue on the bassis of which, as Schopenhauer says, we can equire into the essential nature of every other phenomenon in the external world. We find thus that any object which is an idea in one respect, is also like our bodies, in its inner nature, the 'will'.

Schopenhauer is aware of the fact that if a person could regard all the things and beings i.e., other persons, animals, plants and inorganic objects simply as ideas with no other basis for their existence except his own consciousness, it would then lead to Solipcism or 'theoretical egoism' as he puts it. He believes that although such a view can not be demonstrably refuted, it can not stand as a 'serious conviction' except in a mad house. Hence this view needs a cure rather than a refutation, and this cure is found in discovering the will as objectified in the material world. In analysing the reality of the body and its action we go beyond the fact that it is a mere idea and we find nothing in it except the 'will' and with this its reality is exhausted. In the same way the material world besides being an 'idea' of the knowing subject is also in its inmost nature the 'will'. What is naturally true of ourselves can be reasonably inferred to be true of everything else in nature. A man thus recognizes the 'Will' as the ultimate reality or the inmost nature not

27. Wright illustrates the point thus :—
"His (a man's) feet are an objectification of the desire for locomotion, his digestive organs of hunger, his brain of the desire for knowledge. Were it not for the will, he would have no body at all".
Vide : Wright : 'A History of Modern Philosophy' ;—P-369.

only in those phenomenal existences which thoroughly resemble his own, in men and animals, but reflection[28] leads him also to recognize the same inward force germinating and vegetating in plants,-a force through which crystals are formed, that by which magnet turns to the north pole, the force that acts so powerfully throughout matter appearing, for example, in repulsion and attraction, decomposition and combination and even gravitation. All these are different in their phenomenal existence, but in their inmost nature identical with what we know in ourselves as will. 'Will' thus is the inner nature or the kernel of every particular thing existing in every blind force of nature and also in the preconceived action of man. The difference between these two is only in the degree of manifestation, not in the nature of what manifests itself.

Now in order to substantiate the view that the entire universe considered in its essence, is the 'Will' that objectifies itself, we have to demonstrate in some detail Schopenhauer's concept of 'Will' as the ultimate reality in plants, animals and even in inorganic nature. The will, whether assisted by conscious intellect or not, acts in us uninterruptedly and indefatigably. It acts in the body not only during its formation, but exists prior to the body. The will forms and organises the body according to its needs. The will in the embryo transforms a part of the cerebral substance into a retina 'in order to' receive optical phenomena. The mucous

28. "It is this application of reflection alone that prevents us from remaining any longer at the phenomenon, and leads us to the thing-in-itself. Phenomenal existence is idea and nothing more. All idea of whatever kind it may be, all object, is phenomenal existence, but the 'will' alone is a thing-in-itself. As such it is throughout not idea, but 'toto genere' different from it; it is that of which all idea, all object, is the phenomenal appearance, the visibility, the objectification".

—'The World as Will and Idea'—Tran, by Haldane & Kemp;

Book II. P—142-43.

membrane of the thoracic canal is transformed into lungs, because the body 'wills' to assimilate the oxygen of the atmosphere. The capillary system produces genital organs, because the individual in process of formation 'wills' to propagate the species.

When the organisation of animals is taken into consideration, it appears at the first blush that their habits and practices and their mode of life depend on their organisation. Ordinarily it is supposed that the birds fly because they have wings or that the oxen butt because they have horns. But on keen and intelligent observation just the contrary is found. There are animals who are found to manifest the will to use the organs which they do not yet possess. The goats or oxen, for instance, butt before they have horns ; the wild boars attack with that part of their snout where tusks are going to be. Hence, as Weber and Perry very aptly remark,- 'the will is the principle of organisation, the centre of creative evolution'.[29] In fact instances can be multiplied to illustrate the point. Wild beasts, for example, (especially the eagles and condors) that 'desire' to tear their prey to pieces, to live on plunder and on blood, have teeth and huge claws, strong muscles, piercing eyes. There are creatures viz., stags, roe bucks and gazzelles who do not usually 'desire' to fight, but instinctively 'seek' safety in flight and develop instead of organs of defense, a fine sense of hearing, slender and agile legs. The birds of the moor (storks and pelicans) who 'desire' to feed on reptiles have particularly well-developed legs, neck and beak ; owls 'desire' to see in the dark and so have enormous pupils, soft silken down in order not to awaken the animal 'desired' for prey. The porcupine, the hedgehog and the tortoise cover themselves with a shell because they do not 'desire' to flee. The cuttlefish conceals itself in a brownish liquid ; the ai, in order to hide from its

29. Weber and Perry : History of Philosophy ; P-449.

enemies, assumes the appearance of a tree trunk covered with moss. As a rule, particularly in the desert, the animal assumes the colour which least distinguishes it from the surroundings in which it lives, because it 'desires' to escape the pursuit of the hunter.[30] In all these cases the 'will' or more correctly the 'will to be' i.e., the 'will to exist' is the principal guiding factor. Where none of these means suffices the will provides itself with a still more efficient safeguard viz., 'intelligence' which in man supersedes all the others. This intellect is said to be very much powerful a weapon in so far as it can conceal the will under false appearances, while in the case of animals the intent is always manifest and is always of a definite character.

In the vegetable kingdom the same picture is found, for here also the 'will to live' plays the same role, although it is not always easily discernible. Here also everything is 'striving', desire', 'unconscious appetition'. The tree top 'desiring' light invariably tends to assume a vertical position unless it finds it (light) else where, The seed planted in the ground will invariably push its stem upward, its root downward, in whatever position it may be placed. The toadstool performs real feats of strength and wonderful acts of will, breaking through walls, splitting stones, in order to reach the light. Potatoes growing in a cellar infallibly turn their sprouts to the light. Hence in all these cases, as in the animal kingdom, everything is reduced to that 'elementary will' not connected with an intellect i.e., irritability. There is no essential difference between irritability and the faculty of being determined by motives, for the motive regularly produces an irritation which sets the will in motion. The plants turn to the sun by irritation and the animals also do the same. But the only difference between

30. The illustrations are found in detail in the 'History of Philosophy' written by Weber and Perry. Vide P—449-50.

a plant and an animal is that the latter is endowed with intelligence and knows what effect the sun produces on the body. It is only in the case of men and in the minerals,—at the summit and at the base of creation, that the character seems to be full of mysteries and it becomes, therefore, difficult to recognize the 'will' in these two extremes of creation. Every animal or every vegetable has its fixed character and normally it is possible for us to tell in advance what to expect of it. The behaviour of a dog (that it will be faithful) or of a fox (that it will be cunning) or that of a cactus (that it will 'desire' dry surroundings) or that of a plant (that it will bud or bloom at a particular time) can be fairly predicted. With men and minerals the case is not exactly the same, since it requires a prolonged experience to say anything definite about them. Nevertheless, we find in men clearly marked tendencies, inclinations or propensities, while the mineral kingdom also has its constant tendencies. What Schopenhauer wants to imply by all these instances is that 'will' lies at the basis of all things. It is a perpetual desire to be, the never-ending source of the phenomenal world. As long as there is a 'will' there will be a universe. Individuals may come and go (because they are subject to birth and death, growth and decay), but the 'will'—the desire which produces them is eternal. Birth, decay and death do not apply to the 'will', but only to its manifestations.

Relation between Will as thing-in-itself and its phenomenal manifestations.

The manifestation of 'Will' as explained above points to the fact that Will as thing-in-itself is quite different from its phenomenal appearances. Space and time are the principle of individuation (principium individuationis) in so far as it is through them that the 'Will' differentiates itself into diverse objects in different places and at different times, all of which are none the less interconnected according to the law of causation. Every individual thing or person is determined through and through in all its activities, although the causal determination of inorganic objects differs from that of organisms due to stimuli, and of conscious intelligence due to motives. Schopenhauer says that Spinoza was right when he said that if a stone projected through the air had consciousness it would believe that it was moving of its own will. The impulse given it is for the stone what a motive is for a man. What in the stone appears as cohesion, gravitation and rigidity is in its inner nature what we know as 'Will' and what the stone, if it were conscious, would also recognize as 'Will'. Schopenhauer means to say that knowledge and consequent action from motives belong only to the determinate form that the will has in animals and men. But the reality of the stone is the same in essence as that to which we apply the name of will in ourselves. To quote Schopenhauer : "I on the other hand consider the inner being which alone imparts meaning and validity to all real necessity (i.e., effect following upon a cause) as its presupposition. In the case of man this is called character, in the case of a stone it is called quality, but it is the same in both. When it is immediately known it is called 'will'. In the stone it has the weakest and in man the strongest degree of visibility, of objectivity".[31] He who can have the faculty of knowing the innermost being of nature will interpret the forces of vegetation, of crystallisation, of magnetism, of chemical affinity, even of weight etc. as different only in phenomenal manifestation, but in essence the same i.e., 'Will'. Hence only the Will as thing-in-itself is wholly different from presentation and is that of which presentation is a phenomenon, the visibility, the objectivity.

1. Schopenhauer : **'The World as Will and Idea'—Translated by Haldane & Kemp. Book II, P—164-65.**

Differences, there-fore, affect only the degree of appearing, not the essence of that which appears.

It appears from our foregoing analysis that 'Will' as the thing-in-itself which is outside of space and time through which it individuates itself into different objects, is one and indivisible. It does not, in other words. admit of plurality, since plurality indicates subjection to space and time. In the words of Schopenhauer—"It (Will) is free from all multiplicity, although its manifestations in time and space are innumerable. It is itself one, though not in the sense in which an object is one, for the unity of an object can only be known in opposition to a possible multiplicity ; nor yet in the sense in which a concept is one, for the unity of a concept originates only in abstraction from multiplicity ; but it is one as that which lies outside time and space, the 'principium individuationis i.e. the possibility of multiplicity".[32] Schopenhauer is careful to add that it would be wholly untrue to say that in some way or other there is a smaller part of the Will in the stone and a larger part in man, for the relation of part and whole belongs only to space and does not apply to the Will as thing in-itself. The Will manifests itself as completely in one oak as in million oaks. Hence the multiplicity of individuals does not belong to the Will itself, but only to its manifestations. The Will as such exists whole and undivided in every single thing in nature just as the subject of contemplation exists whole and undivided in each cognitive being. Further the individual or the person, as is perhaps evident in the world of existence is not Will as a thing-in-itself, but is only a phenomenon of Will and as such determined, while the 'Will' is free in so far as there is nothing beyond itself to determine it. Then again Will is in itself mere activity without end, a blind striving. Knowledge appears only as the accompaniment of

32. Ibid. ; P-146.

its ascending stages. It follows, therefore, that primarily and prior to individuation the Will is single, unitary and free. Separate individuals are secondary, derivative and determined. In the 'World-will' we are all really identical with one another and with the whole of nature.

Grades of objectification of Will.

A question is sometimes raised : how do we pass from the universal to that which has a particular character or quality ? Of the Will as thing-in-itself, as we have seen, there is not a greater portion of it in a man and less in a stone. The relation of part and whole belongs exclusively to space. The more or less of anything, as already said, touches only the phenomena i.e., the visibility, the ojectification. A higher degree of it is in the plant than in the stone, in the animal than in the plant and so forth. But the 'Will' that is the essence of all is untouched by the degree, since it is beyond plurality, space and time and the relation of cause and effect.

Hence the question just raised is sought to be answered by Schopenhauer with reference to his interpretation of Platonic 'Ideas'. The Will as thing-in-itself first affirms the 'Ideas' before revealing itself into a multitude of perceptible objects and individual things and events in space and time (which are all 'ideas' or 'representations'—translated from 'Vorstellungen'). 'Ideas' for Plato are eternal forms related to particular things as models. Following Plato Schopenhauer believes that the 'Ideas' or universals include all genera and species, class-concepts, universal qualities and principles. These 'Ideas' are unending, spaceless, timeless, causeless, unchanging laws of nature. All phenomenal objects are copies of them or participate in them in some way. Individual men are merely instances of species 'man'. They are born and die and undergo changes, while the species 'man' is enduring. In the same way there is a contrast between all enduring 'Ideas' and the changing particular 'ideas' of the objective world. The universal 'Will' thus has different grades of objectification which are called 'Ideas'. It is through space and time that the Will multiplies the 'Ideas' in innumerable instances as phenomena determined by the law of causality.

The lowest grade of objectification of Will is represented by the forces of inorganic nature. This grade is partly found in those universal forces of nature appearing in all matter e.g., gravity, impenetrability. and partly in those appearing only in different species of matter like rigidity, fluidity, elasticity, electricity, magnetism, chemical properties etc. The higher grades of objectification of Will as 'Ideas' are represented by the different species of plants, animals and men. Any particular plant, animal or man is a specimen or an individuation of the species at a particular time and place in accordance with the principle of sufficient reason. Schopenhauer thus reaches the conclusion that the whole world with all its phenomena is the objectivity of one and indivisible 'Will' or 'Will-to-be'.

Schopenhauer and Buddhism on will to live.

Now this concept of 'will to be' or 'will to live', as developed by Schopenhauer, closely resembles the Buddhistic view of 'Taṇhā' (tṛṣṇā). Hence it seems to be relevant for us to pause and consider the Buddhistic view of Taṇhā that constitutes an important stage in their wheel of causation (dvādaśnidāna). Schopenhauer does not accept the doctrine of momentariness on which the structure of Buddhism is built, but he subscribes to their view of causation as explained in their theory of dependent origination (Pratītya samutpāda vāda).

Buddha (like Schopenhauer) simply accepts the facts of experience and rules out the possibility of any ultimate cause whence this world of multiplicity may be derived. Adopting the empirical method Buddha holds, there is no 'being', but only 'becoming'. The supreme reality for him is the law of change and that is causality. On this point, it may be noted, Buddhism widely differs from the Upaniṣads.[33]

We shall now consider the import of the doctrine of Pratītya samutpāda that accounts for the coming into being of life which is suffering as well as its cessation. The term 'Pratītya-samutpāda' or dependent origination implies that every point-instant of reality arises in dependence upon a combination of point instants to which it necessarily succeeds, it arises in functional dependence upon a totality of causes and conditions which are its immediate antecedents.[34] The formula in which the theory or causation is expressed, is—'this being, that appears' (Asmin sati, idaṁ bhavati). There is no real production, but only interdependence. In opposition to the realistic and materialistic theories the Buddhists declare that things arise not from one's own self, nor from another self, nor haphazardly. They arise in functional dependence upon other causes.

---

33. Dr. Radhakrishnan makes this point clear. He says : "The Upaniṣads do not posit a mere being exclusive of becoming. They do not regard the world of becoming as an unrelated procession of states. It may be appearance, but yet it is the appearance of reality. The Upaniṣads exclude the idea of absolute change by calling attention to the fact that there is a permanent underlying the flux.

* * *

Buddha does not say that all change involves a permanent that changes, nor does he say that change alone is permanent as some of his followers interpret him. He is indifferent to the 'being" of things and finds the reality relevant to our practical interests in growth".

—Dr. S. Radhakrishnan : 'Indian Philosophy ; Vol. I, P-37.

34. Vide : F. Th. Stcherbatsky : 'Buddhistic Logic'—Vol. I, P-119.

There is no causation in the sense of one eternal stuff changing its forms in the process of evolution, because the conception of an eternal stuff, for the Buddhists, is a misnomer. Nor should causation be understood to mean the sudden bursting of one substance into another. The realistic idea of causation implying the simultaneous existence of the cause and effect– one producing the other is also ruled out by the Buddhists, for according to them cause can exist no more when the effect is produced. The effect only follows upon the cause and is not produced by it when it is said that a cause 'produces' an effect; it is only an inadequate conventional expression (Saṁketa), a metaphor (Upalakṣaṇam). Hence the Buddhists contend that the result arises in functional dependence upon this or that thing (tat tadāśritya utpadyate). The effect thus springs up immediately after the existence of the cause and there is no interval providing the cause any scope for 'work' or 'operation'. The mere existence of the cause constitutes its work. In other words, efficiency is synonymous with existence (artha kriyākāritva lakṣaṇaṁ sat). When the question is raised: 'What then is meant by operation of a cause producing the effect ?'—or what exactly is the 'dependence' of the effect upon its cause ?—the answer is, in the words of Stcherbatsky, 'we call dependence of the effect upon its cause the fact that it always follows upon the presence of that cause, and we call 'operation' of the cause the fact that the cause always precedes its effect'.

To follow the import of the doctrine of 'pratītya Samutpāda', as Buddha himself said' is to realize 'dhamma', for it is upon this fundamental principle that the other teachings of Buddha rest. The doctrine is explained by the Buddhists with the help of twelve successive causes or 'nidānas' each of which conditions the next. This series of these terms or nidānas expresses an interrelation among them and explains that the past present and future of an individual are closely interlinked. Further, this chain of causes and effects also brings out the idealistic character of the outer reality. In order, therefore, to follow the full implication of the contention that our life and all its sufferings originate from 'desire' or 'will', we have to consider the idealistic explanation of reality as adduced by the Buddhists.

According to the early Buddhists nothing exists independent of human mind. The world of multiplicity which is normally supposed to be outside the knowing mind is, in fact, flow of different mental states and processes. The five causal states or nidānas with the help of which the Buddhists try to explain their position are vijñāna, saḍāyatan, sparśa, vedanā and nāmarūpa. By vijñāna is meant the ego-sense that acts as a knower and is set apart from the outer world. In order to know the object certain auxiliary factors are necessary and Saḍāyatan (six sense organs) operate as auxiliary factors. Apart from five sense organs of sight, hearing, smell, taste and touch there is mind which is considered to be the internal sense organ. Now for the awareness of the object there must be a 'contact' between these sense organs and the object. This is indicated by Sparśa, and this again gives rise to sense-feeling or 'Vedanā'. Thus the contact between the knowing subject and the known object results in the awareness of the flow or reality (viśvapravāha) and this is indicated by the term 'nāmarūpa'. 'Nāma' comprises four states viz., (i) vedanā signifying sense-feeling (ii) saṁjñā—meaning perceptual knowledge facilitated by the sense feeling, (iii) saṁskāra—meaning a sort of tendency to work and (iv) vijñāna-meaning intellect that helps one know the object. Rūpa means that which has a sensible form, and all sense-objects with their embodied form fall within this category (Rūpyati iti rūpaḥ). Thus it becomes understandable why 'nāmarūpa' is considered a continuous flow of conscious states and processes. What is ordinarily regarded as the outer world on the basis of a knower-known relation is, in Buddha's view, virtually a continuity of a series of mental states, and this series of everchanging mental states is constituted by the aforesaid four mental states which again operate as a result of contact of two factors viz., conscious intellect or knower on one hand and the sense-object (rūpa) on the other. Hence 'nāmarūpa' virtually stands for this world of reality meaning, as we see, a continuous flow of everchanging conscious states (cetanāpravāha). Now from this flow of conscious states generate the 'will to live'.[35]

This 'will to live', according to the Buddhists, is the ground of our existence and its negation is salvation. Schopenhauer holds that our greatest sin is to have been born in this world. The inkling of this idea is found in the causal chain of the early Buddhists. Avidyā or ignorance that constitutes the first factor in the series consists in accepting the unreal as real and this produces a 'tenacious clinging' to life and prompts one to live and enjoy the world. Ignorance also generates egoism which leads an individual to consider himself separate from the rest of existence, and thus the false desire in him is all the more accentuated. In fact ignorance and false desire are the theoretical and practical sides of one and the same fact. "The empty abstract form of false will is ignorance and the concrete realization of ingnorance is false will".[36] Excepting ignorance or avidyā and jarāmaraṇa or old age and death-which appear respectively as the first and the last factor in the chain of causes, the other ten nidānas are regarded as ten 'Karmas' or acts guiding or determining our existence. The second link in the chain which is known as Saṁskāra (Predisposition or tendency) actually indicates good or bad action deserving reward or punishment here or here after. In wider sense

35. Vide : Dr. Hiranmoy Bandopadhyay : Gautam Buddher Dārśanik cintā'.

36. Dr. S. Radhakrishnan : 'Indian Philosophy'—Vol. I, P-367.

of the term, as Radhakrishnan interprets, it means the 'will force' or 'spirit energy' which determines the new existence. This train of thought is again forcefully presented in 'Taṇhā' that constitutes an important phase in the causal nexus. Taṇhā literally means thirst or longing. It is an earnest longing for life—a potent cause of life together with all its sufferings. Our existence is due to our thirst for being. We also suffer because of our thirst for pleasures, In the series of causes the early Buddhists try to show how our strong and insatiable thirst results in sufferings and sorrows of all sorts and thus leads us from birth to birth, Thus so long as man is possessed by the 'thirst for life' (that corresponds to Schopenhauer's 'will to live'), he is bound to be tossed about in the dark unfathomable depths of Saṁsāra.

From our foregoing analysis it becomes clear that Schopenhauer comes very near to Buddhism on some important points. He accedes to the general outline of the idealistic explanation given by the Buddhists. His concept of all-pervasive 'Will' corresponds to the Buddhistic view of taṇhā which is the ground of all existence. The pessimistic tinge of Buddhism is also found in him. Finally, just as the Buddhists prescribe the way to nirvāṇa by arresting the transitive character of causation, so also Schopenhauer has indicated the way of escape from sufferings ultimately through the total denial of the will, which, however, need not be dilated upon in the present context.

The question of supreme reality has been taken up with all earnestness by almost all the philosophers since the ancient times down to the present day. This reality which the Eleatics call the 'One and the All', Spinoza calls 'Substance', Schelling the 'Absolute' or the 'World Soul', Schopenhauer calls 'Will'. The systems of Schelling and Spinoza have already been dealt with. We shall, therefore, touch upon the Eleatic philosophy here to see how far, if at all, Schopenhauer subscribes to the view of the Eleatics.

The Eleatics and Schopenhauer.

Of the four exponents of Eleaticism.[37] Permenides was the chief and real protagonist of this school, although he seized upon the germs of thought latent in Xenophanes who is admittedly the founder of the school. With his reformative zeal Xenophanes was chiefly preoccupied with propagating his religious views rather than any philosophical doctrine. His principal aim was the moral development and amelioration of the common people. Having trounced the degrading conception of Gods and Goddesses of the early Greeks he introduced a monistic tendency of thought by declaring that God is one and non dual, is 'all-eye, all-ear, all-thought'. God is supposed by him to control the world not from outside as an external being, but He is one eternal and all-pervading. As a matter of fact the world according to Xenophanes is God, a sentient being though without the sense-organs. His system, properly speaking, has a pantheistic rather than a monotheistic colouring. But to the question – how the multiplicity came into existence from his conception of world-god, Xenophanes could not give any satisfactory reply. Thus the relation between the one i.e., God and the many, between the eternal and the non-eternal is left unexplained in the system of Xenophanes. This problem is only set on foot by the Eleatics for the first time in the history of European thought.

The essence of the philosophical system of Permenides is found in the first part ('the way of truth') of his philosophic didactic poem captioned—'On Nature', the other part being 'the way of opinion'. The first part comprises the discussion on the concept of 'Pure Being' which, according to Permeni-

37. (1) Xenophanes—born in about 576 B. C,
(2) Permenides—about 514 B. C.
(3) Zeno—489 B. C.
(4) Melisus—440 B. C.

des, is absolutely real. Its opposite is 'non-being' or 'becoming' which is equated with the sensible world undergoing changes. This non-being is supposed to be illusory, for reality is only ascribed to 'Being'. The character of this 'Being' is described for the most part in a series of negatives.[38] In Permenides the distinction between 'sense' and 'reason' is distinctly pronounced. The world of multiplicity, of change, presented to the senses is, to him, an illusion. The 'Being' which is the only truth is discoverable by reason. Now this Being, as it appears, has been identified with God. But one of the observations made by Permenides viz., that 'Being' is spherical or globe-shaped and that it occupies space, led some critics to give a materialistic interpretation of the system of Permenides.[39] Without entering into the controversy as to whether Permenides is a materialist or an idealist, it is enough for us to take note of the fact that his concept of Being gives adequate evidence of his monistic trend of thought, which annuls the world of sense as illusion. The view of Permenides is buttressed up by Milesus who, however, differs from the former on one point. Milesus believes that 'Being' is not globe-shaped or finite,

38. "There is in it no change, it is absolutely unbecome and imperishable. It has neither beginning nor end, neither arising, nor passing away.

* * *

There is for it no past, no present and no future. It is undivided and indivisible........ It is unmoved and undisturbed, for motion and disturbance are forms of becoming and all becoming is excluded from Being. ....of positive character Being has nothing. ....Its only quality is so to speak 'isness'."—W. T. Stace ;—A Critical History of Greek Philosophy. P—44-45.

39 "Permenides is not, as some have said, the father of idealism. On the contrary, all materialism depends upon his view".—Burnet : 'Early Greek Philosophers'—Ch. IV, Sec. 89.

Hegel, Erdmann, Schwegler etc. however, interpret the system of Permenides as an idealistic one.

but it extends illimitably through space. As for Zeno, he accepts the principal current of thought initiated by Permenides and goes on demonstrating vigorously the falsity of the idea of multiplicity and motion. His arguments, however, seem to be 'childish puzzles' and not at all convincing.

Schopenhauer no doubt accepts the 'monistic principle' of the Eleatics, but he differs from them at the same time on certain fundamental points. He does not agree with them in holding that this 'one and all' or 'Being' is God. The concept of 'Being' so laboriously developed leads the the Eleatics, as many critics hold, to a sort of dualism. As a matter of fact to call the world of plurality an illusion is not certainly to explain it. To the question—how this illusion arises, there is no convincing answer. They are thus faced with two worlds, viz., the true world or the world of Being and the false world i.e., the world of becoming, lying side by side without any link to show how the one arises from the other. The reason for this dualism seems to be due primarily to the utter barrenness of the first principle. The concept of Being is a featureless, characterless concept, completely empty and abstract. If multiplicity is excluded upto the hilt, the concept of Being naturally becomes barren and abstract This conception of abstract monism is undoubtedly alien to Schopenhauer, for he does not regard the world of multiplicity as illusory. He, as we have already seen, recognizes the relative reality of the outer world. He conceives 'will' as the essence of the world of multiplicity. The objective manifestation of the 'Universal Will' in space and time points to the unitary essence of all things, Hence all that we can say is that Schopenhauer accepts the monistic trend of thought of the Eleatics only as a principle. But in the actual formulation of this principle Schopenhauer and the Eleatics are poles asunder.

Schopenhauer's voluntarism as contrasted with certain other voluntaristic theories of the West.

Schopenhauer's concept of the all-pervading 'Universal Will' makes his theory of idealism demonstrably voluntaristic which, however, leads him to pessimism. In the history of western thought we come across some philosophers-not in all cases idealists, who are found to put emphasis more upon 'will' than upon 'intellect' and so are voluntarists. It is necessary for us to consider in brief a few such systems, for this will help us know that voluntarism does not necessarily lead to pessimism. We shall start our review with the system of the famous German thinker Leibnitz (1646-1716).

The dualism of extended or unconscious and inextended or conscious substance as developed in the Cartesian school is opposed by Leibnitz. According to him if matter is nothing but extension, as Descartes thought, we shall be unable to explain 'attraction,' 'repulsion' and many other sensible phenomena. In the same way, if mind is conceived to be nothing but conscious thought, many minute perceptions of which we are not conscious, particularly those in a state of profound dreamless sleep or in a swoon, will remain inexplicable. Hence Leibnitz proceeds to develop the notion of 'force' as the ultimate reality. Extension, for him, presupposes an effort or force that extends itself,-a power both of resistance and expansion. Matter is essentially resistance which again involves activity. So the essence of corporeality is not extension, but the force of extension or active force. True metaphysics does not recognize the inert lifeless matter as enunciated by the Cartesian Physics. A substance that does not act or that which is not the expression of force is inconceivable. Only what is active is real and there is action every where. Now this force in itself is essentially inextended and imperceptible and hence immaterial. Only the effects of force are perceptible. Since force constitutes the essence of matter, it may sound paradoxical to say that matter is in reality immaterial in essence. But it is with this paradox that Leibnitz overcomes the dualism of the physical and the mental worlds. Being inextended force is indivisible, simple and original. As against Spinoza's one substance, Leibnitz speaks of many substances, for according to him there are as many simple, indivisible and original forces as there are things. Now these original forces he calls 'monads' which are properly speaking metaphysical points differing from physical points in that they have no extension, and from mathematical points in that they are objective realities. Again they are said to be real like physical points and exact like mathematical points. These monads have been declared by Leibnitz to be 'windowless' so that each monadic unit costitutes a separate, self-sufficient and independent world of its own. But when the question is raised : What becomes of the universe and its unity ? Leibnitz, we think, can not advance any convincing reply. Nevertheless, he finds the synthetic principle in the analogy of monads and in his notion of 'pre-established harmony'. He is of opinion that though each monad differs from all others there is a-sort of family resemblance among them is so far as they are all endowed with perception and 'desire' or 'appetition'. This desire or appetition closely resembles Schopenhauer's 'will'. All monads whatever stage they may belong to, are 'forces', 'entelechies' and 'souls'. Leibnitz thus gives a spiritualistic tint to his pluralistic theory of monads by holding that souls alone exist, for the so called extension is only a confused perception, sensible manifestation of immaterial force. In other words, everything swarms with life. When the question is raised-viz., how can a stone or a plant or any being inferior to man think ?—Leibnitz opines that the perceptions of lower beings or those of the so-called inanimate objects are infinitely minute and confused, while those of men are clear and conscious. What is true of our soul is true in a measure of all monads. All monads are thus spiritual or psychic forces. There is in them something analogous both to our sensations and to our conations or tendencies to action. These perceptions or tendencies only differ in degree of clearness and distinctness. In the lowest monads everything is confused resembling sleep. Such dormant life fs found in plant. In animals there is consciousness which is called perception together with memory : in man consciousness becomes still clearer which is called 'apperception'-this being a reflexive awareness of the inner state.

With these fundamental tenets Leibnitz proceeds to show that there is a law of continuity by virtue of which the monads form a graduated progressive series from the lowest to the highest, from the dullest piece of inorganic matter to God. God according to him, is the highest and perfect monad, pure activity, the monad of monads. The principle of continuity demands the existence of a supreme monad. His theory of supreme monad, however, is not at all warranted by the definition of monad he has given earlier. But he wants to demonstrate that the harmony governing the universe is a harmony pre-established by God. In fact Leibnitz tries to gloss over the inconsistency involved in such a notion. He only tries to establish that all monads are nonetheless created by God and hence they are neither absolutely primitive and eternal, nor absolute, but they depend on a divinity,-'the primitive unity or the original simple substance of which all monads, created or derived are the products and are born so to speak, from moment to moment, by continual fulgurations of the Divinity'.[40] This observation is not, strictly speaking, pantheistic (although it comes very close to it, for God here is conceived as a real God distinct from the universe. Lei-

40. Vide : Latta : 'Monadology'.

bnitz's theological position on the whole bears greater resemblance to theism than pantheism. In his theological essays he attempts to reconcile his religious views with his philosophical doctrine. Here we find that his voluntaristic idealism is connected with an optimistic world-view. God, the perfect Being as He is, does not undergo any change or development to which all other monads are subject. He created the world of monads (a view which contradicts Leibnitz's earlier contention that God and monads are co-eternal) according to a plan and chose this world as the best possible world. His choice is not groundless but determined by the principle of goodness or moral necessity. He is also determined by logical necessity, for the fundamental laws of thought are binding on Him as well as man. Here Leibnitz has to face some questions : Why this particular world as it is presented to us was chosen by God ? Why again is this world full of so many evils and imperfections ? Why are so much suffering and ennui, oppression and rancour between man and man found in this world ? How can, in a word, this world of evil be accounted for ? In answer Leibnitz contends that an analysis of God's nature makes us understand that there could not have been a better world than this in which we live. God is omnipotent, omniscient and kind. Had it been possible for Him to create a better world He would have certainly done it, for by virtue of his omniscience He could have known it. Leibnitz acknowledges that the existence of evil apparently contradicts his viewpoint. But he observes at the same time that a world free from all imperfections is inconceivable and can not be the best possible world. Referring to the inherent limitations of the finite individuals and also the impediments they have to face, Leibnitz says, there is and must be the physical evil or all pains and sufferings. But these evils, he thinks, help in reforming and training us. Moral evil or sin is never desired by God. It is the natural result of 'freedom' of action human beings enjoy. Further Leibnitz, with the help of some analogies, tries to prove that evil is a foil to goodness enhancing the beauty of the latter. Evil, to him, is only a spur that goads us to good action. Evil is nothing positive. Like the dark shadow of a picture or a discord in a music it helps to bring about the beauty and glory of the good. In fact each monad constantly aspires after something better and has within it an inherent appetition to be free from passivity. These arguments of Leibnitz (which are sometimes highly rhetorical) in explaining evil may not always stand to reason. But he is firmly of opinion that evil is only an imperfection and it exists finally for an all round welfare of all. Thus viewed, his system appears as an optimistic system of voluntaristic idealism.

J. G. Fichte (1762 –1814) :—Almost a similar view point is traceable in the idealistic system of Fichte according to whom the fundamental reality is 'Ego'. Although he is influenced by Kant, he is found to have made certain modification of Kantian theory. According to Kant the materials of knowledge i.e., unorganised sensations or intuitions are given to the mind and organised by the categories of the understanding. Fichte thinks that there can be no 'given' to the Ego ; rather everything including time, space, substance and all the Kantian categories are produced by the activity of the Ego. According to him it is unnecessary to assume the thing-in-itself with the exception of the Ego. We are aware of our own selves in our experience and it is sufficient to posit a larger or universal Ego outside of experience which is said to be the source not only of the forms of our minds by which the sensations are organised into the objects of experience, but also of the sensations themselves. Now this Ego which is always present as the presupposition of all experience, is not any individual ego, mine or yours, but it is the larger Ego which has posited separate individuals and set up in opposition to individual wills an external world of which we become aware through our sensations. This Ego is Common Mind or Will whose nature consists in pure action. In Fichte's system the metaphysical principle and the ethical principle are identified. The 'real reality', according to him, is described in different terms viz., 'Good', 'Active Reason', 'Pure Will' 'Moral Ego' etc. The ultimate principle from which we come and towards which we strive is not 'being' but 'duty'; it is an ideal which is not, but which ought to be. What Fichte means is that 'Being' as such has no value. The universe is to be understood as the manifestation of 'Pure will'—the symbol of the moral 'Idea' which is the real thing-in-itself, the real Absolute. This Absolute or God as he calls it, objectifies itself in the phenomenal world which exists only for moral purposes in order that the individuals here can find the scope for performing their duties and realizing their vocations. Referring to the 'Primacy of practical reason' Fichte tries to show how the dualism between the theoretical and the practical reason is overcome. The faculty of understanding or the theoretical reason which divides the ego into subject and object is the auxiliary of practical reason, the organ of will or the servant of freedom. In other words, understanding simply becomes a phase in the development of freedom. Knowledge is only a means, a secondary thing, and action is the principal and final goal of being. The non-ego or the phenomenal world of senses and temptations stands as an obstacle which the ego sets itself in order to overcome it and thus to realize its essence i.e., freedom.

From these basic features of Fichte's system (the detailed account of which being redundant for our purpose), it appears that his is a voluntaristic theory very much akin to Schopenhauer's. But the fundamental difference between them is that while Schopenhauer is pessimistic, Fichte is optimistic in his outlook. He is alive to the fact that the absolute autonomy of reason which the ego pursues as an ideal, is never fully attained. But this conflict between the empirical and the ideal reality proves that the individuals are destined for an immortal lot and it is the source of their progress also. That which we call evil is the result of misuse of freedom and it is our bounden duty imposed on us by the Supreme Will to mitigate this evil. Hence all that exists in the world is meant for the well-being of mankind.

William James (1842-1910) & Henry Bergson (1859-1941) :—It is necessary to mention in this connection that even after the departure of Schopenhauer from the history of philosophy there appeared some thinkers (not idealists) whose systems are found to have enunciated voluntarism without leading to any pessimistic conclusion. Their views indicate a sort of meliorism seeking a compromise between optimism and pessimism. William James of America and Henry Bergson of France may be referred to as two chief exponents of such voluntarism. Both W. James and Bergson agree in holding the view that the world is full of so many evils and grisly phenomena that the verdict of the idealists like Leibnitz and Fichte does not seem to be readily acceptable. But they contend at the same time that we need not throw up the sponge and succumb ultimately to the hapless and gruesome goal which is supposed by Schopenhauer to be in store for us.

Both W. James and H. Bergson oppose materialism and mechanism in so far as both of them find the centre of reality in the field of life and mind. Both again oppose traditional spiritualism in that they interpret life and mind in terms of their observed or felt existence. The difference between them, however, is that for Bergson, these common terms retain a stronger favour of life, while for James they retain a stronger favour of mind. For Bergson's reality the most adequate term is 'activity', for that of James it is 'experience', James's preoccupation with psychology and the influence of the British empirical school on him are chiefly the reasons of his difference from Bergson. It is no doubt a fact that James is disposed to construe consciousness after the manner of the British empirical tradition as a manifold of distinguishable states traceable to sense experience, he nevertheless insists upon its activity and unity. The activity of consciousness, for him, is selective, interested and teleological. Thus mind, for him, is not just a mirror 'reflecting the environment ; it is an effective agency that seeks to satisfy its desires. It chooses to which of the presented stimuli it will respond in order to fulfil its purposes. Mind is thus primarily teleological in character and not a mechanistic product of the organism. James's theory of knowledge is developed from this psychological standpoint and is dominated throughout by its two main characteristics viz., (i) its emphasis on the categories of interest and practice, and (ii) its reduction of relations, substances and other so-called transcendent elements to the continuities of sense experience. The former motive leads to James's voluntarism and pragmatism, and the latter to his radical empiricism.

W. James does not conceive reality as something ready-made and complete from all eternity. It is rather in the making, unfinished and a flux. He applies pragmatism as a 'method' in ascertaining truth in all areas including philosophy. He finds pluralism pragmatically preferable to monism. Monism, he thinks, presents a block universe and robs us of our freedom of will or moral responsibility, individual efforts and aspirations. Pluralism on the other hand takes perceptual experience at its face value and the concrete perceptual flux, and offers in our activity-situations perfectly comprehensible instances of free will. This view of pluralism is, according to him, quite compatible with his melioristic interpretation of the universe.[41]

---

41. "It is clear that pragmatism must incline towards meliorism. Some conditions of the world's salvation are actually extant, and she

James is found to have been attracted and amazed by the endless variety of religious experience and belief. Although he does not fully agree with them all, he perceives, nevertheless, some truth in every one of them and demands an open mind toward every new hope. He holds the view that in upholding polytheism the ancient thinkers appear to be wiser, for it may be truer than monotheism to the astonishing variety of the world. Such polytheism, he says, 'has always been the real religion of common people and is so still to day'.[42] These observations have led the critics to declare that James is somewhat indefinite about his conception of God. We can not, however, doubt his firm faith in God[43] and his idea of Him which is in keeping with his melioristic world-view. He speaks of God as a part of the universe, a sympathetic and powerful (though not all-powerful) helper, a conscious personal and moral being as we all are, with whom we come into communion as certain experiences show. God is not, according to him, the guarantor of goodness of the world, but a powerful ally in our efforts to combat the evil. This conception of God naturally harmonizes with James's meliorism. In his 'Varieties of Religious Experience' James is found to stick to the view that the practical needs of religion require a God to exist in a realistic sense, independent of us, yet friendly to us and our ideals. In his later essay 'The will to believe' he affirms our 'right to believe' in God even without absolute proof, because by accepting God we can gain enrichment in our lives and inspiration to effective conduct which otherwise we should lack.

can not possibly close her eyes to this fact : and should the residual conditions come, salvation would become an accomplished reality".—William James : 'Pragmatism' ;

Vide : 'Pragmatism and Religion'—P-185.

42. William James : 'Varieties ot Religious Experience'—P-526.

43. "I myself believe that the evidence for God lies primarily in inner personal experiences".—W. James : 'Pragmatism', – Some metaphysical problems pragmatically considered.—P-78.

To return to Henry Bergson again, we find that his dualistically tinged metaphysics agrees with William James on certain fundamental points, but it asserts that the correct approach to reality which is ceaseless changing, is not to be gained through reflective thinking, but through intuition. In his dissertation 'Time and free will' Bergson maintains that reality is 'Duration' i.e., a continuity in time, not broken up into parts by which our intellect tries to interpret it when it measures intervals of time in terms of space, and that our life in a space-less time is in a sense free and undetermined. In his principal work 'Creative Evolution' he speaks of duration as 'a continuous progress of the past which gnaws into the future and which swells as it advances'.[44] Now this 'duration' is constituted of two factors,—one is matter which is inactive and existing in space, and the other is consciousness or vital force ('Elan Vital') existing in all living beings and with full vigour and prominence in man. This 'Elan Vital' is free and active, and the inner urge of it to manifest itself makes the world process dynamic. Evolution, according to Bergson, is a creative process going on in time and not determined beforehand by any omnipotent and omniscient creator. It is rather governed spontaneously by the 'Elan Vital' which ever presses onward, overcoming the obstacles put by 'matter' in its course. This explanation, briefly speaking, gives us a convincing account of Bergson's voluntarism. But as we have indicated, his voluntarism does not lead to pessimism as is the case with Schopenhauer. The concept of 'vital impulse' is equated by Bergson, with the concept of God which is, however, different from the traditional theological concept. In 'The two Sources of Morality and Religion' Bergson develops this idea. Without dilating on the point it is sufficient for our purpose to note that in this treatise he gives us in clear terms a melioristic view of the universe in the spirit of William James. The

44. Vide: H. Bergson: 'Creative Evolution';—Introduction.

second or higher source of morality and religion which he calls 'intuition' enables us to have an insight into the vital impulse or God operative in evolution, and thus it helps us develop an altruistic attitude. Bergson thus believes that the progress in human society can be furthered and all evils averted by our own efforts.

Schopenhauer's pessimism.

Some of the voluntaristic systems discussed above make it clear that voluntarism is not necessarily connected with pessimism. Schopenhauer does not appear to be very much inconsistent in his viewpoint. But it is equally true that his pessimism is not implied in his voluntaristic idealism. His pessimistic conclusions are based mainly on two grounds, viz., (i) his analysis of the nature of 'Will' and ii) empirical evidence. In all grades of its objectification from the lowest inorganic forms to the highest organic forms, the Will is controlled by no aim. Striving is its sole nature which no attaining can put to an end.[45] It is not, therefore,

45, The confusion that sometimes arises of the will as the thing-in-itself with its manifestations is made clear by the following observation of Schopenhauer himself :—

"Every particular act of will of a knowing individual (which is itself only a manifestation of will as thing-in-itself) has necessarily a motive without which that act could never have occurred....... Hence the motive determines only the act of will of a knowing being at this time in this place and under these circumstances as a particular act, but by no means determines that that being wills in general. ....Therefore every man (because he has some permanent aims and motives guiding his conduct) can give account of his particular actions, but if he were asked, why he wills at all, or why in general he wills to exist, he would have no answer, and the question would indeed seem to him meaningless. ....In fact freedom from all aim, from all limits belongs to the nature of the will which is endless striving". Schopenhauer ; 'The World as will and Idea'—Translated by Haldane and Kemp ; Book—II, P—213.

capable of any final satisfaction. This endless striving of the will-to-be, the will-to-live, the will-to-conquer, the will-to-reproduce, we see everywhere and see hindered in many ways. A particular desire arises from some want or deficiency and when it is fulfilled the pain is temporarily removed and no positive pleasure or happiness is attained. Again every satisfaction lays the seed of some new desire. Thus there is no end to individual wishes. Why is this ? Schopenhauer's answer is that it is all due to the fact that 'Will' is the lord of all worlds—the endless source of all life. Everything is but a manifestation of this Will. Therefore no one single thing can ever give it satisfaction. This apart, when a particular desire, be it sensuous or intellectual, is satisfied, it results in a sort of boredom. When again it is not satisfied, a sense of uneasiness continues. Thus a man's life swings like a pendulum backwards and forwards between uneasiness and boredom. There is a constant transition from desire to satisfaction and from satisfaction to a new desire. So much for Schopenhauer's analysis of desire.

By way of empirical evidence Schopenhauer points out numberless instances of macabre and calamitous incidents of human history. History, according to him, is merely an interminable series of murders, robberies, intrigues and lies, and if you know one page of it, you know them all. The so-called human virtues viz., the love of labour, perseverence, temperence, frugality and the like are nothing but refined egoism. Human life surveyed as a whole, seems to him a tragedy. The over-arching, never-satisfied wishes, the frustrated travails, the pulverized and abandoned hopes, grave errors piled up throughout life together with increasing anguish or trauma and death at the close—are always a tragedy. Optimism, for Schopenhauer, is not merely absurd, it is rather a cruel mockery to speak of optimism in the face of the unspeakable miseries of mankind.[46] We are, in his

46. The rejection of optimism by Schopenhauer and his adherence to

opinion, like shipwrecked mariners who struggle and struggle with their backs to the wall to save their wearied bodies

---

a pessimistic world-view do not stand the test of logical scrutiny. There are critics who do not accept his analysis. Wright, for example, observes and rightly :—"The pessimism in Schopenhauer may be claimed to be based on a false analysis of desire, It simply is not true, in the opinion of most philosophers, that pleasure is purely negative, that it is merely the removal of pain. The joy in life is something positive. ....Schopenhauer is right that nothing desired will permanently satisfy any body, and that whenever a person has some success he desires to make further progress.—The remedy, however, is not to cease endeavours, but ever to seek new ends which previous attainments have brought within one's horizon. Thus man advances from year to year in the life of the individual and from age to age in the history of the species".—Wright : 'A History of Modern Philosophy'.—P-381.

As to the empirical evidence Schopenhauer, in our view, seems to have overlooked the brighter aspects of human life and human history and thus he appears to give hyperbolic statements in explaining the import of human experience.

It must be noted in this connection that Schopenhauer's personal life was full of so many unhappy and undesirable incidents that it might have been very difficult for him to nurse an optimistic outlook on life. Will Durant aptly remarks : "At the bottom of Schopenhauer's unhappiness was his rejection of normal life". (Vide :-W. Durant—'Story of Philosophy ; P-378). In fact his was not a perfectly normal life. He spent almost all his life in a boarding house as a bachelor. He could not develop a happy relation with his mother whom he deserted for more than one reason during the last twenty four years of her life. Further, Schopenhauer could not control his strong sensual impulses which drove him into a series of irregular amours of which he was ashamed. He is said to have become greatly relieved when old age delivered him from the temptations of the flesh. (Vide :-Wright : 'A history of modern philosophy',—P-359). Again when he was at the university of Berlin his lectures were little attended, while Hegel in the same period was at the zenith of glory. This made him disgruntled, It is alleged that he was sickened at the sight of the sufferings of the poor in central Europe during the economic depression subsequent to the Napoleonic wars. All these factors were largely responsible for his having resorted to pessimism.

from the terrible waves only to be engulfed at last. To him 'world' and 'evil' become almost synonymous terms.

Way of escape sought.

Now a few words may be added on Schopenhauer's suggestions regarding the way of escape from the world of perpetual sufierings. In the third book of the 'World as Will and Idea' Schopenhauer develops his views on aesthetics. Here he contends that man can, in his brief aesthetic experiences, (i.e. in the contemplation of the beautiful and the sublime in nature and art) forget his individual self and his desires and thus by abolishing his subordination to the 'will' he can fix his mind directly on the timeless platonic 'Ideas'. Schopenhauer is aware that the relief sought here from the gnawing pains of self-conscious individual desires is purely temporary. Hence he proceeds to elaborate his views on ethics and religion in the fourth book of the 'World as Will and Idea' and also in the 'Basis of Morality'. He holds here first that greater relief than what is obtained in aesthetic experience, is gained through morality the basis of which is sympathy. It is in sympathy that we forget for the time our egoism and recognize our own fundamental identity with those whom we pity so that the sufferings of others become our sufferings also. This is true in all acts of justice and still more true in benevolence. But since all such altruistic feelings can not solve the difficulties of life permanently, Schopenhauer urges upon the unhappy man to follow a sort of asceticism. This he indicates by what he calls 'the denial of the will to live'. He says that this line of thought is also entertained by the Buddhists, the Christian saints and certain mystics of other religions. The denial of will-to-live is facilitated by certain ascetic practices viz., fasting, self-flagellation, celibacy and the like. It is the best way to deny the will-to-live altogether so that the 'Will' can no longer manifest itself in the finite individuals who constantly strive and suffer. If the will to live can thus be denied or completely eradicated from a person's mind, he can enter into a state of blessedness which the Buddhists call the state of 'Nirvāṇa'.

Impact of the Upaniṣads on the concept of Will.

From what has been discussed so far, it becomes evident that Schopenhauer adopts and explains the pantheistic spirit of the Upaniṣads in his analysis of the concept of 'Will'. As a matter of fact the association with pantheism Schopenhauer accepts in principle though the term 'pantheism' may not appear to be congenial for him. The concept of 'Will' or the universal force is in his system one and all and it is through the operation of this 'Will' that the entire universe is sought to be explained. This force is the basic reality, while the individuals of the species representing diversity have a secondary role. Schopenhauer thinks that the Upaniṣadic concept of 'Tattvamasi' (that thou art) supports his contention. He holds that unity is the essence and not the diversity. The individual is subordinated to the basic reality. He expressly states in his principal work: "The Hindus were deeper than the thinkers of Europe, because their interpretation of the world was internal and intuitive, not external and intellectual, the intellect divides everything, intuition unites everything; the Hindus saw that the 'I' is a delusion, that the individual is merely phenomenal and that the only reality is the Infinite One – 'that art thou'. Whoever is able to say this to himself with regard to every being with whom he comes in contact – whoever is clear-eyed and clear-souled enough to see that we are all members of one organism, all of us little currents in an ocean of will he is certain of all virtue and blessedness and is on the direct road to salvation".[47]

The Upaniṣadic concept of 'Brahman' and Schopenhauer's concept of 'Will' should not, however, be interpreted as absolutely identical. The fundamental difference that does not escape our notice is that 'Brahman' in the Upaniṣads is conceived as Ānandam or Rasavān (blissful existence) who creates this universe and pervades it for tasting aesthetic joy. Schopenhauer's concept of 'Will' has no such objective and it is due primarily to his pessimistic bent of mind. His 'Will' is completely blind to the interests of the individual. It uses the individuals only as an instrument, as a means for the perpetuation of species and the maintenance of the flow of life. In this sense Schopenhauer's view is teleological. But apart from this, we can not be blind to the striking points of resemblance between Schopenhauer's thought and that of the Upaniṣads. For a clearer understanding of Schopenhauer's viewpoint it is necessary to refer to and analyse an important observation made by Schopenhauer himself. He says : "With the Eleatics, Scotus Erigena, Bruno, Spinoza and Schelling, I accept the one and the all, the doctrine of the unitary essence of all beings ; only I am careful not to add : all is God, and so I differ essentially from the pantheists. The god of the pantheists is an X, an unknown quality by means of which they aim to explain the known ; my 'Will' on the other hand is a fact of experience ; I proceed as all true science must proceed from the known to the unknown. My method is empirical, analytic, inductive ; that of the pantheistic metaphysicians synthetic and deductive. Pantheism is synonymous with optimism ; in my system, however, the evil in the world is frankly conceded and its significance fully recognized".[48]

47. The excerpt is from 'The World as Will and Idea'—Vol-I, quoted by Will Durant in his 'The Story of Philosophy'.—P 368-69.

48. This excerpt, taken from Schopenahuer's 'The World as Will and Idea'—Book II, is quoted by Weber and Perry in their 'History of Philosophy',—P-456.

When Schopenhauer thus differentiates his philosophy from pantheism he obviously refers to some forms of pantheism as conceived in the west according to which the material world is sought to have been deduced from the concept of one substance or God. That is why he says that those systems are deductive while his philosophy is inductive. In fact his philosophy does not seek to explain the ultimate cause or causes of the world ; rather it confines itself to the facts of inner and outer experience which are accessible to every body and points out the true and intimate connection existing between these facts. Hence his philosophy without drawing any conclusion concerning what lies beyond experience, merely explains the data of sensibility and self-consciousness and strives to understand only the immanent essence of the world. He holds that it is the business of the dogmatic metaphysicians and transcendentalists to keep on asking 'Why' and 'Whence' and they forget that 'Why' means by what cause, that there are no causes and effects outside the time-succession and that therefore the 'Why' has no meaning in the sphere to which the forms of time and space can not be applied. Hence Schopenhauer offers us an empirical metaphysics[49] and standing on the ground of experience he boldly declares this reality which constitutes the basis of being and its substance by its right name 'Will'. This 'Will is that which is intuited or known immediately in experience and is, therefore,

49. Schopenhauer explains in clear terms the method adopted by him and the task of philosophy in general when he says : "My philosophy, at least does not by any means seek to know whence or wherefore the world exists, but merely what the world is"......... "The capacity for philosophy eonsists just in......the knowledge of the one in the many, and the many in one. Philosophy will, therefore be a sumtotal of general judgements whose ground of knowledge is immediately the world itself in its entirety without excepting anything.—Vide : Schopenhauer's 'The World as Will and Idea'—translated by Haldane and Kemp.—Book I ; P-108-109.

exclusively fitted for the explanation of the rest. What is unknown should always be explained by what is better known and not conversely.

The basic approach to reality in the Upaniṣads is, as we have seen, both intuitive and intellectual or cognitive, but according to Schopenhauer, it is purely intuitive. Even after acknowledging this difference it is possible for us to maintain that in the analysis of their fundamental contention both the Upaniṣads and Schopenhauer come very close to each other. In fact Schopenhauer appears to have developed a deep respect for the pantheistic spirit of the Upaniṣads and this is evident not only in his eulogistic statements about the Upaniṣads, but also from his detailed analysis, as we have seen, of an all-pervading force or Will. Our opinion on this point stands corroborated by an important observation made by MaxMüller : "That Schopenhauer should have spoken of the Upaniṣads as 'products of the highest wisdom' ('Ausgeburt der hochsten weisheit'), that he should have placed the pantheism there taught high above the pantheism of Bruno, Malebranche, Spinoza and Scotus Erigena as brought to light at Oxford in 1681, may perhaps secure a more considerate reception for those relics of ancient wisdom than anything that I could say in their favour".[50] Schopenhauer has spoken of the essential identity of all that is mundane by virtue of the objective manifestation of a universal Will almost in the spirit of the Upaniṣads where the Supreme Spirit or Brahman is said to permeate the entire existence. It is, therefore, neither an exaggeration nor a distortion of truth if we say that the study of the Upaniṣads prompted Schopenhauer to accept and follow the pantheistic doctrine enunciated there in.

The Upaniṣadic doctrine like Schopenhauer's is also voluntaristic. The Brahmavāda of the Upaniṣads, as we

50. Maxmüller : 'The Sacred Books of the East'—Vol-I, Introduction.

have explained in the previous section, conceives the supreme reality as an all-pervading force (very much like Schopenhauer) which 'desired' to be many[51] and thus manifested itself in the world of perception for tasting 'ānanda' ('joy'-that is comparable to aesthetic emotion). It is also thus voluntaristic wedded to an objective. The only difference here is that Schopenhauer's voluntarism leads him to a pessimistic conclusion and finally to seek absolute relief by way of the denial of 'will to live'. But the Upaniṣadic concept is sublime and unique of its kind. It is neither pessimistic nor optimistic. Its objective is to derive aesthetic joy by producing a work of art which is the universe. It is from the concept of 'Ānandam' that all beings originate, all live for it or go unto it or enter into it after death.[52] This cosmic spirit revealed as 'Ānandam' or 'Amṛtam' is known or realized by the learned.[53]

---

51. (i) "So'kāmayata–Eko'ham bahusyāṁ prajāyeye'ti".—Taittirīya ; 2.6.
(ii) "Ātmā vā idam eka evā'gra āsīnnā'nyat kiñcana miṣat sa īkṣata lokānnu sṛjā iti".—Aitareya—2.1.
(iii) "Tadaikṣata bahu syāṁ prajāyeye'ti tattejo'sṛjata". —Chāndogya ; 6.2.3.

52. "Ānando' Brahme'ti vyajānāt, Ānandāt hi eva khalu imāni bhūtāni jāyante. Ānandena jātāni jīvanti. Ānandaṁ prayantya'bhisaṁviśanti"—Taittirīya, 3.6.

53. (i) "Tat vijñānena paripaśyanti dhīrā Ānanda rūpam amṛtaṁ yadvibhāti,—Muṇḍaka—2.2.8.
(ii) Rabindranath Tagore gives a wonderful poetic rendering of this idea in the following lines :—

"I participated in many games
in the toy-land of the one
Who assumes diverse forms ;
I had a view of the one who is unique
with wide-open eyes".

—'Jābār Din', The Gītānjali (142).

CHAPTER—VII

Theosophy of Madame Blavatsky (1831—1891).

Introduction.

In our survey of the impact of the Upaniṣads it is necessary for us to refer to the contribution of the Russian lady Madame Helena Petrovna Blavatsky who appeared as one of the striking world figures in the last quarter of the nineteenth century. Her thoughts and ideas as found in the field of theosophy bear much evidence of her acquaintance with the thoughts of the ancient saints and seers particularly those of the Upaniṣads which she attempted to follow to a considerable degree. A true iconoclast by temperament, Madame Blavatski flouted the orthodoxies, whether of religion, science or philosophy and tore to pieces the conventional wrappings which hid the 'Real' from the view. However reviled by the people, Blavatsky with her uncompromising zeal and iconoclastic attitude proceeded to work in the service of humanity.

Theosophy and theosophical society.

The commendable achievement of Madame Blavatsky was the foundation of the 'Theosophical Society' in the United States of America. She had been there in 1873 and plunged into the spiritualistic movement then flourishing in America.[1]

1. In the formation of the theosophical Society H. P. Blavatski was assisted by Col. Henry Olcott—a man highly honoured and well-known in public life in America. They came to India in 1875. and here laid the first firm foundation of their work. The three principal objectives of the theosophical society were :—

The confidence of the scientists was rudely shaken when they failed to explain by scientific methods the strange phenomena happening around men. H. P. Blavatsky tried, as we come to know, in two ways to indicate the explanation of them, viz. first, by the practical demonstration of her own powers and secondly, by declaring that there was an age-old knowledge of the deeper laws of life, studied and guarded by those who could use it safely and beneficently. In order to substantiate her declaration, Madame Blavatsky wrote 'Isis unveiled' in 1877 and 'The Secret Doctrine' (a new explanatory version of and a corollary to 'Isis unveiled') in 1888. Before we come to discuss how the teachings of the Secret Doctrine are reflected in it, let us see the principal tenets of theosophy and the theosophical society as announced by Blavatsky.

The name 'Theosophy'[2] writes Blavatsky, dates from the 3rd century of our era and began with Ammonius Saccas and his disciples who started the 'Eclectic Theosophical System'. The object of this system was to inculcate certain great moral truths upon its disciples and all those who were lovers of truth. Here also the motto adopted by the theosophical society was —'there is no religion higher than truth' ('Satyāt nāsti paro' dharmaḥ'). The chief aim of the

---

(i) to form a nucleus of universal brotherhood of humanity without distinction of race, creed, sex, caste or colour ;
(ii) to encourage the study of comparative religion, philosophy and science ; and (iii) to investigate unexplained laws of Nature and the powers latent in man. This Society spread rapidly from country to country, strongly upheld by men and women to whom its declared service to humanity, the breadth of its platform, the clarity and logic of its philosophy and the inspiration of its spiritual guidance, made convincing appeal. Vide :—'A Sketch of Madame Blavatsky's Life'—as recorded in the 'Secret Doctrine',—Vol. I. P—15-16.

2. Vide : 'The Key to Theosophy'—by H. P. Blavatsky.

founders of the eclectic theosophical school was to reconcile all religious sects and nations under a common system of ethics based on eternal verities. The purpose of Ammonius Saccas was naturally to urge the Christians, the Jews and Idolators to lay aside their contentions and strifes in view of the fact that they were all in possession of the same truth under various vestments and were all the children of a common mother. This is also the contention of modern theosophy. Ancient theosophists claim as do the modern that the Infinite can not be known by the finite self, but that the divine essence can be communicated to the higher spiritual self in a state of ecstasy. Real ecstasy is explained by H. P. Blavatsky by referring to the definition of it given by Plotinus as the 'liberation of the mind from its finite consciousness, becoming one and identified with the Infinite'. Blavatsky thinks that this is the highest condition and is reached only by the few. It is also identical with that state which is known in India as 'Samādhi'. A true theosophist, she says, must put in practice the loftiest moral ideal, must strive to realize his unity with the whole of humanity and work ceaselessly for others.[3]

The fundamental contentions of the Secret Doctrine : an eclectic approach and elements borrowed from the Upaniṣads.

With this preliminary it will now be convenient for us to follow the fundamental teachings of the Secret Doctrine and see how far H. P. Blavatsky voices the spirit of the Upaniṣads. In fact it must be noted at the beginning, as Madame Blavatsky herself concedes, that what she offers is nothing original, but a 'nosegay' of different views. She is correct. Her approach is purely eclectic. It is virtually a hotch potch

3. Ibid : P—16.

of eastern and western ideas, although she borrows more liberally from Indian thought.

The three fundamental propositions are sought to be established in the Secret Doctrine. First, there is an Omnipresent, Eternal, Boundless and Immutable principle on which speculation is impossible, since it transcends the power of human conception and can only be distorted by the efforts to describe it through language. It is beyond the range and reach of thought,—in the words of the Māṇḍukya 'unthinkable' and unspeakable.[4] To render this idea clearer Madame Blavatsky says that the absolute reality should be adopted as a postulate which precedes all manifestation. It is the Infinite and Eternal cause, the rootless root of all that was, is or ever shall be. It is devoid of all attributes and is essentially without any relation to the manifested finite being. It is 'Beeness' rather than 'Being',—'Sat' in Sanskrit and is beyond all thought or speculation.

The second proposition of the Secret Doctrine explains the absolute universality of the law of periodicity, of flux and reflux, ebb and flow, which physical science has observed and recorded in all departments of Nature. 'The alternation of Day and Night, Life and Death, Sleeping and Waking—is a fact which is universal and without exception and it is, therefore, easy to comprehend that in it we see one of the absolutely fundamental laws of the universe'.[5]

The third important teaching of the Secret Doctrine is that there is a fundamental identity of all souls with the Universal Oversoul and this Oversoul, Blavatsky thinks, is the obligatory pilgrimage for every soul.

Now in explaining the fundamental root cause of the universe Madame Blavatsky appears to hold the view that One Reality—the Absolute or Parabrahman is of the nature

4. The Secret Doctrine—Vol. I, P—79.
5. Ibid : P—82.

of absolute consciousness, i. e., 'that Essence' which is out of all relation to the conditioned existence of the finite world. It is here that she reflects the concept of undifferentiated Brahman as explained in the Māṇḍukya Upaniṣad.[6] When, however, we think of the manifested universe with its duality of matter and spirit (otherwise spoken of as object and subject or substance and consciousness respectively), we can not, as Blavatsky says, regard spirit and matter as independent realities, but as two symbols or aspects of the Absolute or Parabrahman which constitutes the basis of the conditioned being whether subjective or objective.[7] All manifestation thus proceeds from this Absolute which is the source and origin (fons et origo) of 'Force' and of all individual consciousness and supplies the guiding intelligence in the vast scheme of cosmic evolution. Hence all individual consciousness and the different grades of differentiation of matter are rooted in the Absolute. The subject and the object, the spirit and matter are but the aspects of the

---

6. Cf. "Adṛśyaṁ avyavahāryaṁ agrāhyaṁ alakṣaṇani acintyaṁ avyapadeśyaṁ ekātma pratyayasāraṁ prapañco'paśamaṁ śāntaṁ śivaṁ advaitaṁ caturthaṁ manyante".—Māṇḍukya—7.

7. This idea is developed in the following passage :—

"The most distinct and the one prevailing idea, found in all ancient teaching, with reference to Cosmic Evolution and the first creation of our Globe with all its products, organic and inorganic,......is that the whole Kosmos has sprung from the Divine Thought. This Thought impregnates Matter which is co-eternal with the One Reality : and all that lives and breathes evolves from the Emanations of the One Immutable, Parabrahman—Mūlāprakṛti, the eternal One Root".—The Secret Doctrine,—Vol. 2—Section 3.

Thus it appears that when Blavatsky speaks of the universe as the periodical manifestation of Parabrahman through Mūlāprakṛti, she obviously refers to mūrta Brahman; and has in her mind the Sāṁkhya concept of 'mahat'—the first step forward of Pradhāna (i.e. Prakṛti in its creative role). She thus appears to borrow an element from Sāṁkhya philosophy.

One Unity in which they are synthesized.[8] Sri Krishna prem and Sri Madhava Ashish explain the point when they say : 'There is no part of man as there is no part of the cosmos which has not emerged from the unitary source. Within us and around us we experience nothing but aspects of divine consciousness.'[9]

Madame Blavatsky refers repeatedly in her dissertation to the accumulated wisdom of the ancient seers, particularly of India and points out that the flashing gaze of those seers has penetrated into the very kernel of matter and recorded the soul of things there, where an ordinary profane observer, however learned, would have perceived but the external work of form. But modern science does not believe in the 'Soul of things', and hence rejects the whole system of ancient cosmogony. Blavatsky is of opinion that the chief difficulty which prevents men of science from believing in divine as well as nature spirits is their materialism. She is however careful to add here that neither the occultists nor the theosophists reject the views and theories of modern scientists only because these views are opposed to theosophy. The theosophists, in fact, are the first to recognize the intrinsic value of science. "But when its high priests resolve consciousness into a secretion from the grey matter of the brain, and everything else in Nature into a mode of motion, we protest against the doctrine as being unphilosophical, self-contradictory and simply absurd, from a scientific point of view, as much and even more than from the occult aspect of the esoteric knowledge".[10] Again the principal impediment which may hinder a spiritualist from believing in 'matter' is the general ignorance of the exact

---

8. Vide : The Secret Doctrine—Vol. I, P—80-81.
9. Sri Krishna Prem and Sri Madhava Ashish : 'Man the measure of all things'. P-25.
10. The Secret Doctrine, Vol—I, P-336.

nature of matter. Blavatsky thus seeks to resolve the contradiction existing between science and philosophy by holding the view that everything in the universe is imbued with life. She says that we men must remember that simply because we do not perceive any mark of consciousness, say in stones, we have no right to say that no consciousness exists there. There is no such thing as blind or dead matter, nor is there any blind or unconscious law: She thus becomes an upholder of panpsychism. Nature, taken in its abstract sense, can not be unconscious, as it is the emanation from and thus an aspect, on the manifested plane, of the 'Absolute Consciousness'. "Where is that daring man", asks Blavasky, "Who would presume to deny to vegetation and even to minerals, a consciousness of their own ? All he can say is that this consciousness is beyond his comprehension".[11] This view is shared by Friedrich Paulsen, a famous German idealist.[12] In fact the theory of panpsychism finds acceptance even among the modern natural scientists who discard the idea of absolutely dead and rigid bodies. Blavatsky thus indicates that the same mental thread runs through the material phenomena, and the human mind is the highest development on the earth of the mental processes that animate the entire nature.

A believer in teleology, Madame Blavatsky thinks that the

---

11. Ibid : Vol—I, P-320.
12, Cf. "From the beginnings of Greek Philosophy to our day, the philosophical, that is, universal view of reality has gone beyond the physical—astronomical notion and has regarded it as necessary to associate with reality in general and in particular, an inner, ideal, mental principle. Plato and Aristotle, Spinoza and Leibnitz, Schelling and Schopenhauer, Lotze and Fechner, however else their thoughts may diverge, all agree that the mental element does not play the part of an isolated side-issue in the world ; that on the contrary 'everything corporeal' points to something else, an inner, intelligible element, a being for itself which is akin to what we experience within ourselves".

—Friedrich Paulsen : 'Introduction to Philosophy',—P-93.

whole order of Nature evinces a progressive march towards a higher life. There is also a design in the action of the apparently blindest forces. The whole process of evolution with its endless adaptations is a proof of this. The immutable laws that weed out the weak and the feeble species to make room for the strong, and which ensure the survival of the fittest, though apparently cruel in their immediate action, are all working towards the grand end. The very fact that adaptations do occur or that the fittest do survive in the struggle for existence, shows that what is called unconscious Nature is in reality an aggregate of forces.

What appears from the foregoing discussion is that Madame Blavatsky comes very near the contentions of the Upaniṣads and the Advaita Vedanta. We have already seen that referring to the ancient Indian thought she says that the central point discussed there from which everything emerges, around and towards which everything gravitates and upon which is hung all its philosophy, is One Homogenous, Divine Substance—Principle, the One Radical Cause. It appears as a substance on the plane of the manifested universe, which according to her, is an illusion.[13] But it remains a 'Principle'—a root cause in the beginningless and endless, abstract, visible and invisible space. It is impersonal and omnipresent Reality containing everything and is latent in every atom of the universe itself.[14] This observation obviously goes to account for the fact that Madame Blavatsky has a leaning to the pantheistic

13. "All that which is, emanates from the Absolute which by reason of this qualification alone, stands as the one and only Reality,—hence everything extraneous to the Absolute, the generative and causative Element, must be an illusion most undeniably." 'The Secret Doctrine'—vol. I,—P-335. Vide : Vol. 2, Part-3, Section-14.

14. (i) Cf. "Sarvaṁ Khalvidaṁ Brahma tajjalāniti"—Chāndogya Upa. 3. 14.1.

(ii) Vide : 'The Secret Doctrine'—Vol-1, P-317 & Vol. 2, Sec-3.

world-view as advocated in the Upaniṣads. But the fundamental difference between her system and that of the Upaniṣads lies in the fact that she favours illusionism ('māyāvāda' in the spirit of the Advaitin) which, as we have seen, is not a decided view of the Upaniṣads. She distinctly holds the view that the universe with everything in it is māyā, since everything is evanescent here 'from the ephemeral life of a fire-fly to that of the sun'. Compared to the eternity and immutability of the One Divine Reality, the mundane things with their fleeting and ever changing forms, must be necessarily in the mind of a philosopher a will-o'-the wisp. This universe appears to be real only to the conscious beings who are as unreal as it is in itself. What Madame Blavatsky means is that the experience on any plane is an actuality for the percipient being whose consciousness is on that plane, though the said experience, regarded from the purely metaphysical standpoint, may be conceived to have no objective reality. This attitude naturally indicates that Blavatsky has adopted the advaitin standpoint. It must be noted, however, that in 'explaining' illusionism Blavatsky's arguments differ from those of an advaitin. Her concept of māyā is not exactly the same as it is with Śaṁkara. To Śaṁkara the universe is māyā in the sense that it gives us a distorted view of reality by making what is intrinsically one appear as many. To Bavatsky it is māyā because it is in flux. This is, therefore, an element which she has borrowed from the Buddhistic philosophy. Hence it appears that she has not given a faithful reflection of the Upaniṣadic spirit in developing the idea of the Absolute in its relation to the finite world.

In fine we must take note of certain other points on which Madame Blavatsky appears to echo the Upaniṣadic thought. She maintains, for example, that the universe is regulated by the Absolute from within and not from without, and that there is a fundamental identity of all souls with the Universal Oversoul or Absolute. To realize this Absolute, she says, is obligatory for us, and this is possible not through any logical reasoning or speculation, but through mystical intuition.[15] These ideas she has clearly borrowed from the Upaniṣads, for according to them the Ātman or Brahman is Antaryāmī, that is, it regulates everything from within the world.[16] The universe is planned and controlled by a superior pervasive intelligence which is Brahman.[17] He who realizes his essential identity with this Brahman through prolonged contemplation, can mitigate all sorrows, infatuation and bereavement arising out of ignorance.[18]

---

15. Commenting on the 'Stanzas of Dzyan' as recorded in the 'Secret Doctrine' Sri Krishna prem and Sri Madhaba Ashish make a very pertinent observation which may be mentioned in this connection : "Such texts are not the sterile postulates of the laboratory, but teachings for the soul, based on mystical experience and intended to be corroborated by mystical experience. The truths of the soul are to be experienced, not just speculated about".

—Sri Krishna Prem and Madhava Ashish,
—'Man the measure of all things', P—21.

16. "Yaḥ pṛthivīmantaro' yamayati eṣa te ātmā antaryāmi amṛtaḥ".
—Bṛhadāraṇyaka, 3.7.3.

17, "Saḥ paryagāt.........paribhūḥ sayambhū yāthā
tathyataḥ vyadadhāt śāśvatībhyaḥ samābhyaḥ".
—Īśa ; 8.

18. "Yasmin sarvāṇi bhūtani
ātmaivābhūd vijānataḥ,
tatra ko mohaḥ kaḥ śoka,
ekatvamanupaśyataḥ".
—Īśa ; 7.

SECTION 3

IMPACT ON THE NINETEENTH CENTURY WESTERN LITERATURE

CHAPTER—VIII

ENGLISH POETS

Introduction.

We have explained and analysed so far the impact of the Upanişadic pantheism on the philosophical systems of the nineteenth century. Now in this section we shall rivet our attention upon the literary mart of the western world, for pantheistic thought, as we have found in the Upanişads has also been remarkably poetized by some of the poets of outstanding merit belonging to this century. We find in their poetic productions an astonishing similarity in thought with the Upanişads, although it is not a fact that every one of them was acquainted with the Upanişadic teaching. We shall, therefore, refer to them and explore the close resemblance and also the extent of the Upanişadic impact—direct or indirect as the case may be. Our enquiry will start with two English poets viz., Wordsworth and Shelley.

William Wordsworth (1770—1850)

In the early nineteenth century Wordsworth occupied and exalted position among the English romantic poets. A considered opinion about him is that he is the greatest interpreter of Nature in English poetry and in certain respects he appears to be without any peer among the English poets. His attitude to Nature differed fundamentally from that of others in that he was not simply content with admiring the external and scintillating charm and loveliness of Nature. He probed deep into Nature's mystic meaning. Since his early childhood Wordsworth had experienced the benign influence of external nature. When he was an imma ture boy he wandered like a child of Nature among the hills and dales, the meadows and streams of lake districts where he was born and brought up. The steady clouds, the charming flowers of the meadows, the stars, the streams and such other lovely things of Nature moulded his being. The poet is prolific in recording his indebtedness to Nature. He expressly declares that all that was good in him—his little nameless, unremembered acts of kindness and love and his entire moral existence was the result of the salutary influence Nature had exerted on him. Nature was to him the anchor of his lofty and purest thoughts. But for her assuaging influence on his character the poet could not have surmounted his hours of trouble. His traumatic state of existence following the disappointment in the French Revolution might have turned him a sour misanthrope. But Nature only, as the poet himself says, saved him from his possible degeneration and acted to him as a friend, philosopher and guide. Thus to Wordsworth, Nature was not a dead, inert, material substance. The poet discovered in her a living soul or an active principle. We find a wonderful poetic rendering of this idea in the poem 'The Excursion'.[1] Wordsworth's poetry, as David Nichol Smith rightly points out, 'makes no division between man and the world in which he lives. He thinks of all created

1. "To every Form of being is assigned
An 'active' principle—however removed
From sense and observation, it subsists
In all things, in all nature ; in the stars
Of azure heaven, the unending clouds,
In flower and tree, in every pebble stone
That paves the brooks, the stationary rocks,
The moving waters, and the invisible air".

things, human or inanimate as parts of one great whole, filling their appointed place, moving in their established order'.[2]

In his famous autobiographical poem 'The Prelude' Wordsworth exhibits the development of his own mind as a poet. This poem reveals him both as a poet of Nature and as a poet of Man. Here also it is of things pervaded by a spirit that the poet speaks in the opening lines of Book XII. It is again of Nature conceived as a unitary being and an inspirer of emotions and moods that he speaks in the opening lines of Book XIII. As a matter of fact throughout 'The Prelude' the poet speaks of Nature as things and places animated either by an all-pervading spirit or by spirits of their own. His dominant conception, however, is that Nature is a body possessed of a 'Soul'. There is a spiritual presence in things—a conscious spiritual life which animates all objects. It pulsates in the clod ; it breathes in the rock ; it murmurs in the brook ; it throbs in the sea ; it moves in the cloud ; it inhabits the stars ; it rolls in all things and is the soul of all. Thus we find that instead of a crass materialism or crude deism with a transcendent God, Wordsworth gives us a spiritual interpretation of reality and proceeds to speak of an all-pervading spirit or God maintaining the reality of both God and the finite things.

The famous poem of Wordsworth—'Tintern Abbey'[3] occupies a distinctive position in the whole corpus of English romantic poetry. It deserves our special consideration, for here we find the Wordsworthian creed concerning Nature

2. Wordsworth : Poetry and Prose ; Introduction—
by David Nichol Smith.

3. The full title of the poem reads :—"Lines composed a few miles above Tintern Abbey on revisiting the banks of the Wye during a tour, July 13, 1798". The poem was written in 1798 and was included as the last piece in the "Lyrical Ballads" published that year in collaboration with S. T. Coleridge.

and Man and their relation set to a beautiful and impassioned music. It is virtually Wordsworth's autobiography in miniature illustrating the evolution of his soul and the various stages of his attitude towards Nature and also explaining the conception of an all-pervading soul which, as we shall see, is in perfect conformity to the cosmic conception of Brahman illustrated in the Upaniṣads.

The occasion of the poem is the revisiting of the river Wye near Tintern Abbey in 1798. The poet feels that these 'beauteous forms' of Nature are now as impressive as they were when he visited the spot five years before. Wordsworth reiterates hts unflinching faith in the purifying and chastening power of Nature on man, because by virtue of this healing influence the poet has been able to preserve his cheerful spirit during his years of tribulation. His love of Nature, therefore, continues unabated. While recording his indebtedness to Nature the poet also reviews the changes that have been wrought over him. Now when he revisits the former scenes, these attractive surroundings yield not only a sense of 'present pleasure', but also the feelings and thoughts that lead to a remoter charm. The first stage of his attitude to Nature was marked by a sort of wild and thoughtless gaiety of a boy, which however had vanished subsequently giving place to a burning passion for all that was beautiful in Nature. "The sounding cataract haunted me like a passion", says Wordsworth. When he beholds Nature he often hears "The still sad music of humanity, nor harsh, nor grating though of ample power to chasten and subdue." There is, in other words, nothings repugnant or discordant about the 'still sad music of humanity'. Further we also find something more in the final stage of his attitude to Nature. He says that he is conscious of the presence of a universal soul animating all things and linking up everything in the universe. It is just his poetic insight that reveals to him 'a presence' that disturbs him 'with the joy of elevated thoughts'. He has a deep poetic feeling or profound consciousness that there is an immanent and active spirit pervading the world of man and the world of external nature. This idea is given a grand poetic expression in the following lines of 'Tintern Abbey':—

"And I have felt
A presence that disturbs me with the joy
Of elevated thoughts, a sense sublime
Of something far more deeply interfused,
Whose dwelling is the light of setting suns,
And the round ocean and the living air,
And the blue sky, and in the mind of man:
A motion and a spirit, that impels
All thinking things, all objects of all thought
And rolls through all things".[4]

Here Wordsworth with the insight of a true poet and a mystical philosopher attempts to explain the conception of Supreme Reality. It is on the strength of the view of immanence of this Spirit both in Nature and in man, and the conception of it as actively animating the entire existence so superbly conveyed by the poet in the aforesaid lines, that we can consider Wordsworth a pantheist.

In order to substantiate our view we have to make a critical survey of the opinion of some of the critics who do not subscribe to the contention that Wordsworth is a pantheist. Prof. E. H. Sneath, for instance, is in favour of regarding the Wordsworthian view as theistic, and not as pantheistic. He is of opinion that a thorough-going pantheism identifies Nature with God or Absolute and this God or universal spirit is never spoken of by a pantheist as 'dwelling' in the natural phenomena or in the minds of men. Things and minds do not exist apart from the Absolute. They have no essential being, no separate individuality according to

4. 'Tintern Abbey'—Lines 93-102.

pantheism They exist only as modes of one ultimate Being. To quote Prof. Sneath: "Wordsworth's conception of a Spirit present in things and in the mind of man,—a Spirit which is the impelling power of both—is very far removed from such a philosophy".[5] Referring to Wordsworth's recognition of the existence of three distinct natures viz,. (i) a universal presence, (ii) a world of corporeal things and (iii) a world of finite spirits, Sneath again says: "He (Wordsworth) does not identify the universal Spirit with the 'light of setting suns' nor with 'the round ocean', nor with 'the living air', nor with 'the blue sky', nor with 'the mind of man'. He merely affirms that these are its 'dwelling' and that Spirit is their impelling power. Pantheism is not involved in such a statement. The poet is merely giving expression to his faith in the immanence of the Spirit in the world — a faith which is in thorough accord with theism".[6] Again it is also pointed out by Sneath that the ethical tone of Wordsworth is quite distinctly pronounced in the poem 'Tintern Abbey Lines'. When the poet felt 'a presence' in Nature his love for her augmented a great deal and he found in her an anchor for his noblest thoughts, a 'nurse', a 'guide', a guardian of his heart and the soul of his moral being. To the poet Nature always ministers to the intellectual, aesthetic and moral needs of man. But according to pantheism there can be no moral life in God or man, for morality presupposes the conception of self-determined personality, and pantheism precludes the possibility of personality. To a pantheist all being is governed by the inner law of necessity and therefore there is no such thing as self-determining being.[7]

In our view it is improper to regard Wordsworth as a theist and not as a pantheist for the simple reason that he

---

5. E. H. Sneath: 'Wordsworth: Poet of Nature and Poet of Man'. P—131.
6. Ibid: P—131.
7. Ibid; P—130.

did not identify the world of reality with God or Absolute in the spirit of a thorough-going pantheist. It must be carefully noted that the non-recognition of identity between God and the world does not necessarily amount to rejection of pantheism. A sympathetic understanding with the poetic insight of Wordsworth (as revealed in his poems, particularly in 'Tintern Abbey') enables us to hold the view that he was a pantheist in spite of the fact that he did not propagate a carefully reasoned system of a thorough-going pantheism in the light in which Prof. Sneath understands it.

In interpreting Wordsworth what we must bear in mind is that he was above everything else a poet and not a metaphysician. As a poet, very naturally, he thought in terms of images and not in syllogisms. Nevertheless, there is a philosophical thinking in his poems. J. C. Smith is absolutely on the dot when he observes: "His (Wordsworth's) philosophy was the soil in which his poetry flowered"[8] Even Prof. Sneath also does not demur to this when he says: "He (Wordsworth) was pre-eminently a poet—a philosophic poet, pre-eminently an intuitionist. Virtually all of his poetry so far as it deals with basal conceptions, is intuitional in character. He seldom 'reasons', he 'sees'. He is a seer rather than a philosopher".[9] Hence in evaluating Wordsworth's poetry we should be careful to note that he reaches the heart of things not by cold intellectual processes, —by analysis and dissection, but by a peculiar mystical insight or intuition. Now if we do not forget this distinctive Wordsworthian trait, we can not indict Wordsworth for not expounding a strictly systematic metaphysical theory of

8. J. C. Smith : 'A Study of Wordsworth'. Chapter VII, P-89.
9. E. H. Sneath : 'Wordsworth-poet of Nature and poet of Man'.
The view that Wordsworth was primarily a poet and not a philosopher, is also shared by A. C. Bradley ; Vide : Oxford Lectures on Poetry'. 'Wordsworth'—P-129.

a relation of things to the Absolute Spirit. Hence when he speaks of a Spirit 'dwelling' in natural objects, or of 'a motion and a spirit that impels all thinking things...... and rolls through all things',—all that he means is that the entire world is pervaded by a universal Spirit. This concept of the divine immanence in the world constitutes the main strength of pantheism.[10]

It appears from above that it is neither very easy nor quite relevant to seek any definite answer to the question as to whether Wordsworth was 'purely' a theist or a 'tho rough-going pantheist. The critics are, in fact, very much divided on the point.[11] What is relevant and possible for us

---

10. Prof. Sneath could not ignore this view although he interpreted Wordsworth as having a definite leaning to theism. Vide: E. H. Sneath—'Wordsworth—poet of Nature and poet of Man'. P-132

11. Prof. Sneath is of opinion that Wordsworth was, in his later years, gradually led to a dependence on orthodox Christian faith much more than on his Nature faith for power to comfort and sustain the afflicted human soul. He says: Now he (Wordsworth) sees with the eye of a Christian faith and with the eye of reason rather than with the eye of mystical intuition".—Ibid; P-297.

Prof. Dowden, however, points out that even here Wordsworth 'found the Divine Presence abroad in nature and in the spirit of man and refused to narrow it to a paddock, Anglican or other'. Vide: Dowden: The Poetical Works of William Wordworth; Vol—I, P-Lxi; 1892.

Referring to Wordsworth's attitude to Christianity Coleridge said of him in 1798: "He (Wordsworth) loves and reverences Christ and Christianity. I wish he did more.".

J. C. Smith observes in this connection that Wordsworth may well have passed through a stage which could fairly be called pantheistic. To quote his words: "It might fairly be doubted whether the author of 'Tintern Abbey' conceived of 'something far more deeply interfused' as a transcendent and personal Deity....Poems of this period from 'Tintern Abbey' to 'Immortality Ode' contain nothing that is definitely Christian. It is not that they never refer to the central mysteries of Christian faith—The Incarnation, the Atonement, the Resurrection, but that the whole way of salvato hold is that in a particular period of Wordsworth's poetic career the pantheistic creed was distinctly pronounced. And this pantheism in the sense that there is an all-comprehensive Spirit or Absolute pervading the entire existence, is demonstrated in the lines of 'Tentern Abbey'. This contention is very much akin to the Upaniṣadic view born of the cosmic conception of the Absolute we have dealt with in the first section of our work. Wordsworth, in the spirit of the Upaniṣads, recognizes the relative reality of the universe and does not consider the multiplicity an illusion as the thorough-going pantheists normally do. The method of approaching the Absolute according to the Upaniṣads, is, as we have seen, both intellectual and intuitive, while Wordsworth speaks only of intuitive apprehension. Wordsworth's thoughts, it may be noted incidentally, appear to be very much similar to that of the contemporary German idealists. But there seems to have been no direct borrowing on Wordsworth's part. He is understood to have known nothing of German metaphysics beyond what he might have heard from Coleridge. "Writing to Crabb Robinson in 1840 he thanked that he never read a word of German

tion which they imply has no place for these mysteries—J. C. Smith : 'A study of Wordsworth',—P-92. Wordsworth in his view returned to orthodoxy later. To quote him again : "For Wordsworth, to return to orthodoxy meant to return to the Church of England. ....His study of English History including the study of Church History which afterwards yielded the 'Ecclesiastical Sonnets', convinced him that the Church of England was the appointed guardian of England's soul, and his own observation had taught him that in many parts of the country only the clergy of the Established Church stood between the people and barbarism. Having returned to the Anglican Church Wordsworth accepted most of her dogmas. ....As the years went on he identified himself more and more closely with the interests of the Church, temporal as well as spiritual".—J. C. Smith : 'A Study of Wordsworth'—P-100.

metaphysics".[12] As to Wordsworth's knowledge of the Upaniṣads we do not get any evidence of his acquaintance with Duperron's French or Latin translation or with any other translation of the Upaniṣads. It is only in the evolutionary process of Wordsworth's attitude to Nature that we find the poet reaching a pantheistic world-view. "The main movement carries the poet from the sensory to the emotional and the mystical, from matter-of-fact observation (sensory and psychological) to mystical insight and cosmic vision".[13] Wordsworth thus speaks of a universal Spirit as knitting together in a splendid harmony all the things of the world. This awareness or vision of a universal soul enables him to perceive the underlying unity in all things. It is here that the poet perfectly reflects the Upaniṣadic spirit.

P. B. Shelley (1792—1822).

William Wordsworth and S. T. Coleridge are found to have dominated the first part of the English romantic poetry and in the second part we come across Byron, Shelley and Keats. Here we shall make a passing reference to Shelley's thoughts as revealed in his famous poem 'Adonais' which is relevant to our enquiry.

'Adonais' is an elegy[14] written by Shelley in 1821 on his

12. Ibid : P—89.
13. Vide : 'Critics on Wordsworth',—Edited by Raymond Cowell. Albert S. Gerard's essay on 'Exploring Tintern Abbey'.
14. Following the form of pastoral elegy, this poem imitates and sometimes echoes two famous Greek elegies of the 1st century B. C. Viz., Bion's Lament for Adonis' and the 'Lament for Bion' supposed to be written by Moschus, but really by an anonymous pupil of Bion. The name 'Adonais' is Shelley's invention, a modification of 'Adonis'. The impression in the poem (lines 316-342) that Keats's premature death was caused by the effect on him of

fellow poet Keats who had died of consumption in Rome. Shelley, in fact, was not a close friend of Keats. His emotion expressed in the poem 'Adonais' is not so much a personal grief as sorrow at the loss to poetry. "He seems to have had no great admiration for any of Keats's poems except 'Hyperion'. In the others he found only promise. But he nad been eager in oflers of service to keats for he saw that Keats was a pcet devoted to his art, and in 'Adonais' he wrote of the glory of that art, and the mystery of death as much as of Keats himself".[15]

Following the convention of pastoral elegy Shelley employs not only the imagery of the shepherd's life, but introduces certain traditional features also, for example, the expostulatory question addressed to some higher power,[16] the laments of Nature for the dead,[17] and the procession of the mourners.[18] From the beginning we find Shelley making lamentation with solemn music for the departed soul of Keats. Gradually Shelley's imagination expresses itself in the first pastoral allusion.[19] At the thirty eighth stanza

---

the savage criticism of his 'Endymion' in the 'Quarterly Review' is not probably true. Keats is understood to have manfully refused to be daunted by the adverse criticism of a poem he himself thought of but poorly, and in fact all his great poems were written after the attacks upon him. The hostility of the critics, however, diminished the chances of his earning his living by poetry and may have reduced his power of resistance to the disease he suffered from.

15. A. Clutton Brock : Shelley the Man and the Poet'.—P-261.

16. "Where wert thou, mighty Mother, when he lay,
When thy son lay, pierced by the shaft which flies
in darkness ? Where was lorn Urania
Where Adonais died ?

17. 'Adonais'—Lines 188-144.

18. 'Adonais'—Lincs 262-315.

19. "Oh weep for Adonais ;—The quick Dreams,
The passion-winged Ministers of thought,
Who were his flocks, whom near the living streams

of the poem (Adonais) we find a sudden change from grief to something like joy. The complete reversal of tone, from grief to joy in the final portion of 'Lycidas'[20] is a new feature introduced by Milton and is copied to a certain degree by Shelley in his 'Adonais'. Like Milton, Shelley also thinks of impersonal immortality of man, which under the influence of Platonism achieves a new significance. Because of absence of intimacy with Keats Shelley's emotion of bereavement does not swell very much and he has been able to communicate his feelings and thoughts in a much restrained way.[21] At the fortieth stanza we note that the pastoral convention drops away and the poem becomes a hymn to the glory of art and the mystery of death.[22] The burden

---

of his young spirit he fed, and whom he taught
The love which was its music, wander not.—
Wander no more, from kindling brain to brain,
But droop there, whence they sprung ; and mourn
Round the cold heart, where, after their sweet pain,
They ne'er, will gather strength, or find a home again.
(L—73-81)

20. Cf. "So Lycidas sunk low, but mounted high,
Through the dear might of him that walked the waves......
(—Milton's Lycidas ; L—172-173.)

In ancient Greek pastoral elegies this note of hope and joy is not found, for man there meets the inevitable darkness of death.
But here the indication from darkness to light,
from death to immortality is hinted at by Milton.

Shelley also holds the view :—
"Nor let us weep that our delight is fed
Far from these carrion Kites that scream below ;."
—Adonais ; L—334-35.

21. "Peace, peace ; he is not dead, he doth not sleep—
He hath awakened from the dream of life—
(L—343-44).

22. "He has outsoared the shadow of our night ;
Envy and calumny and hate and pain,

—'Oh, weep for Adonais''! — changes into :

"Mourn not for Adonais ! Thou young Dawn,
Turn all thy dew to splendour, for from thee
The spirit thou lamentest is not gone."

Shelley seems to have nursed a view of life analogous to the doctrine of māyā. Phenomenal life, for him, is of the nature of illusion, a dream, and death is a waking from this dream to reality. This view that the visible universe with its multiplicity of phenomena, misrepresents the final reality which is not manifold but undivided unity, is expressed in the passage :

"The one remains, the many change and pass;
Heaven's light for ever shines, Earth's shadows fly;
Life, like a dome of many-coloured glass,
Stains the white radiance of Eternity,
Until Death tramples it to fragments".

(Lines 460–64)

Platonism in Shelley is clearly marked in this view. But it would be a mistake to suppose that Shelley lives consistently on that plane. Though the world is illusion, it has a kind of fairy tale reality in whose dominion his poetry is often willing to linger, indeed in which poetry must linger.[23]

The thought in the poem 'Adonais' takes a sudden turn, as we have already indicated, from lamentation to a sort of immortality foretold for Adonais, and this defiant assertion of immortality leads the poet at once to the conception of a Supreme Being or God (for which 'Beauty', 'Love' and such other abstract terms are mostly used by Shelley) pervading the universe. After death Adonais has become a part

And that unrest which men miscall delight,
Can touch him not and torture not again" ;
(—Adonais, L—352-55).

23. Cf. Graham Haugh : 'The Romantic Poets'. Ch. IV, P-147.

of the spirit that governs the universe. This is given a poignant poetic expression thus :—

"He is a presence to be felt and known
In darkness and in light, from herb and stone,
Spreading itself where'er that Power may move
Which has withdrawn his being to its own ;
Which wields the world with never-wearied love,
Sustains it from beneath, and kindles it above".
(Lines 373-78)

Now as with Wordsworth so also with Shelley, we do not find any evidence of his direct acquaintance with the Upaniṣads. Nor can it be said that Shelley has maintained consistently the pantheistic viewpoint all through. But from a consideration of the thoughts introduced in the poem 'Adonais', it can hardly be doubted that the belief in an all-embracing Absolute Spirit has been shared by him and it is here that he closely approaches the pantheistic world-view of the Upaniṣads.

CHAPTER—IX

Ralph Waldo Emerson. (1803—1882)

Introduction.

Of the host of American thinkers of the nineteenth century famous for their prodigious contribution, Emerson is one who holds an illustrious position for his keen interest in the moral and spiritual development of man. In his long and eventful life Emerson composed a good number of poems and essays which bear the mark not only of his literary talent, but of the depth of his religious and philosophical thinking as well. His poems, however, contain some stylistic and structural defects which a more meticulous craftsman would have avoided. As a matter of fact Emerson cared very little for prosodic perfection or melodic effects as he was intent primarily upon the idea he wanted to convey.[1] But in spite of the structural defects of his poems Emerson holds a central place among American men of letters because the message he wanted to communicate to mankind remains as vital and stimulating to day as it was to the men of his day-

Idealistic outlook.

Emerson's was a theory of spiritualistic idealism. Strongly resenting the barbarism and materialism of the age he

1. Emerson himself was conscious of his deficiency as a poet and he acknowledges it in one of his letters addressed to a friend :—

"I feel it a hardship that with something of a lover's passion for what is to me the most precious thing in life, poetry, I have no gift of fluency in it, only a rude and stammering utterance". (Vide : Letters of R. W. Emerson—edited by R. L. Rusk ; New York, 1939).

berated the people of his time when they in their mad materialistic pursuits were oblivious of the need of their moral and spiritual uplift.[2] He believed with all his heart and accordingly asserted repeatedly through his essays and lectures that spirit overlies nature and that man has only one proper choice. Alive to the world of Nature in which man exists and with which man comes in regular contact, Emerson nursed no hostility to Nature. To quote him : "I do not wish to fling stones at my beautiful mother, nor soil my gentle nest. I only wish to indicate the true position of Nature in regard to man".[3] Natural objects were thus only the mediate things to him and not ultimate realities. The telling observations[4] he made in course of his lectures on Nature point to the fact that his choice of the ideal over the material or mind over matter as presenting the higher reality, was considered and deliberate. This way of thinking made Emerson what we call an idealist. It must be noted however, that his thoughts and ideas as reflected in his essays give rise to a hot controversy among the critics, and he has been interpreted and re-interpreted in various ways since his time down to the present day. Emerson's views lying scattered in his works are largely responsible for generating this controversy. Prof. H. A. Pochman and G. W. Allen

---

2. Cf. "Man must never lose in his material quests, his longing for the touch of the divine". –Rabindranath Tagore : 'Religion of Man'.

3. Vide : Emerson's lectures on 'Nature'.

4. A few such observations are worth mentioning :—

   (i) Every natural fact is a symbol of some spiritual fact'. (ii) 'The laws of moral nature answer to those of matter like face to face in a glass'. (iii) 'The axioms of Physics translate the laws of Ethics'. (iv) 'Every natural process is a version of a moral sentence'. (v) 'Be it (Nature) what it may, it is ideal to me so long as I can not try the accuracy of my senses'.—Vide : Lectures on 'Nature' delivered in 1836.

have elaborately dealt with this point.[5]

What, in fact, Emerson never relinquished was his genuine faith in goodness, in the distinction between right and wrong, and in the Supreme Spirit inherent in man. 'His

5. "His (Emerson's) idealism was subtle enough to accept both mind and matter, even while endeavouring at various times during his life, to reconcile or identify the two with each other. An uphappy dualist, he sought throughout his life to unify this world,—to make it monistic—to reduce the dualistic enigma of mind and matter to unity. To this end he searched the scientists from ancient to modern times no less than the idealistic philosophers from Plato to Kant and beyond. He sought to reconcile science and religion or as he put it to make his 'religion philosophical' and his 'philosophy religious'. In the process he rejected neither the natural nor the spiritual. ....But he alienated both the orthodox theologian and the strict scientist. Neither forgave him for what he conceded to the other. To the theologian he was a heretic, infidel, atheist; to the scientist, a transcendental dreamer, a mystical soothsayer. an impractical idealist.
These irreconciled elements in Emerson are not the only faults that men have found with Emerson. There are other inconsistencies that he did not bother to harmonize. He had no patience with what he called 'foolish consistency'. He declared: 'I delight in telling what I think, but if you ask me how I dare say so, I am the most helpless of mortal men'. ......He defied tradition and authority, and he wrote in the mood of the moment, from inspiration. ....Hence it often turned out that what he said in one connection contradicts what he said in another. Accordingly the seekers after paradox have found it easy matter to make him out 'conservative or liberal, or radical, orthodox or infidel, moralist or amoralist, belligerent or pacific, patriot or traitor. And on the basis of a single or isolated passages, he is all these and more too."
But whatever difficulties Emerson the lecturer or the essayist presented to his followers, and however many conflicts he failed to settle in his own mind, he was consistent on one point. He believed implicitly in the moral principle as supreme and absolute. His God seemed to many people of doubtful divinity, but no one doubted Emerson's faith in goodness. In deed goodness and Godliness were very nearly synonymous with Emerson".—Henry A. Pochman and Gay Wilson Allen: 'Masters of American Literature'. Vol—I, P 675-76.

exaltation of man is praise to the God in man, and the self he describes is the higher self whose paternity is divine. What he rhapsodizes in the 'Essays' are his occasions of spiritual enlargement. A self-realization of this high order provides the thematic unity of the essays, and gives them their electric and liberating effect'.[6] Hence without entering into the quagmire of controversy, what is relevant for us is to analyse some of his remarkable writings where the gleanings of his thought can be discovered to have profound kinship with Indian scriptural texts. In our analysis it will also be evident that Emerson makes no pretension in candidly acknowledging his debt to the Indian scriptures.

Emerson and the Upaniṣads.

We shall first take up Emerson's famous poem 'Brahma'.[7] In the first four lines of the poem he voices almost literally a verse from the Bhagavadgītā and the Katho' paniṣad. He who considers this self as a slayer or he who thinks

6. Vide : Emerson's Essays –Introduction,—S. Paul.
7. The original poem reads :—

"If the red slayer thinks he slays,
or if the slain thinks he is slain,
They know not well the subtle ways
I keep, and pass and turn again.

Far or forgot to me is near ;
Shadow and sunlight are the same ;
The vanished gods to me appear ;
And one to me are shame and fame,

They reckon ill who leave me out ;
When me they fly, I am the wings ;
I am the doubter and the doubt,
And I the hymn the Brahmin sings.

The strong gods pine for my abode,
And pine in vain the sacred seven ;
But thou meek lover of the good !
Find me, and turn thy back in heaven".

that this self is slain, is mistaken in grasping the truth, for 'It' does not slay nor is 'It' slain.[8] The entire poem explains the concept of Brahman in the spirit of the Upaniṣads. It is, as in the Upaniṣads, a unifying and all-pervading spirit. This interpretation stands corroborated not only by Emerson himself, but also by the observations made on the poem by certain other eminent scholars and critics. Prof. Frederic J. Carpenter points out that the concept of 'Brahma' was developed by Emerson out of snatches of the ancient Hindu scriptures. Prof. Norman Foerster has observed that the poem is both easier and harder than it is commonly regarded : easier because, as Emerson said of people who are puzzled, "If you tell them to say Jehovah instead of Brahma they will not find any perplexity, and harder because it requires for a full understanding, a richer religious and metaphysical background than most people possess". Emerson himself liked the interpretation given to the poem by an unnamed 'little girl' of Concord who declared that she found no difficulty in understanding the poem. "It simply means", she said', "God everywhere".[9] Emerson again says elsewhere that in all nations there are minds which incline to dwell in the conception of the fundamental unity. This tendency finds its highest expression in the religious writings of the East, and chiefly in the Indian scriptures.[10]

As in the poem 'Brahma' so also in many essays Emerson hinges upon the concept of an all-comprehensive Soul,

---

8. Cf. Ya enaṁ vetti hantāraṁ yaścainaṁ manyate hatam,
Ubhou tou na vijānīto' nāyaṁ hanti na hānyate".
—The Gītā : II, 19,
Almost an identical sloka is found in the Kaṭha Upaniṣad ;
Kaṭha—1.2.19.

9. Vide : 'Masters of American Literature', Vol-I. Edtd. by Prof. H. A. Pochman & Prof. G. W. Allen.—P-789.

10. Vide : Emerson's essay on 'Plato'.

and here we find direct references to the different sayings of the Upaniṣads. He concludes his essay on 'Immortality' with a reference to the Yama-Naciketā episode of the Kaṭha Upaniṣad, and this amply illustrates his breadth of vision and also his courage of conviction in recognizing and acknowledging his debt to the Upaniṣadic conception of Reality and the way to realize 'It'.

A way of life that Emerson time and again defended was to live sincerely and become 'a genuine man'. He sketched long before in the notes of a sermon that a genuine man must (i) believe in himself, (ii) speak the truth, (iii) think the truth and (iv) act the truth. In fact 'Truth' and 'Spirit' are the dominant words of Emerson's essays and the horizon they extend before us fades into the 'Reality' that alone promises man a true fulfilment. His entire work is a diary of a continuing discovery of self – to find within oneself, in inner experience the current of the 'Universal Being'. It is to partake of spirit to act with the power of God. For self-reliance, Emerson assures us, is nothing if it is not a dependence on and obedience to this overwhelming tide. The essay, therefore, that complements 'Self - Reliance' is the 'Oversoul'.[11] We shall now analyse this essay wherein his central thought has been given remarkable exposition.

The very title of the essay viz,. 'Oversoul' indicates that it is almost a literal translation of the Sanskrit term 'Paramātman' (Supreme Self) and there can not be even a speck of doubt that Emerson was strongly imbued with the spirit of the Upaniṣads. The thought contained in the essay is akin to the thought found in the different ancient Upaniṣads. Referring to this Oversoul Emerson writes :– "I dare not speak for it. My words do not carry its august sense; they fall short and cold. Only itself can inspire whom it will, and behold, their speech shall be lyrical and sweet

11. Vide : Emerson's Essays. Introduction, by Prof. Sherman Paul.

and universal as the rising of the wind".[12] In similar words Yama, the Lord of Death speaks to Naciketā in the Kaṭhoʼpaniṣad. One who does not develop the higher spiritual faculties or has not turned away from evil conduct, whose senses are uncontrolled, who is not tranquil, whose mind is not at rest, can not attain the 'Self' simply by intellectual knowledge.[13] Again there are passages where Emerson says: "The philosophy of six thousand years has not searched the chambers and magazines of the soul. In its experiments there has always remained, in the last analysis, a residuum it could not resolve. Man is a stream whose source is hidden. Our being is descending into us from we know not whence. The most exact calculator has no prescience that somewhat incalculable may not baulk the very next moment. I am constrained every moment to acknowledge a higher origin of events than the will I call mine. ....We live in succession, in division, in parts, in particles. Meantime within man is the soul of the whole, the wise silence, the universal beauty, to which every other part and particle is equally related, – the eternal 'One'. And this deep power in which we exsit, and whose beatitude is all accessible to us, is not only self-sufficing and perfect in every hour, but the act of seeing and the thing seen, the seer and the spectacle, the subject and the object are one. We see the world piece by piece, as the sun, the moon, the animal, the tree; but the whole of which these are the shining parts is the 'Soul'".[14] Here the relation between the phenomenal world and the Supreme Self is demonstrated in the Upaniṣadic spirit. Swami Paramānanda has explained this pcint with adequate clarity. "The ancient

12. 'The Oversoul'—Essays of Emerson; edited by Sherman Paul.

13. Cf. "Nāyamātmā pravacanena labhyaḥ na medhayā na bahūna Śrutena."—Kaṭha;

14. Essays of Emerson; Edited by S. Paul. P—149-50.

Vedic scriptures abound in passages describing almost in identical terms the relation of the phenomenal world with the unseen One and the connection of the soul with its origin —the one without a second. Nowhere does Vedānta deal with the universe as a combination of unrelated fragments; it sees all things as parts of a great whole and it tries to bind all these parts together in that whole, yet without destroying the entity of each individual soul".[15] Emerson thus follows the Upaniṣadic pantheism in its true spirit.

Emerson again follows closely the Keno' paniṣad when he records his thought thus : "All goes to show that the soul in man is not an organ, but animates and exercises all the organs, is not a function like the power of memory, of calculation of comparison, but uses these as hands and feet; is not a faculty but a light; is not the intellect or the will, but the master of the intellect and the will, is the vast background of our being in which they lie,—an immensity not possessed and that can not be possessed......" The Keno'paniṣad begins with almost the same definition of Atman or Self. According to this Upaniṣad Self is 'the ear of the ear, the mind of the mind, the speech of the speech, the life of the life, the eye of the eye. It is that which can not be thought by mind, but by which the mind is able to think; that which is not seen by the eye, but by which the eye is able to see; that which can not be heard by the ear, but by which the ear is able to hear.[16] In order to bring out the nature of 'Oversoul' and its relation to man, Emerson says, "What we commonly call man, the eating, drinking, planting, counting man – does not, as we know him represent himself, but misrepresents himself. Him we do not respect; but the soul whose organ he is,

15. Swami Paramānanda : 'Emerson and Vedānta,—Chapter III, P—48-49.

16. "Śrotraṣya śrotraṁ manaso' manaḥ yadvāco' ha vācaṁ sa' u prāṇasya prāṇaḥ. cakṣuṣaścakṣuratimucya dhīraḥ pretyāsmāllokādamṛtā bhavanti –Kena, 1 2.

would he let it appear through his action, would make our knees bend".[17] All that Emerson means to say is that to the eating, drinking or sleeping man his entire life is contained in his physical being, and 'that' by which he is living, acting or thinking is overlooked. This state of consciousness inevitably misrepresents us leading us to all selfish desires and passions, egotism and vanity, competitions and rivalry. But the real man within knows that his true being is of God. Emerson reflects and quite precisely, the spirit of the Śvetāśvatara Upaniṣad in the following passage:–"The influence of the senses has in most men overpowered the mind to that degree that the walls of time and space have come to look solid, real and insurmountable ; and to speak with levity of these limits is, in the world, the sign of insanity. Yet time and space are but inverse measures of the force of the Soul. A man is capable of abolishing them both". ...."See how the deep, divine thought demolishes centuries and millenniums, and makes itself present through all ages. Is the teaching of Christ less effective now than it was when first his mouth was opened ? The emphasis of facts and persons to my soul has nothing to do with time. And so, always the soul's scale is one; the scale of the senses and the understanding is another. Before the great revelations of the soul Time, Space and Nature shrink away".[18] Emerson here sounds very much the teachings of the Śvetāśvatara Upaniṣad which holds that prior to creation (i. e., revelation of Self), there was no day, no night, neither

17. Yadvācānabhyuditaṁ yena vāgabhyudyate, tadeva Brahma tvaṁ viddhi nedaṁyadidamupāsate. Yanmanasā na manute yenāhurmano' matam tadeva Brahma......yaccakṣuṣā na paśyati yena cakṣūṁsi paśyati, tadeva Brahma ; yat śrotreṇa na śṛṇoti, yena śrotramidaṁ śrutam tadeva Brahma,.........Kena ; 1.5, 1.6, 1.7, 1.8.
Vide : ; 'The Oversoul'—Essays of Emerson, edited by S. Paul, —P-151.

18. Ibid ; P—152-53.

existence nor non-existence.........When He (Ātman) shines everything shines after Him; by His light everything is lighted. He makes all, He knows all, self-caused, the knower, the regulator of all time.[19]

Emerson, like the Upaniṣadic sages, had a conviction that theoretical knowledge is not dependable in so far as it leads to an ever-increasing tangle of diversity, while direct vision or even a small amount of knowledge based on direct apprehension leads to fundamental unity. Emerson thus declares: "The mind is one and the best minds who love truth for its own sake think much less of property in truth. Thankfully they accept it everywhere, and do not label or stamp it with any man's name, for it is theirs long before-hand.......The action of the soul is oftener in that which is felt and left unsaid, than in that which is said in any conversation" ('Oversoul'). Emerson here sounds the same universal note which runs through all Vedic teaching, that 'truth' is not the exclusive property of any one group of people, but is the common property of the entire human race and is equally open to all who claim it. As to the direct vision or realization of the Supreme Self Emerson, as we have already indicated, speaks in deference to the Upaniṣadic message. Man, he says, never seeks communion with the Supreme soul with a view to attaining any worldly success,—health, wealth or prosperity.[20] A strong urge or love for the soul leads him Godward. The ignorant always resorts to the way that brings immediate and tangible results. He moves outward while the wise moves inward. Thus corresponding to two paths—one leading to God and the other to the worldly objects there are two classes of people. On them Emerson reflects thus: "One class speaks from within or from experience as parties

19. Vide: The Śvetāśvatara Upaniṣad; Chapter IV & VI; 4, 18, 6.14.
20. Cf. 'Na vittena tarpaṇīyo' manuṣyaḥ'—Kaṭha—1.1.27.

and possessors of the fact ; and the other class, from without as spectators merely or perhaps as acquainted with the fact on the evidence of third persons. It is of no use to preach to me from without. I can do that too easily myself. Jesus speaks always from within and in a degree that transcends all others. In that is the miracle".[21]

This attitude as envisaged by Emerson has been emphatically demonstrated by the Indian sages since the Vedic age till the present day.[22] Erudition has never been considered by them an essential qualification of a spiritual teacher. He must be one whose brain should not be loaded with theories about God. On the contrary he is required to have a direct acquaintance with truth. To quote Emerson: –"The tone of seeking is one, the tone of having is another".[23] Emerson, in fact, has written copiously on the fact that so long as man is conscious of his little self, he remains self conceited and hankers after earthly 'possession'. But when his consciousness expands and he comes to discover the cosmic self within him, when in other words, spiritual seeking becomes an all-absorbing passion of his soul, he is inevitably released from all the doctrinal and creed-bound beliefs and is brought face to face with the cosmic soul. Emerson reiterates his conviction that the eternal self resides in the heart of every mortal.[24] In the spirit of the Upaniṣads he holds again : "Ineffable is the union of man and God in every act of the soul. The simplest person. who in

21. Essays of Emerson,—edited by S. Paul ; P-161 (The Oversoul).
22. Cf. "The special mental attitude which India has in her religion is made clear by the word 'Yoga' whose meaning is to effect union. Union has its significance not in the realm 'to have', but in that 'to be'."—Rabindranath Tagore : Religion of Man'—Spiritual Union.
23. Emerson's Essays : edited by S. Paul ; P-160.
24. Cf. 'Eṣa [devo' viśvakarmā mahātmā sadā janānām hṛdaye sanniviṣtaḥ ! –Śvatāśvatara, 4.17.

his integrity worships God, becomes God. ....When we have broken our God of tradition and ceased from our God of rhetoric. then may 'God' fire the heart with His presence".[25] In the Upaniṣads we find a similar passage—'When the mind is concentrated and turned within, the mortal perceives the glory of the immortal self and rejoices because he has obtained that, which is the cause of all true joy'.[26]

What appears from our foregoing analysis is that the kinship in thought between the Upaniṣads and many of Emerson's writings is not a matter of inference only. Emerson himself frequently acknowledges his debt to the ancient Indian scriptures. In his essay -'Worship' he says : "We owe to the Hindu scriptures a definition of Law which compares well with any in our western books : 'Law it is which is without name or colour or hands or feet, which is smallest of the least, and largest of the large ; all and knowing all things ; which hears without ears, sees without eyes, moves without feet and seizes without hands'. This is a free rendering of a passage of the Śvetāśvatara Upaniṣad.[27]

Emerson reviews the mighty attainments of ancient Greece and Rome and also of ancient and mediaeval Europe and writes in his essay – 'Progress of Culture' :—"But if these works still survive and multiply, what shall we say of names more distant, or hidden through their very superiority to their co-evals, - names of men who have left remains that certify a height of genius in their several directions not since surpassed, and which men in proportion to their

25. Emerson's Essays ;—S. Paul ; P-164.

26. Cf. "Eko' vaśī sarvabhūtāntarātmā
ekaṁ rūpaṁ bahudhā yaḥ karoti,
tamātmasthaṁ ye'nupaśyanti
dhīrāsteṣaṁ sukhaṁ śāśvataṁ netareṣām".
—Kaṭha-2.2.12.

Cf. Kaṭha—1.2.20 ; Śvetā—3.20 ; Taittirīya - 2.7.2. etc.

27. Cf. Śvetāśvatara Upaniṣad ; 3.19.

wisdom still cherish, -as Zoroaster, Confucious, and the grand scriptures only recently known to the western nations-of the Indian Vedas, the Institutes of Manu, tne Purāṇas, the poems of the Mahābhārata and the Rāmāyana"? This pregnant interrogation put by Emerson is a distinct mark of his appreciation of ancient Indian thought. Swami Paramānanda[28] has aptly observed that Emerson was thoroughly imbued with the message of the Vedas and the Upaniṣads and accordingly he recognized the loftiness and beauty of their pantheistic outlook and ethical teachings.[29]

In fine it must be noted that Emerson had discovered certain profound truths in his own soul,[30] and because

---

28. Vide : Swami Paramānanda : 'Emerson and Vedānta'—Ch.I. P-21.27.
29. This view is corroborated by Emerson himself in his essays. A few important excerpts are worth mentioning here.
Even after appreciating the beauty and excellence of the ethical teachings of the western countries of ancient times Emerson says : "Later when Confucius and the Indian scriptures were made known, no claim to monopoly of ethical wisdom could be thought of".
"It is within this century that England and America discovered that their nursery tales were old German and Scandenavian stories ; now it appears that they came from India and are the property of all the nations descended from the Aryan race, and have been Warbled and babbled between nurses and children for unknown thousands of years".
(Quoted from the essay—"Quotations and Originality.)
Again Emerson writes : "The favour of the climate making subsistence easy and encouraging an outdoor life, allows to the Eastern nations a highly intellectual organisation,—leaving out of view at present the genius of the Hindoos (more oriental in every sense), whom no people have surpassed in the grandeur of their ethical statement". (Essay on-"Persian Poetry)".
30. All that Emerson recorded in his essays was deeply felt by him. His writings were not, therefore, merely the intellectual analysis of what he thought, but a faithful record of what he felt inwardly. Possibly for this reason he is found to have been preoccupied in his essays mostly with the ethical questions rather than with metaphysical problems. His 'Philosophy is a way of living not a system of thought. His writing is the record of his own 'man thinking'.—

of his personal experience it was easy for him to accept and appreciate with delight the same truth he discovered elsewhere. Like the ancient sages of India Emerson felt in his heart of hearts that the discovery of 'Paramātman' in all beings together with the realization of this Supreme Cosmic Being helps one develop a unitary outlook and Steer clear of all barriers due to caste, colour and creed, and enjoy Supreme 'Bliss' and 'Infinitude'. At this stage man becomes free from all pangs of earthly life such as disease, death and bereavement.[31] This evidently indicates a faithful reflection of the Upaniṣadic spirit. Hence Emerson's indebtedness to the Upaniṣads is beyond all doubt.

Vide : Robert E. Spiller : 'The Cycle of American Literature' P-37, 42.

31. Cf. "Yasmin sarvāṇi bhūtānyātmaivābhud vijānataḥ, Tatrā ko' mohaḥ kaḥ śoka 'ekatvamanupaśyataḥ".
— Īśa Up.-7.

CHAPTER—X

WALT WHITMAN. (1819–1892).

Introduction.

The poetic talent of Walt Whitman has arrested the attention of innumerable scholars and critcs of different lands. His "Leaves of Grass"—the whole corpus of his poetic productions (the different editions of which were published between 1855 and 1892) contains themes that invariably invited a formidable array of critical studies, favourable or adverse in and outside America. He has become a legend as it were, a pivotal figure in the international literary movement. The poetic theory outlined in the preface to the 1855 edition of'Leaves of Grass', describes his personal ambition. The bard who is 'to be commensurate with a people', to 'incarnate' its geography and life and to span his country from east to west, is of course himself. The poet who believes that 'all beauty comes from beautiful blood and a beautiful brain' is confessing a personal ambition —even a dedication of himself to an ideal—to live and to record a beautiful life.

Our purpose here is to see how Whitman, who is looked upon by many as a poet of the body, transgresses his sensuality and on the metaphysical plane reaches pantheism which is very much akin to the Upaniṣadic doctrine, and to find out how far he has been inspired by the Upaniṣads in this regard.

Whitman and transcendentalist movement in America.

When Whitman appeared in the literary firmament of America, a distinctive tendency to transcendentalism was in the air and Whitman was ostensibly inspired by this spirit advocated mainly by Waldo Emerson, Henry David Thoreau, Theodore Parker and others. These thinkers came together in 1830's and 40's and generated not a definite systematic creed or school of philosophy, but a fermentation of ideas and attitudes stressing the moral and spiritual needs of the people, which served as a major stimulation of literary activity or philosophical thinking in the United States during the American Renaissance.[1] These thinkers were profoundly influenced by Kant's 'Critique of Pure Reason' where Kant, in attempting to establish the limits of human understanding, concluded that finite mind can have a scientific knowledge of phenomena only. He did not deny the reality or the existence of 'something' behind phenomena, but asserted that it was unknowable. Kant admitted, however, the human need for belief in such ultrarational ideas as God, Immortality, Freedom etc. Now this line of Kantian thinking stimulated the speculative minds especially of America to explore this 'unknowable' region. W. F. Taylor has summarized the result by declaring that the transcendentalists were the mystics. They hoped to 'transcend' the phenomenal realm and receive their inspiration towards truth at first hand from the Deity unsullied by any contact with matter. Spiritual verities alone were of great importance to the transcendentalists and these were immediately imparted to the soul from God. Yet God, the Oversoul was revealed also in nature which was a beautiful web of appearances veiling the spirituality of the universe, a living garment, half-concealing, half-revealing the Deity within.[2] Of the transcendentalists it was Emerson to whom Whitman was more indebted for

1. Cf. F. O. Matthiessen :—'American Renaissance : Art and Expression in the age of Emerson and Whitman'.

2. Vide : Walter F. Taylor :—'A History of American letters' ; P—145-46.

the fundamental ideas in his earliest 'Leaves of Grass'. Despite the fact that on certain occasions he tried to minimise his debt to Emerson, he arrived ultimately at an open and almost undeviating allegiance both to Emerson as a person and to Emersonian ideas in general.[3] One such idea, dominant not only in Emerson, but in all other contemporary thinkers in America is 'other worldliness'. This attitude however does not mean attenuation of this earthly existence. It indicates a craving for release from the imperfect empirical life to a higher plane of being where the spiritual aspirant realizes the Soul to be the absolute reality. The term 'other worldliness' has almost the same connotation for the ancient Indian thinkers, for it implies to them also that the empirical world is not final and that the highest good can be found only in a higher realm which is spiritual, where man realizes his soul to be divine and supreme. Having reached this spiritual world, however, one does not condemn this lower world of existence as false and unreal.[4] In the Bṛhadāraṇyaka Upaniṣad Maitreyī in her zeal for the knowledge of the 'Supreme Soul' reveals this attitude.[5] Thoreau, another American transcendentalist typifies this attitude in his 'Walden' and urges us not to fix our heart on that which is transitory.[6] Some of the clo e parallels between Whitman's thoughts and the ideas of the contemporary transcendentalists are perhaps due to the fact that Whitman also like them wrote as a mystic as we shall explain presently. We shall also explain how Whitman in the spirit of some of his contemporaries as also like that of the Upaniṣadic thinkers seeks to discover the Eternal

---

3. Vide : John B. Moore : 'The Master of Whitman'—Studies in Philology XXIII, 77.
4. Dr. S. Radhakrishr an explains the point clearly in his 'Eastern Religion and Western Thought'. P-75.
5. Cf. The Bṛhadāraṇyaka Upaniṣad ; 2. 4.
6. Vide : Henry David Thoreau- Walden, Ch. I.

Infinite Being in which all worldly objects are virtually anchored. As a matter of fact he could not evade the influence of this group of thinkers in general and of Emerson in particular who, we come to know, wrote for the magazines and newspapers which Whitman read and to which he also contributed during 1840's. These American thinkers became genuinely interested in the literature and religion of Asia, especially of the Hindoos. Sanskrit was then taught at Harvard, and India was frequently discussed in newspapers and popular magazines-to judge by the large number of clippings which Whitman amassed in his own scrap books.[7]

Mysticism in Whitman Evolution of his thoughts and ideas.

The point we should take note of at the outset is that Whitman's is no systematic and coherent philosophical system. The thoughts and ideas of his 'Leaves of Grass' may be considered philosophical by many. But he did not belong to any definite school. The poet himself did not, in fact, want to be a formal metaphysician. To quote his words : "I will not be a great philosopher and found any school, and build it with iron pillars, and gather young men around me, and make them my disciples".[8] Whatever may be the opinions of the scholiasts we can, nevertheless, trace an order or more precisely an evolution of his ideas.[9]

---

7. Vide : Whitman's 'Notes and Fragments',, Part IV, items—210-236, 332-339, 395.
8. Vide : Emory Holloway : Uncollected Poetry and Prose of Walt Whitman . Manuscript Note Book for 1847, II, P-66.
9. John Addington Symonds says : "It is useless to extract a coherent scheme of thought from Whitman's voluminous writings ......But though he may not be reducible to system, we can trace an order of his ideas."—John A. Symonds : 'Walt Whitman – a study'. P-42. Matthiessen confirms this view when he says : "No arrangement or rearrangement of Whitman's thoughts can resolve the paradoxes or discover in them a fully coherent pattern. He was incapable of

We find a consensus among almost all the critics and biographers[10] according to whom Whitman was a mystic. The term 'mystic' is undoubtedly ambiguous and it is sought to be explained in different ways by different thinkers. It must further be noted that the mystics of all lands and ages do not always present identical views. Similarities may be found among them, but the dissimilarities also can not be overlooked. Rudolf Otto is right in holding that in spite of much formal agreement. mystical experience is capable of great diversity, Its content can be curiously varied. The moods and feelings which it arouses can differ from one another even to the extent of being diametrically opposed.[11] But in spite of diversity of interpretation it is not impossible to determine the fundamental trait of mysticism which in some way, as we shall find here, is traced in Whitman. Mystics desire, above all else, to come some how into direct contact with the supernatural. To seek an infallible standard or proof of the accuracy of this sort of experience is of no avail, for mystical experience is something unique of its kind. Dr. Rufus M. Jones, a widely accepted authority on mysticism perhaps aptly analyses this experience when he says : "The fundamental fact of first hand mystical experience, the direct encounter with the living revealing God in the depths of the soul, is pretty much of the same type in all ages, in all lands and in all religions.

---

sustained logic, but that should not blind the reader into impatient rejection of the ebb and flow of his antithesis. They possess a loose dialectic of their own".—F.O. Matthiessan : 'American Renaissance'—P-526.

10. Some notable critics and their works are :—
    i) Dr. Richard Maurice Bucke :—'Walt Whitman'.
    ii) John Addington Symonds :—'Walt Whitman—a study'.
    iii) Emory Holloway :—'Uncollected Poetry and Prose of Walt Whitman'.
    iv) Edward Carpenter : —Days with Walt Whitman'.
11. Cf. Rudolf Otto. 'Mysticism—East and West'—P-39.

What varies is the interpretation of experience through the attempt to communicate it and to make others see the significance of the inward event".[12] There are two profoundly different ways of knowing a thing, as Bergson puts it : 'The first implies that we move round the object ; the second that we enter into it'.[13] The mystic resorts to the second means.

In 'Leaves of Grass' and also in his prose writings Whitman has given the description of experiences which are mystical in the sense we have indicated above. One such remarkable description is found in ,Song of Myself'[14] for

---

12. Vide : Rufus M. Jones : Review of Jewish Mysticism by C. Scholen' —'Harvard Theological Review'—XXXVI,—1943.

13. Quoted by Russell in his 'Mysticism and Logic and other essays' from Bergson's 'Introduction to Metaphysics. P-1.

14. "I believe in you my soul. the other I am must not
abase itself to you,
And you must not be abased to the other.
Loafe with me on the grass, loose the stop from
your throat,
Not words, not music or rhyme I want, not custom
or lecture, not even the best,
Only the lull I like, the hum of your valved voice.
I mind how once we lay such a transparent summer morning,
How you settled your head athwart my hips and gently
turned over upon me,
And parted the shirt from my bosom-bone and plunged
your tongue to my bare-stript heart,
And reach'd till yon felt my beard, and reach'd
till you held my feet.
Swiftly arose and spread around me the peace and
knowledge that pass all the argument of the earth,
And I know that the hand of God is the promise
of my own,
And I know that the spirit of God is the brother
of my own,
And that all the men ever born are also my brothers,
and the women my sisters and lovers,
And that a kelson of the creation is love,

here we find a complete picture of almost all the phases of a mystical experience 'from the communication with the 'Soul' and the sensation of being penetrated and permeated by the supernatural, to the belief that the experience has brought with it clairvoyant knowledge and spiritual wisdom. Typical of the mystics are the resultant convictions of equality with God, brotherhood with all people, and love as the foundation of the whole universal creation'.[15] In fact these ideas resulting from a mystic vision[16] constitute the principal theme of the poem mentioned. In the 1855 preface to the Leaves of Grass Whitman declared : 'The poets of the cosmos (the kind of the poet he was trying to be), advance through all interpositions and coverings and turmoils and stratagems to first principles'. In 'Passage to India' he predicted-'Nature and Man shall be disjoined and diffused no more, the true son of God (i. e., the poet) shall absolutely fuse them'.[17]

But an enriched conception of Soul or the spiritualistic tendency which leads the poet to pantheism, does not appear to have been a decided conviction from the beginning. Whitman is generally interpreted as a poet of the body.

And limitless are leaves stiff or drooping in the fields,
And brown ants in the little wells beneath them,
And mossy scabs of worm fence, heap'd stones,
elder, mullein, and poke-weed".
—Section-9, Song of Myself

15. Gay Wilson Allen : 'Walt Whitman Handbook'—P-250.

16. Like all mystics Whitman regards this vision or intution as incommunicable. For example,—

"There is something that comes home to one now and
perpetually,
It is not what is printed, preach'd discussed,
it eludes discussion and print,—
It is not to be put in a book, it is not in this book...
(—A Song For Occupations, sec. 2)

17. Vide : The concluding lines of sec. 5, 'Passage to India'.

The poems in 'Song of Myself' give us his conception of soul no doubt, but there are, in these poems, adequate references to his eulogy to body. In a notebook Whitman says: "I am always conscious of myself as two—as my soul and I: and I reckon, it is the same with all men and women'.[18] In the first line of the poem quoted by us from 'Song of Myself'—'the other I am'—refers obviously to the physical self. This position naturally prompts us to touch upon the evolutionary process of Whitman's fundamental ideas on body and soul.

The 1855 edition of 'Leaves of Grass' makes it abundantly clear that Whitman sings rapturously of the body and carnal sensation. The terms—'body' and 'soul' recur almost simultaneously and seem to have the same resonance or the same richness of suggestion at this period. The poet says—'I am the poet of the body and I am the poet of the soul'. ('Song of Myself'; Sec. 21). The poet even goes to the extent of ascribing to the body a halo of divinity as it were when he says—

"The man's body is sacred and the woman's
body is sacred,
No matter who it is, it is sacred"......

* * *

This is the female form,
A divine nimbus exhales from it
from head to foot,
It attracts with fierce undeniable attraction,
I am drawn by its breath as if I were
no more a helpless vapour... "[19]

In 'Song of Myself' the poet introduces himself unambiguously as 'turbulent, fleshly, sensual, eating, drinking

18. Vide: Emory Holloway: 'Uncollected Poetry and Prose of Walt Whitman' II, P-66.

19. Vide: 'Children of Adam' (Leaves of Grass) Sec. 6 and 5.

and breeding, and says,—'I believe in the flesh and appetites'.[20] But these utterances should not prejudice the readers so as to regard Whitman as an out and out sensual poet. Roger Asselineau drives home the point when he says: "For him (Whitman) the body is not simply an end in itself, but a means. It does not represent the goal, but the starting point. He very quickly leaves it behind and, transcending material appearances, reaches a spiritual reality—the soul, of which the body is the outward manifestation. In other words, his sensuality instead of remaining exclusively carnal, opens out and is sublimated. The spirit in order to be manifest, can not do without matter and, of course, all mysticism depends on and is accompanied by emotions of the flesh".[21] It appears, therefore, that during 1855-56 Whitman had a keen awareness of the purely sensual source of his mystical intuitions. Hence he does not conceal the physical concomitants of his mystical states. The poet even goes further, and ignoring all conventional modesty and social taboos, he speaks of the sexual origin of his mysticism and sings of the body accordingly.[22]

---

20. Vide : 'Song of Myself'—Sec. 24.
21. R. Asselineau : 'The Evolution of Walt Whitman',—Vol. 2, P-4.
22. (i) "If I worship one thing more than another
It shall be the spread of my own body
or any part of it,
Translucent mould of me it shall be you!
Shaded ledges and rests it shall be you!
Firm masculine colter it shall be you!
... ...
You my rich blood! you milky stream
pale strippings of my life".
—'Song of Myself'—Sec. 24.
(ii) "Welcome is every organ and attribute
of me, and of any man hearty and clean,
Not an inch nor a particle of an inch
is vile,

It is thus during the first stage of his career as a poet (roughly speaking, from 1855 to 1860) that Whitman's mystical thought is expressed mostly with the carnal sensations as its basis. But with the passage of time and advancement of his thought, the sensations lost their sensuality. In other words, at the later stage of Whitman's career as a poet, his mystical fervour subsists, but the sensuality is calmed, purified and sublimated.[23] It may be noted, however, that in spite of his progressive spiritualization the poet does not, even in his old age, repudiate the sensuality of his youth outright, nor does he forget what he owed to his body. He only appears to have been averse to narrow puritanism or asceticism.[24]

But in view of the importance Whitman attaches to body, he should not be understood to have propounded a materialistic theory. It is true that the poetry of the body impregnates 'Leaves of Grass'. It is also true that the eulogistic passages on body are there[25] which may appear to many to

---

and none shall be less familiar
than the rest".
—'Song of Myself'—Sec. 3

(iii) Vide also—the 1860 edition of 'Leaves of Grass' where Whitman devoted two entire groups of new poems to carnal love viz., 'Children of Adam' and 'Calamus'.

23. Whitman happens to have re-written in 'Old Age Echoes' under the title—"To Be At All"—a passage which already figured in section 27 of 'Song of Myself' in the first edition of 'Leaves of Grass'. The subject is the same, but the triumphant tone of sensuality has departed. This naturally corroborates our observation.

24. Whitman's declaration to a Philadelphia journalist on March 3, 1880, runs thus:—"The theologians to a man teach humility and that the body is the sinful setting of the immortal soul. I wish men to be proud of their bodies, to look upon the body as a thing of beauty, too holy to be abused by vice and debauchery",—Quoted by Henry Bergman in his 'Whitman on his Poetry',—P. 163-64.

25. A few such passages may be quoted here:—

(i) "Was somebody asking to see the soul?
See your own shape and countenance,

be confusing and sometimes even contradictory, and for that reason it may appear somewhat difficult to assess the poet's attitude to spiritualism. But these passages are not, in fact, professions of materialistic faith. It is true that under the influence of violent sensations,—particularly intense tactual sensation, to which the poet seems to have been subject from time to time, he becomes very much sensitive to the material aspect of the world. But materialism as an ontological theory signifies that 'matter' is the only reality and consciousness is a byproduct of it. Whitman never upholds this view. It is, therefore, a misconception to regard him as a materialist in the sense in which it is generally understood in philosophy. What we find on the contrary, is that he is very much conscious of the existence of soul from the beginning, and the mystical emotions into

---

Persons, substances, beasts, the trees, the
running rivers, the rocks and sands.
All hold spiritual joys and afterwards
loosen them ;
How can the real body ever die and be buried ?

* * *

Behold. the body includes and is the meaning,
the main concern, and includes
and is the soul :
Whoever you are, how superb, and how divine
is your body, or any part of it" !
—'Starting from Paumanok', Sec. 13.

(ii) "And if the body were not the soul,
what is the soul" ?
—'I sing the Body Electric' ; Sec. 1,
('Children of Adam').

(iii) "O I say these are not the parts and poems
of the body only, but of the soul,
O I say now these are the soul" ;
—Sec. 9—'I sing the Body Electric'.

(iv) "I accept Reality and dare not question it,
Materialism first and last imbuing".
—'Song of Myself'—Sec. 23.

which his sensations have soon blossomed out, put him in contact with an order of suprasensible reality which he cannot but interpret in terms of spiritualism. As the following passage shows :—

"The real life of my senses and flesh
transcending my senses and flesh,
My body done with materials, my sight
done with my material eyes
Proved to me this day beyond cavil that
it is not my material eyes which finally see,
Nor my material body which finally loves,
walks, laughs, shouts, embraces,
procreates".[26]

Whitman thus feels the need of admitting the existence of a spiritual principle along with matter. As a consequence we find that the poet is sometimes torn between two equally plausible solutions, each of which corresponds to his temperament. Neither materialism nor spiritualism is rejected by the poet. But at this period (1860) a short poem which disappeared from the book later,indicates a complete reversal of his postion :—

" I have said many times that materials
and the soul are great, and that
all depends on physique ;
Now I reverse what I said, and
affirm that all depends on the aesthetic
or intellectual.........
And I affirm now that the mind governs -
and that all depends on the mind".

In the 'Song at Sunset' composed at this period the poet exclaims :—

"How the water sports and sings !
(Surely it is alive !)

26. 'A Song of Joys'—Lines 100-104.

How the trees rise and stand up with
strong trunks, with branches and leaves!
(Surely there is something more in each of
the trees, some living soul.)
O amazement of things - even the least particle!
O Spirituality of things!"[27]

The poet even goes to the extent of doubting matter and the testimony of his senses. His observations in 'Of the Terrible Doubt of Appearances' do not escape our notice:—

"May-be the things I perceive, the animals,
plants, men, hills, shining and flowing waters,
The skies of day and night, colors, densities,
forms, may-be these are (as doubtless they are)
only apparitions, and the real
something has yet to be known".[28]

The belief in the existence of an immortal soul even in inanimate things is found to have been expressed by the poet as early as 1855.

—"I swear I think now that everything
without exception has an eternal soul".[29]

But his faith in 'matter' during this period is perhaps strongest. The ambivalence of the poet is clearly marked at this stage. The reason is that he appears to have passed through a profound moral crisis of a sexual origin in the years which preceded the 1860 edition of 'Leaves of Grass'. Matter betrayed him in refusing to satisfy the aspirations of his flesh. Hence is probably the reversal to soul. Whatever the origin of this change in point of view may have been, the poems written in and after 1860 put emphasis on 'Spirit' or 'Soul' and not on 'body'. The tendency

27. 'Song at Sunset'—from 'Songs of Parting', L—35-39.
23. Vide: 'Of the Terrible Doubt of Appearances' from 'Calamus'—1860.
29. 'To Think of Time'—Sec. 9.

towards spiritualism is thus reinforced with an emphatic and constant recurrence of the word 'Soul' which becomes the 'actual Me' of the poet.[30]

Pantheism in Whitman.

Now it will be convenient for us to discover and explain the doctrine of pantheism Whitman propagates in his poems of 'Leaves of Grass'. It is, however, held by some critics that 'Panpsychism' is perhaps a more satisfactory term for Whitman's thought than 'Pantheism'. But they do not and perhaps can not deny the applicability of pantheistic note to Whitman's thought. Prof. G. W. Allen explains the point by saying that it is perhaps contradictory to Whitman's thought to be both pantheistic and panpsychic, for the former is usually thought of as universal spirit or God pervading the nature, where as the latter teaches that each atom, particle etc. has a distinct soul. But since there is an all-embracing kinship or unity among these souls, the distinction is very subtle, - so much so, that Whitman ignored it outright.[31]

Our analysis made so far, indicates that Whitman's 'I' implies a generic and cosmic conception of self rather than his personal existence. This cosmic soul is deified by the poet and is said to pervade the universe. To put it otherwise,—everything that exists in nature necessarily pertains to the essence of an all-pervasive cosmic soul. In upholding the concept of an immanent God incarnated in each creature Whitman from the very beginning of his career as a poet breaks with the traditional Christian conception of a transcendent God.[32] An unmistakable pantheistic

30. Vide : 'Passage to India',—Sec. 8.
31. Vide : G. W. Allen : 'Whitman Handbook'—P 256-57.
32. That Whitman was very much violent in his attacks on Christian

tendency can be traced even in the 1855 edition of 'Leaves' of Grass' when he proclaims in 'Song of Myself' (Section 48) :—

"I hear and behold God in every object,
* * *
I see something of God each hour of the
twenty four, and each moment then,
In the faces of men and women I see God,
and in my own face in the glass,
I find letters from God dropt in the street,
and everyone is sign'd by God's name."

During this period the poet professes to be the successor of the ancient founders of religion and thereby resolves to surpass them all—'accepting the rough deific sketches to fill out better' himself. The poet expresses the pantheistic spirit with much brilliance and vigour in the following passage :

"A vast similitude interlocks all ......
All souls, all living bodies though they be ever
so different, or in different worlds,
All gaseous, watery, vegetable, mineral processes,
the fishes,the brutes......

---

priests and Churches, is quite evident in the following remark he made :—

"There will soon be no more priests. Their work is done. They may wait a while, ...perhaps a generation or two dropping off by degrees. A superior breed shall take their place. A new order shall arise and they shall be the priests of man, and every man shall be his own priest".—Preface to the 1855 edition of 'Leaves of Grass'.

Further, he appears to be more harsh when he writes to Emerson on this point thus :—The Churches are one vast lie ; the people do not believe them, and they do not believe themselves ; the priests are continually telling what they know well enough is, not so, and keeping back what they know is so". (Quoted from a letter of Whitman addressed to Emerson in 1856).

All identities that have existed or may exist
on this globe or any globe......
This vast similitude spans them, and always
has spann'd,
And shall for ever span them
and completely hold and enclose them".[33]

Later Whitman tries to give a precise intellectual meaning to his mystical revelation by inventing a new term - 'Santa Spirita' which, according to him, stands for 'universal life'. Thus in 1865 he writes in 'Chanting the Square Deific'—

"Ethereal, pervading all......
Essence of forms, life of the real identities,
permanent, positive (namely the unseen),
Life of the great round world, the sun
and the stars, and of man......
I the general soul......"(Sec. 4)

Whitman at times speaks in a language that may create an impression that he is perhaps returning to the orthodox conception of a transcendent divinity. But as a matter of fact he remains faithful till the end of his life to the pantheistic conception. The passages bearing adequate testimony to this are :—

(i) "You unseen force, centripetal,
centrifugal, through space's spread......
What central heart—and you the pulse vivifies all ?
* * *
Holding the universe with all its parts
as one - as sailing in a ship"?

33. This quotation is from a poem entitled by Whitman 'Clef Poem', meaning, according to the poet, that it gives the key to the mystery of the universe. (Vide : 'On The Beach At Night Alone'.) This thought again is borne out in certain other poems of this period. For example :—"Strange and hard that paradox true I give,
Objects gross and unseen soul are one". etc. etc.
—Vide : 'A Song For Occupations' Sec. 5.

(-'You Tides with Ceaseless Smell'– written in 1885)
(ii) "Thou that in all the life and death
of us, in action or in sleep !
Thou laws invisible that permeate them and all,
Thou that in all, and over all, and through
and under all,
Thou ! thou ! the vital universal giant force
resistless, sleepless, calm,
* * *
How ill to e'er forget thee" !
—'A Voice From Death' (from- 'Good-bye My
Fancy' -written in 1889.)

(iii) "Allah is all, all, all – is immanent in every life and object".- 'A Persian Lesson' – written in 1891. This pantheistic view, it may be noted, was neither adhered to, nor so zealously preached by any other American thinker in the nineteenth century as was done by Whitman and Emerson.[34]

34. Almost all the contemporaries of Whitman were emphatic on the moral development of the people based primarily on the Christian conception of God. A brief reference may be given to Theodore Parker who was one such truly Christian thinker holding his belief in immanence as well as transcendence of God. A candid cxpression of his faith is found in one of his letters addressed to his nephew :— "I believe there is one God who has existed from all eternity with whom past, present and future are alike present ; that He is almighty, good and merciful. I believe the books of the Old and New Testament to have been written by men inspired by God for certain purposes. ......I believe that Christ was the son of God, that he came to preach a better religion by which men may be saved." (Life of Theodore Parker – Page 30.31). Parker explicates his religious creed in detail in Booh II of his 'A Discourse of Matters Pertaining to Religion'. He says, "Jesus fell back on God aiming to teach absolute Religion, absolute Morality. ......Philosophical spiritualism liberates us from all personal and finite authority and restores us to God—the primeval fountain, whence the Church, the scriptures and Jesus have drawn all the water, of

Now this immanent God whom Whitman sometimes calls 'Nature', sometimes 'Santa Spirita' or again 'Life Spirit' including all beings ('Life of the real identities') as is evident from his different writings, is not a static spirit or an immobile presence, but a perpetual becoming. As a matter of fact when the poet wrote his first 'Leaves of Grass' he was surrounded as it were, by the mysterious living forces circulating not only through animals and men but also through inanimate objects. The entire universe appeared to him from the start essentially as a vital impulse or an irresistible current without beginning or end ceaselessly impelling the enormous mass of creation towards the future.[35] The poet often represents this vital impulse of the world as a universal sexual desire. But as we have indicated earlier, his senses calmed down quickly and his sexual obsession finally ceased. The dynamic conception of the world as a constant becoming professed as early as 1855 in the poems of 'Song of myself', is retained right upto the end of his life. His poems and also his prose writings bear strong evidence to that.[36] This life-force perceived

---

life, wherewith they fill their urns. Thence only shall mankind obtain Absolute Religion and Spiritual well-being". (A Discourse of Matters Pertaining to Religion'. Book II, Ch-VII, P-320).

35. "All goes onward and outward and nothing collapses"
—'Song of Myself' (Sec. 6)

There is that in me—I do not know what
it is, but I know it is in me.......
it is eternal life...
It is Happiness".—'Song of Myself'– Sec. 50.

"Urge and urge and urge,
Always the procreant urge of the world.
Out of dimness opposite equals advance,
always substance and increase,
always sex"—Ibid.

(The expression—"always sex" was added in 1856.)

36. A few references to the later writings of Whitman are given in

by the poet in the immensity of space, and also in infinity of time appears to be a closer parallel to Bergson's 'Elan Vital' than Emerson's pantheistic 'Oversoul'which we have already discussed.

Leaves of Grass, the Upaniṣads and the Gītā.

Before we come to Whitman's indebtedness to oriental literature, we shall enumerate the striking resemblance in thought between his "Leaves of Grass", and the Upaniṣads and the Gītā.

The first important parallel is traced on the concept of self. In the Upaniṣads as well as in the Gītā the self

---

this connection :—

"Ever the mutable,
Ever materials changing, crumbling,
recohering..... "

(—Vide : Eidolons',—1876).

* * *

"Unseen buds, infinite, hidden well,
Under the snow and ice, under the darkness,
in every square or cubic inch,
Germinal, exquisite, in delicate lace,
microscopic, unborn,

* * *

Urging slowly, surely forward,
forming endless,
And waiting evermore, for ever more behind".

(Vide : 'Unseen Buds'—in 'Good Bye My Fancy'—1891.)

Referring to—'The Great Unrest of which we are part' (Specimen days) he says :—

"Indeed, what is Nature but change,
in all its visible and still more its
invisible processes" ?

(—Vide : 'The Complete Prose of Walt Whitman', edited by Malcolm Cowley (1948), P-194.)

is a spiritual reality. It is Brahman incarnate in the body and is permanent, indestructible, eternal and all-pervading.[37] In the same way Whitman's 'Me' or 'Myself' symbolizes man in his universality, and the cosmic 'I' merges with all creation considering himself to be the spirit of the universe. The 'I' in Whitman's 'Leaves of Grass', as we have explained, does not signify the circumscribed self or any particular individual. The poet transcends the ramifications of his particular individual self and seeks identification with the universal, the Divine.[38] There are passages in 'Song of Myself' which undoubtedly echo the voice of Lord Krishna of the Gītā. Insisting on the disinterested performance of duties Lord Krishna urges Arjuna to take part in the battle and thus the Lord of the Gītā holds equal both gain and loss, victory and defeat, joy and pain.[39]

---

37. (i) "Yaccāpi sarvabhūtānām vījaṁ
tadahamarjuna,
Na tadasti vinā yat syānmayā bhūtaṁ
carācaram".
—The Gītā, 10/39.

(ii) "Tvamakṣaraṁ
Sadasattatparaṁ yat".
—Ibid, 11/37.

(iii) 'Tvayā tataṁ Viśvamanantarūpa"
-Ibid, 11/38.

38. "Come, said the Muse,
Sing me a song no poet yet has chanted,
Sing me the universal".
—'Song of the Universal'. (1874).

39. Cf. "Sukhe duḥkhe same kṛtvā
lābhālābhau jayā jayau
tato' yuddhāya yujyasva......."
—The Gītā, 2/38.

"Duḥkheṣu anudvignamanāḥ,
sukheṣu vigataspṛhaḥ,
Vītarāga bhayakrodhaḥ sthitadhīr—
munirucyate".—Ibid, 2/56.

In the same way Whitman tries to equal all opposites when he says :—

"With music strong I come, with my
cornets and my drums,
I play not marches for accepted
victors only, I play marches for
conquer'd and slain persons".

*   *   *

"Have you heard that it was good
to gain the day ?
I also say it is good to fall, battles are
lost in the same spirit in which
they are won".[40]

Again the poet says :-

"It is for the wicked just the same
as the righteous,
I make appointment with all,
I will not have a single person slighted
or left away,
The kept-woman, sponger, thief are hereby invited
There shall be no difference between
them and the rest'.[41]

Thus all people irrespective of their stations in society are welcomed by the cosmic self whom the poet seeks to represent. The correspondence between the Gītā and 'Leaves of Grass' becomes more evident when the poet representing the Divine Self- says :—

"I rise from age to age and take
Visible shape and move a man
with men
Succouring the good......"
(The Song Celestial)

40. 'Song of Myself'—Sec. 18.

41. 'Song of Myself', Sec. 19
Cf. "Śuni caiva śvapākeca paṇḍitāḥ
Samadarśinaḥ"—The Gītā, 5/18.

We are here invariably reminded of the declaration of Lord Krishna who promises to descend upon the earth to protect the good and redress all wrongs, and undo the evil whenever the cause of righteousness is in jeopardy.[42] In projecting experience through the filament of his ego, Whitman, in fact, goes beyond the limits of ordinary experience, and his poetic vision leads him, as we have seen, to discover the universal or cosmic self as the ultimate reality pervading the entire existence.

As a result of self-knowledge which implies identification of the individual and universal self, Whitman believes, there emerges a consciousness that "I am all". He who knows the 'actual self' i. e., the reality beneath his empirical being, knows himself to be the permeating essence of the cosmic existence outside, because his own self is the self of all. The poet thus comes to feel that he is himself the cosmic whole. He describes himself as "Walt Whitman, a Kosmos". He thus contains everything, even all contradictions within himself. He is 'of old and young, of the foolish as much as of the wise",......

"Of every hue cast am
I, of every rank and religion,
A farmer, mechanic, artist, gentleman,
sailor, quaker,
Prisoner, fancyman, rowdy, lawyer,
physician, priest".[43]

The all-pervasiveness of Brahman or Cosmic Self is demonstrated in the Upaniṣads in the same way when it is stated there:—'.He sees all things, becomes all things ; though one, He becomes threefold, fivefold, sevenfold, ninefold, twenty, hundred, thousand fold".[44] Again it is said : .He

42. Cf. The Gītā ; Ch. IV. 7, 8,
43. 'Song of Myself—Sec. 16.
44. The Chāndogya Upaniṣad ; 7.26.2.

indeed is below, is above, is to the west, to the east, to the south, to the north. He indeed is this whole world'.[45] The Upaniṣads and the poems of Leaves of Grass' are thus found to follow the same line of thought when both declare with equal emphasis that one's real self is the cosmic self, and knowing it one knows all. At the stage of enlightenment one thinks and feels cosmically.[46]

Furthermore, Whitman seems to echo the voice of the Upaniṣads as also of the Gītā in his method of realising the cosmic soul. In his continued effort for self-elevation Whitman adopts after the Hindu thinkers a meditative discipline (Dhyāna yoga). When he speaks of 'self-mastery' or his endeavour to 'lift the self by the self' he appears to speak in the same vein as is found in the Gītā.[47] The poet repeatedly insists, in the spirit of the Upaniṣads, on a mental discipline which can help one develop the intuitive faculty which alone ultimately takes one to the deep-lying essence beneath. The Gītā enjoins on us a life of detachment and renunciation with our eyes fixed on the beyond. In the Bṛhadāraṇyaka Upaniṣad Yājñavalka impresses upon us that the objects of the world are loved not for themselves, but for the 'self' that is in them, for the eternal they contain. 'Verily a husband is not dear that you may love the husband, but that you may love the self is a husband dear.[48] Reflecting this spirit Whitman says:—

> ',Each is not for its own sake,
> I say the whole earth and all the stars
> in the sky are for religion's sake".
> ('Starting from Paumanok', - Sec. 7)

45. Ibid. ; 7.25.1.
46. The Bṛhadāraṇyaka Up.—1.4.7.
47. "Bandhurātmātmanastasya yenā'tmaiv'ātmanā jitaḥ—The Gītā, 6/6.

* * *

'Jitātmanaḥ praśāntasya paramātmā samāhitaḥ'—Ibid, 6/7.

48. Vide : The Bṛhadāraṇyaka—2.4.5.

The attitude of renunciation and detachment forms the dominant note of Whitman's 'Song of the Open Road' where the poet presents himself as a pilgrim and a wayfarer and the universe itself as a road for the travelling soul. The poet recognizes the fugitive character of the objects of the world and refuses to be allured by them. He says :—

"Allons ! we must not stop here,
However sweet these laid up stores,
however convenient the dwelling,
we can not remain here,
However sheltered this part and however
calm these waters, we must not
anchor here".[49]

Like the truly wise sages of the Upaniṣads Whitman also feels that our outward expansion and material aggrandizement are not the marks of greatness of character of an individual or of a nation. Material prosperity can not satisfy the inner craving of man. ('Na vittena tarpaṇīyo' manuṣyaḥ'). Hence true religion begins with renunciation, and so long as man does not recognize this, spirituality will remain at a distance and the so-called achievements in the field of democracy and civilization will end in a fiasco. Whitman thus keeps on insisting like the seers of the Upaniṣads that moral purification by way of abjuration of all greed, attachment, selfishness and such other egoistic tendencies, is indispensable prerequisite to meditation or contemplation which finally leads to the realization of the true nature of self. Dr. V. K. Chari has, in his 'Whitman in the light of Vedāntic Mysticism', made a penetrating analysis on meditation resorted to by Whitman. He makes it clear that the American transcendentalists had a special respect for the Hindu method of meditation (Dhyāna Yoga). Henry David Thoreau also practised yoga and there are explicit references

49. 'Song of the Open Road'—Sec. 9.

to it in his 'Walden',[50] Regarding Whitman, Dr. Chari writes in his treatise: "Whitman is conscious of a certain trance-like state leading to the suspension of the conscious intellect and accompanied by a strange feeling of exaltation and joy and a transformation, as it were, of the whole being; a state in which the mystic experiences a new awakening, the awakening of the spiritual vision and, like the sage in the Upaniṣads, understands the being whose essence is joy".[51] There are, in fact, some evidences that Whitman underwent the meditative experiences akin to the Hindu yogic practices. There is a passage in one of his note books indicating the method of his meditation,—a type of the "self-teaching exercises" which Whitman appears to have undergone deliberately.[52]

Whitman again in the Upaniṣadic spirit accepts the reality of the world of multiplicity, In the Upaniṣads we

---

50. "I know of no more encouraging fact than the unquestionable ability of man to elevate his life by a conscious endeavour."—'Walden. ; Ch. II.

*　　　*　　　*

'By a conscious effort of mind we can stand aloof from actions and their consequences ; and all things—good or bad, go by us like a torrent. We are not wholly involved in nature".—Ibid ; Ch. IV.

51. Dr. V. K. Chari :—'Whitman in the light of Vedantic Mysticism ; Ch. IV. P—104.

52. "Abstract yourself from this book ; realize where you are at present located, the point you stand that is now to you the centre of all. Look up overhead, think of space stretching out, think of all the unnumbered orbs wheeling safely there, invisible to us by day, some visible by night, ... spend some minutes faithfully in this exercise. Then again realize yourself upon the earth, at the particular point you now occupy ...... Seize these firmly in your mind, pass freely over immense distances. Turn your face a moment thither. Fix definitely the direction and the idea of the distances of separate sections of your own country, also of England ...... and such like distant places". - 'Complete Writing of Walt Whitman', Vol. VI, Part-II. (Quoted by Dr. Chari in his book)'

have seen that in illustrating the pantheistic concept of Brahman, the world is not regarded as unreal or illusory. Whitman also does never consider the world of multiplicity as illusory or chimerical. In combating the idealistic philosophy that advocates illusionism, Whitman writes in his note book :—

"I am the poet of reality,
I say the earth is not an echo.
Nor man is an apparition ;
But that all things seen are real,
* * *
I have split the earth and the hard
coal and rocks and the solid bed
of the sea,
And went down to reconnoitre there
a long time,
And bring back a report,
And I understand that those are positive
and dense every one
And that what they seem to the child
they are........"[53]

Whitman's concept of experience, as is evident from his innumerable poems, has truly been cosmic in amplitude excluding or denying nothing. Real truth, according to him, should be all-inclusive and it does not shut out any element as alien. Hence his triumphant voice :—

"And henceforth I will go, celebrate
anything I see or am,
And sing and laugh and deny nothing". As a matter of fact Whitman takes keen interest in all aspects of human life. He is fully alive to the duties of a poet who, according to him, is not a mere visionary or a dreamer living in an

53. 'Uncollected Poetry and Prose of Walt Whitman'—Emory Holloway ; II, P—69-70.

ivory tower divorced from the grim realities of life. In an age when most of the English romantic poets flee from the reek and squalor of life, when Emerson takes shelter in the country solitude and Thoreau at the 'Walden Pond', Whitman devotes himself to sprawling New York in its iron age and sings song for engines, trades factories and occupations, and finds in them 'eternal meanings'. The task of poetry for him is not so much to idealize as to see things in their true colours. He thus sets forth his realistic creed thus: "In these 'Leaves' everything is literally photographed. Nothing is poetized, no divergence, not a step, not an inch, nothing for beauty's sake, no euphemism, no rhyme, an awful adherence to the truth".[54] Like Shelley who says that the poets are 'the unacknowledged legislators of the world' Whitman also believes that a truly great poet as the 'arbiter of the diverse' or the 'equalizer of his age' must play a significant role in shaping the destiny of the people. Such a poet is Whitman himself who as a spiritual democrat, finds in the ideal of true democracy the possibilities of universal peace, toleration and brotherhood. Such a great leveller and the uncompromising apostle of equality and fraternity, pleading moral and spiritual regeneration of common man in his 'Democratic Vistas,[55] attaching

54. Vide : 'Complete Writings of Walt Whitman'—Vol—VI, Part—I.

55. The great clue to progress in human civilization is indicated in the Poem—'I was Looking A Long While', which reads :—

"I was looking a long while for
Intentions,
For a clew to the history of the past
for myself,
and for these chants, and now
I have found it,
It is not in those paged fables
in the libraries,
(them I neither accept nor reject,)

due importance even to animal as well as inanimate world, enunciates a theory which can be anything but illusionism. In fact Whitman has, as a result of the inner expansion, felt that the entire world with all its variety is contained within the cosmic self, but he does not, on that account, doubt the existence of external objects. There is thus a strong undercurrent of realism which forms the basis of his philosophical thinking.

Another interesting parallel thought between the Upaniṣads and Whitman can be discovered in their respective attitude towards evil. The Upaniṣads, while recognizing human life throbbing with all its good and evil aspects, insist on our adopting a comprehensive or synthetic outlook. The ancient seers of our country believed that since we fail to perceive the existence of an all-comprehensive Absolute and look at things from a narrow and circumscribed outlook, we are apt to be tormented by sorrows and sufferings, disease and death and so many numberless evils. But if and when man attains parāvidyā, and rises above all pettiness and pusillanimity of his egoism, and can thus follow the proper import of the pantheistic doctrine, he can develop a wider vision and also a catholicity of heart so as to extend a loving attitude to one and all. Moral evils or sinful activities then completely disappear from the human world. But as to the physical evils or sufferings and troubles which still persist, they do not, as the Upaniṣadic sages observe, affect us. The pangs of separation, death, disease

---

It is no more in the legends than
in all else,
It is in the present—it is this earth to day.
It is Democracy (The purport and
aim of all the past)
It is the life of one man
or one woman to day—
the average man of to day".

and travails do not at this stage of spiritual enlightenment, exert any baneful effect on us. The physical evils exist no doubt, but they exist as a constitutive element of an all-comprehensive Reality whom the sages call Ānandam and these evils then lose their biting or stinging effect on man.[56]

With Whitman evil is a stark reality and it occupies a distinct place in the cosmic scheme. But in the evolution of his thought, as we have seen, evil disappears and does not finally appear to produce its unwholesome effect on man. Here his thought sounds very much the tone of the Upaniṣads.

As early as 1855-56, Whitman gives us an impression that everything in the world is perfect and that this is the best of all possible worlds. Brimming over with joy and passionate optimism, evil also appears as perfect to the poet.[57]

---

56. (i) ',Manasaivedamāptavyam neha nānāsti kiñcana ; mṛtyoḥ sa mṛtyuṁ gachhati ya iha nāneva paśyati". Kaṭha, 2. 1. 11-

(ii) Cf. The Bṛhadāraṇyaka Up.—4.4.19.

(iii) Īśa up.—7.

57. (i) "Pleasantly and well-suited I walk,
Whither I walk I can not define, but I
know it is good,
The whole universe indicates that it is good,
The past and the present indicate that
it is good.
How beautiful and perfect are the animals !
How perfect the earth, and the minutest
thing upon it !
What is called good is perfect and
what is called bad is just as perfect,
The vegetables and minerals are
all perfect ;
and the imponderable fluids perfect ;
Slowly and surely they have pass'd on
to this, and slowly and
surely they yet pass on".
(—'To Think of Time ',-Sec. 8)

There are indeed passages which indicate that Whitman includes evil as well as good and attempts to equalize them. These passages and many other expressions of socially tabooed subjects together with his comradely greeting of harlots and low characters[58] tend to convince the readers that Whitman has denied the existence of evils or refused to make any moral distinctions.

But it is a misconception to hold that Whitman tries to dodge the problem of evil. The passages which tend to mislead the readers have a deeper implication. What the poet wants to impress upon us is that he is the poet of all, and side by side with all that is good or socially amenable, he insists on the inclusion of all that is ugly, crude and repulsive in the cosmic scheme. Maxmillian Beck gives us an enlightening view on this point when he says that there is a fundamental philosophical thesis in all Whitman's writings - that the value of anything that exists, does not lie in its specific quality, in'what'it is, but purely in its own being. There are passages in Whitman's poems which appear to be shocking and tiresome unless understood as a means of emphasizing his infinite delight in 'pure real

(ii) "The Soul is always beautiful,
The universe is duly in order, everything is
in its place,
What has arrived, is in its place and
what waits shall be in its place".
(-"The Sleepers",—Sec. 7)
Cf.—"Song of the Open Road",—Sec. 5.

58 "It is for the wicked just the same as
the righteous, I make appointment
with all",

* * *

"I am not the poet of goodness only,
I do not decline to be the poet of
wickedness also".
Vide :— 'Song of Myself',—Sec..19 & 22.

existence'. He thus speaks of the 'absolute' equality in worth of every real existing being.[59] Hence far from denying

---

59. Cf. Maxillian Beck :— 'Walt Whitman's Intuition of Reality'. —Ethics ; P—14—24.

60. (i) "The pleasures of heaven are with me
and the pains of hell are with me".
—'Song of Myself',—Sec. 21.

(ii) "I see all the menials of the earth
labouring,
I see all the prisoners in the prison,
I see the defective human bodies of the earth,
The blind, the deaf and dumb, idiots,hunchbacks,
The pirates, thieves, betrayers, murderers
slave-makers of the earth,
The helpless infants and the helpless old men
and women".
(—'Salut au Monde' ; Sec. 10)

(iii) The most poignant expression of
the poet's awareness of evil is found in
'I sit and look out' (1860) :—
"I sit and look out upon the sorrows
of the World, and upon all oppression
and shame,
I hear secret convulsive sobs from
youngmen at anguish with themselves,
remorseful after deeds done,
I see in low life the mother misused by
her children, dying, neglected,
gaunt, desperate,
I see the wife misused by her husband,
I see the treacherous seducer of young women,
I mark the ranklings of jealousy and
unrequited love, attempted to be hid,
I see these sights on the earth,
I see the workings of battle, pestilence,
tyranny, I see martyrs and prisoners,

* * *

I observe the slights and degradations
cast by arrogant persons upon
laborers, the poor and upon negroes
and the like ;

evil he accepts it as a part of reality. In fact none can overlook that Whitman's poems abound in his keen awareness of the grim sufferings and turpitude of the world.[60]

Now as a pantheist it has been revealed to him that God is everywhere, but at the same time he perceives evil everywhere around him. The question which naturally obsessed him was – whether it was possible that God should be evil or that evil should partake of God. On reflection Whitman finds a solution to this agonizing problem. Leaning to a spiritualistic solution the poet declares that evil is a temporary accident and not an absolute reality. Soul for him is necessarily good and beautiful and it is matter that temporarily prevents the soul from blossoming out. In keeping with his optimistic outlook he proclaims the final victory of good over evil.[61] He spares no pains to vindicate this spontane-

---

All these-all the meanness and agony
without end I sitting look out upon
see, hear and am silent".

(iv) That the poet himself was subject to so many evils and was tormented for the troubled desires he had cherished, is expressed thus :—

"It is not upon you alone the dark
patches fall,
The dark threw its patches down upon me also,
* * *
Nor is it you alone who know what it is
to be evil,
I am he who knew what it was to be evil'
I too Knitted the old knot of contrariety,
Blabb'd blush'd, resented, lied, stole,
grudg'd,
Had guile, anger, lust, hot wishes,
I dared not speak,........"
(—'Crossing Brooklyn Ferry',-Sec. 6 ; —1856)

61. This and not the total negation of evil, seems to be the decided conviction of the poet. Since evil to the poet is an accident which can be got over in the battle of life, he naturally reaches some such conclusion in 'Starting From Paumanok' (1860 Edition of 'Leaves of Grass') as evil does not 'really' exist.

ous optimism in the teeth of the assaults of life to which he was subject from time to time. Hence in spite of his occasional cry of despair—that we are 'flotsam and jetsam cast up haphazardly on the shore', the poet does not fail to rediscover the consoling notion of an eternal progress. His sense of 'becoming' of the world accepts evil only as a transitory phase which finally disappears with the realization of soul as the abiding reality.[62] The implication of almost all the poems of Whitman is that the intuitive knowledge of the all-pervasive Soul (almost akin to that of the Upaniṣads and Schelling) leads to the love of all creation. sympathy with all creatures and the promotion of happiness (which again is very much like the Upaniṣadic concept of 'ānanda') in one's own self and others.[63] It is this conviction again that helps Whitman withstand his former obsession with the thought of death and he begins to think of his immortality. We need not dilate on the concept of immortality. But what we should note here is that in the height of his spiritual enlightenment he is transported to a state of existence where no evil can affect him.[64] This contention is quite akin to, if not thoroughly

---

62. Whitman develops this idea later in 'Roaming in thought' bearing a symptomatic sub-title : 'After Reading Hegel' (1881) :—

> "Roaming in thought over the universe, I saw the
> little that is
> Good steadily hastening towards immortality,
> And the vast all that is call'd Evil I saw
> hastening to merge itself and become lost
> and dead".

63. Cf. The Gītā :—

> "Sarvabhūtasthamātmānaṁ sarva bhūtāni cātmani,
> Īkṣate yogayuktātmā sarvatra sama darśanaḥ".
> —6/29.

64.
> "I sing the endless finales of things,
> I say Nature continues, glory continues,
> I praise with electric voice,

identical with, that of the Upaniṣads according to which, as we have already seen, an enlightened seer, by virtue of his synthetic outlook, remains unaffected by the evils of earthly life.

Whitman's indebtedness to the Upaniṣads.

From our foregoing analysis it may appear that Whitman has been profoundly influenced by the Upaniṣadic thought. It is no doubt highly controversial as to whether Whitman was really acquainted with the translations of the Upaniṣads. Edward Carpenter admits that there are interesting parallels between the ancient Upaniṣads and 'Leaves of Grass'.[65] But he does not make any positive claim that the Upaniṣads are the definite sources from which Whitman draws his fundamental thoughts. As to his indebtedness to the Bhagavadgītā also the critics and biographers are not quite sure. But none, we think, has been able to rule out the possibility of at least an indirect impact of the Gītā and the Upaniṣads on Whitman.[66] There are certain evidences which prompt us to believe that Whitman must have been acquainted with the Upaniṣadic thought.

For I do not see one imperfection
in the universe,
And I do not see one cause or
result lamentable at last in the universe".

65. Vide : Edward Carpenter : 'Days with Walt Whitman'—(1906), P –94-102.

66. As to the influence of the Gītā on Whitman Prof. Gay Wilson Allen refers to Dr. Dorothy Frederica Mercer's unpublished dissertation on Whitman viz., "Leaves of Grass and Bhagavadgītā : A Comparative Study"—which, Prof. Allen thinks, is a scholarly work, he had the privilege to study. Prof. Allen informs us that Dr. 'Mercer does not claim definitely that the Bhagavadgītā was one of Whitman's actual sources, though she suggests it 'may have been'. —(Vide : G. W. Allen : Whitman Handbook, P—459—60.

We have already noted that in Whitman's time there were certain important men of letters in America chiefly known as American transcendentalists who were genuinely interested in the literature and religion of Asia particularly of the Hindus. Orientalism was very much in the American intellectual atmosphere between 1840's and 50's. Whitman was directly associated with them and, as we have indicated already, he amassed in his scrapbooks the clippings from the newspapers and journals dealing mainly with Indian religion. It is quite likely, therefore, that he could not escape at least some indirect influence of the Hindu thought from them.

Further, in 1856 i. e., after the publication of the first edition of 'Leaves of Grass' (1855), Henry David Thoreau an ardent orientalist went through the book and observed : 'Wonderfully like the orientals - ...... considering that when I asked (Whitman) if he had read them, he answered—'No : tell me about them',[67] Now this interview between Thoreau and Whitman indicates that till then Whitman was not familiar with the Hindu thought and that Thoreau's question only stimulated his curiosity to have some knowledge of the oriental thought. But it is also possible for us to infer that for some reason or other Whitman wanted to suppress before Thoreau his acquaintance with the Hindu thought, for as it appears, it is not a fact that he was completely in the dark about Indian philosophical thinking. In 'A Backward Glance' he claims to have read the ancient Hindu poems in preparation for 'Leaves of Grass' before'.[68]

67. Henry David Thoreau : ,Familiar letters'. Boston, 1894'-Quoted by Bliss Perry in his 'Walt Whitman'-P-121-22.

68. Vide : Preface to 'November Boughs', 1888,-reprinted in Emory Holloway's Inclusive Edition of 'Leaves of Grass ; 1925.

On many other occasions Whitman evinced some knowledge of the Hindu and other oriental translations, although he does not always appear to have expressed this indebtedness in a categorical manner. Many of his poems reveal that he was conversant with the "Shastras and Vedas'.[69] He writes : "I hear the Hindu teaching his favourite pupil the loves, wars, adages, transmitted safely to this day from poets who wrote three thousand years ago".[70] The poems in 'Passage to India' are full of allusions to the 'epics of Asia' and the 'elder religions'. With a respectful compliment to the ancient Indian thought Whitman says that from the vast storehouse of philosophic thought, 'the infinite greatness of the past ' emerges India as an integral symbol of man's quest for the Infinite - India with her 'flowing literatures, tremendous epics, religions, castes, old occult Brahma interminably far back, the tender and junior Buddha ......" (Passage to India, Sec. 6.) In the same poem India is supposed to symbolize 'primal thought' holding key to the 'aged fierce enigmas'. India again is like the elder brother who guides the younger (meaning 'America') into the unkown regions :—

"O thou transcendent,
Nameless, the fibre and the breath,
Light of the light, shedding forth universe
thou centre of them
Thou mightier centre of the true, the good,
the loving,
Thou moral, spiritual fountain—
affection's source thou reservoir,
.............."

('Passage to India', Sec. 8). But this poem is not 'Passage to India only ; it is a passage to more than India' (Sec. 9),

---

69. Vide : 'Song of Myself',—Sec. 43.
70. Vide : 'Salut au Monde'—Sec. 3.

since it recognizes all that is best in the great religions of the world - eastern as well as western.

From a consideration of what has been said above, all that we can say without any fear of contradiction is that Whitman must have had some idea about the thoughts of the Vedas, the Upaniṣads and the Gītā, for otherwise he could not have made such explicit references to Indian thought in his writings. Whitman's poetic genius is undisputed and it is true that all his ideas do not always run parallel to those of the ancient Indian scriptures. But nevertheless we can not deny the interesting and sometimes illuminating parallels between his 'Leaves of Grass' and the Upaniṣads or the Gītā. Nor can we ignore the direct references to India which the poet makes without any prevarication. It will, therefore, be neither unfair nor illogical to say that Whitman has been to a certain degree influenced by the oriental thought, particularly by the Upaniṣads.

CHAPTER—XI

FRENCH POETS

Introduction

We shall close our analysis by referring to some eminent French poets of the nineteenth century who are believed by many to have been acquainted with and influenced by the Upaniṣadic thought. Louis Renou, for instance, thinks that there are not a few writers in France and often writers of considerable importance who have expressed sentiments concerning India which reflect spiritual communion to which the German thinkers stake their claim. Such French evidence is usually rather later than that of the Germans, just as romantic movement in France developed later than in Germany.[1]

We come across three principal French poets in the nineteenth century who may be supposed to have been interested in the ancient Indian thought, and they are : (1) Alphonse de Lamartine, (2) Alfred de Vigny and (3) Victor Hugo. Our analysis, however, will reveal that the pantheistic thought of the Upaniṣads is not traceable in any of these three figures in the field of the French romantic poetry. But there is no reason to suppose that our discussion on them in the present context is irrelevant or redundant. We are prompted to make a brief survey of their poetic productions for the simple reason that there are evidences which unmistakably account for their acquaintance with and deep respect for the Upaniṣads. This is particularly indicated by no less a thinker than Louis Renou. Let us take the case of Lamartine first.

1. Vide : Louis Renou : 'Influence of indian thought on French Literature,. Page—8.

Alphonse de Lamartine (1790—1869).

'Les Méditations Poétiques' (The Poetic Meditations) published in 1820 was the first experiment in romantic poetry that made Lamartine famous. The poems included in this volume cover such themes as early death, sadness in solitude, man's response to nature and nature's indifference, justice and injustice of the creator etc. In spite of certain limitations arising chiefly out of the poet's rhetorical manner of expression, moralising arguments or artificial vocabulary, critics agree on one fundamental trait viz, that the features which appeared in Lamartine's early poems and gave them their novelty were the personal emotions conveyed directly from the author to the reader and not through the intermediary of an imagined third character. As was natural for a romantic poet, Lamartine, whatever the theme of his early poems might have been, treated it in close union with his sincere feeling. The lyrical outbursts of Lamartine's poems—their music, rhythm and flow on which his strength as a romantic poet rests are not our concern here. What we should take cognizance of is that apart from the lyrical charm and beauty of some of his poems in which perhaps he closely resembles Shelley[2], there is a philosophical fervour in his poems. In fact his greatest vein is not that of emotional lyricism in which he holds a distinctive position among the nineteenth century poets, but a philosophical fervour in which emotion and thought are inseparably

2. "Lamartine aspired to be a philosophical poet and with the same character but different gifts he might have become the French Wordsworth. But in fact if he can be compared to any English poet it is rather with Shelley whose bursts of passionate and childlike lyricism he often echoes in a slightly more stilted language".—Vide : Geoffrey Brereton : 'An Introduction to the French Poet',—P—111.

fused.[3] When we thus come to consider his philosophical views as reflected in his 'Poetic Meditations' as also in his later works we can not overlook his optimistic outlook on life and devoutly Christian sentiment. Prof, Dowden aptly remarks : "He was a noble dreamer in practical affairs, and just ideas formed a portion of his dreams. Nature had made him an irreclaimable optimist ; all that is base and ugly in life passed out of view as he soared above earth in his luminous ether. Sadness and doubt indeed he knew, but his sadness had a charm of its own, and there were consolations in maternal nature, in love, in religious faith and adoration ……..The pure and ample harmonies of his verse do not attack the ear, but they penetrate to the soul. All the great lyric themes—God, nature, death, glory, melancholy, solitude, regret, desire, hope, love—he interpreted on his instrument with a musician's inspiration".[4]

Lamartine's only consistent philosophy is a kind of Christian pantheism. The whole of the universe is supposed to be an expression of the deity. In his 'Poetic Meditations' he gives a poetic rendering of this idea in the following lines :—

"That universal star, which ne'er declines
Is God ; that mighty whole, the self adored !
He is - all is in Him ; immensity
And time compose the unmixt element
Of His infinitude. Space is his mansion,
Eternity His age ; day is His glance ;
The world His image. 'Neath His
shadowing hand

3. Cf. L. Cazamian : 'A History of French Literature',—Ch. XIV, P—303.

4. Vide : Edward Dowden : 'A History of French Literature',—Book V, P—369—70.

The universe subsists. Existence flowing
In waves eternal downward from His bosom,
Like a vast river fed by that source boundless,
Escapes, and where 'gins returns to end".[5]

Conceiving God as a personal being the poet in the spirit of a true Christian holds that man should put his firm faith in Him and it is by His grace that a moral regeneration of the people on earth is possible. Hence in the same poem the poet again says :—

"Lo ! Lo ! the God whom every spirit worships,
Whom Abraham served ; of whom Pythagoras dreamed ;
Whom Socrates announced, whom Plato saw
Dimly ; ... ...
And whom at least Christ came to show
to earth,
It is no more that God by mortals fashioned,
That God explained to error by imposture,
That God disfigured by false priests'hands,
Whom our forefathers blindly worshipped
trembling ;
He is alone, is one, is just and good,
Earth sees His work and Heaven knows
His name".[6]

From the experiments made in 'Poetic Meditations', a great work finally grew viz., 'Harmonies Poe´tiques et Religieuses' (Poetic and Religious Harmonies). Published in 1830 this volume not only fulfilled the promise of 'Les Me´ditations Poe tiques', but even went beyond it. The glory of God as pervading and sustaining the entire universe

5. Vide : 'Dieu' (God)–Sec. V–'Les Me´ditations Poe´tiques'—translated by Rev. William Pulling in—Life and Works of Lamartine'.

6. Ibid ; Sec. VI.

is sung with strong devotion in many poems of this work. In the poem 'Cry of the Soul' for example, we find :—

"Lord ! Lord ! thy name alone relief
affords !
'Tis the Echo sole responsive to my heart !
Or those bursts rather (transports void of words),
Are themselves th' Echo of how great
thou art !
Not oft Great Name ! thou sleepest
in my breast.
Not oft thou sleepest on my lips of fire ;
But each time deeper thou art there
impressed,
And my soul's cry is e'er thyself our sire" ![7]

Again in the poem 'Prayer' the poet
says ; —

"Nature... ... ... seems to offer God
in her grand language
The glorious homage of the whole creation
Behold th' oblation boundless universal !
All nature is the temple, earth the altar,
The sky's the dome, and its stars numberless
* * *
Are the blest torches lighted for this
temple ;
* * *
Soul of the universe, Sire, God, Creator,
Lord I believe in thee, 'neath all these
names.
* * *
Th' extent reveals Thy greatness
to mine eyes ;

7. Taken from 'Poetic and Religious Harmonies',—translated by Rev. William Pulling.

The earth Thy goodness and the stars
Thy splendour,
Thou hast produced Thyself in Thy
bright work ;
The universe entire reflects Thine image,

* * *

Sure of Thy love, and witness of
Thy power,
I wait for th' endless day of life immortal
Death with funeral shades in vain
surrounds me,
My reason through his darkness seeth light :
'Tis last step which brings me close to Thee.
'Tis the veil falling, 'twixt Thy face
and mine ;
Haste for me, Lord, that moment so desired,
Or, if Thou in Thy secrets holdst it still
Hear from Heaven's height my cry of need.

* * *

Nourish my frame with bread, my soul
with hope ;
Warm Thou again with Thine all-powerful eye
My spirit darkened by the senses' shade,
And as the solar beams exhale the dews,
For ever in Thy breast absorb my thought".[8]

Geoffrey Brereton[9] observes that no clearer chant to the glory of God had been raised in French literature since 'Le Génie du Christianisme' (the Spirit of Christianity), none in French verse since the choruses of 'Esther' and 'Athalic'. With the ardour of complete assurance Lamar-

8. Quoted from 'Poetic and Religious Harmonies',—translated by William Pulling.

9. Vide - G. Brereton : 'An Introduction to the French Poets'. P—107.

tine hymned in his poems[10] the power and beneficence of the creator and his self-manifestation in trees, stars, sunrise and evening.

Before we make a general assessment of the French poets as related to their possible borrowings from India, let us make a brief survey of the other two notable figures of the 19th century viz., Vigny and Hugo with particular reference to their views on religion.

Alfred de Vigny (1797-1863).

The poetic temperament of Vigny, a sombre figure among the French romantics shows a sharp contrast to the optimism of Lamartine and confident assertiveness of Victor Hugo. Literature was his necessary means of expression, but here in spite of the literary merit of some of his poems, he had more outward failures than successes[11]

Vigny's poems roughly fall into two groups with a long interval between.[12] Since Vigny has been called by him-

10. Vide : 'La Chene' (The Oak), 'L 'Hymne du matin' (The hymn of the morning), 'L' occident' (The West), 'L' Infini dans les cieux' (The Infinite in the Heaven) etc.
11. Extolling the poems of Vigny's first volume L. Cazamian, however, observes :—

    "It (the first volume) contains a dozen masterpieces, any one of which has such originality and concentrated significance that it might in itself suffice to make a writer's fame. The language forged and polished has an exceptional density, each syllable being packed with meaning. What is thus conveyed is the burden of an earnest, intensely meditative mind, of thought steeped in the emotions of a sensitive heart, and waking a thousand human echoes............ ... ... No French verse is fuller, more weighty, more unforgettable than that of Vigny at his best".

    —L. Cazmian : A History of French Literature ; Part VII, Ch- XLV, P -304–05.
12. The early group is represented by the first edition of 'Poems

self first and by most critics since, a philosophical poet, it is necessary for us to enquire into his philosophical theory if there be any. Vigny's own impression of himself is 'une sorte de moraliste epique'. This indicates that he adopts a distinct moral attitude in his poems, although his total poetic output does not reveal that his poems are merely the exemplifications of moral ideas. Nevertheless it is agreed upon by the critics that Vigny is the first among the 19th century French poets in whom a didactic attitude is clearly marked. In 'La Maison du Berger' there is an appeal to the poets to take their rightful place as spiritual and intellectual leaders of the people. This didacticism or the desire to communicate a message is as evident in Vigny's novel and drama as in his poetry. The result is that the ideas conveyed do not necessarily form a coherent philosophy but are coloured by a fairly consistent pessimism. A more or less constant assumption of Vigny is that mankind are the victims of an inescapable fatality, and unhappiness is their normal lot. The nobler the men are, the more they suffer. On whatever plane we like to consider man—moral, political or social, he seems condemned at best to solitude, at worst to isolation. God and nature seem to be indifferent to man. But in contrast to these dark notions, an excellent poem 'La Bouteille a´ la Mer' (The Bottle in

antiques et modernes' (Poems-ancient and modern). Published in 1826 it includes such poems as 'mois' (month), 'Le Deluge' (The deluge) and 'Le Cor' (the Horn) as well as 'Eloa' (which had appeared separately in 1824) and ten poems reprinted from his first slim volume of 1822. Until his middle forties he published a few poems and translation of Shakespeare's 'Othello', 'The Merchant of Venice', 'Romeo and Juliet' etc, and also an historical drama and some short stories In his maturity Vigny began publishing separately. In 'La Revue des deux mondes' (The Review of the two worlds)—The poems of his second main group which need not be mentioned here in detail. The best of his writings are found in 'Les Destinees' (Posthumous) and Journal d'un poete'.

the Sea) offers a crumb of hope to those who can solace themselves with a sort of vicarious and gratuitous optimism. In this poem the idea of God has changed in essence in so far as God is no longer limned here as indifferent or unjust Vigny usually has in mind.[13] As a matter of fact Vigny, as G. Brereton also thinks, had in him a profoundly ingrained religious faith which insisted that the Deity was benign in spite of all the evidence that may be advanced to the contrary.[14] In the last series of his poems viz., 'Les Destinees' Vigny is found to be conscious of the sadness of human fate no doubt, but his pessimism appears to be replaced by an unbreakable courage. He develops an attitude of superhuman charity with no outbursts of bitterness or violence against any living person. A quiet and proud, but not imperious resignation and a tender compassion are the chief characteristics of these pieces. As a moralist Vigny establishes a code of conduct on the cult of honour and exhibits a stoical resignation and proud indifference in response to the 'silence éternal de la Divinité'.[15]

Victor Hugo (1802–1885).

When we come to the literary field of Victor Hugo we are struck by his manysided genius which flourished particularly in the domain of poetry and novel. In his poetry Hugo is perhaps at his best. His poems covering different

13. Cf. P. E. Charvet : 'A Literary History of France',—Vol. 4, P—116—17.
14. Vide : G. Brereton : 'An Introduction to the French Poets' — P—114.
15. This attitude of the poet is revealed in the post script of the poem 'Le Mont des Oliviers'—with a title 'Le Silence', The original poem 'Le Mont des Oliviers' expresses poet's religious despair. Here Jesus seeks God in vain and Judas lurks near.

subjects - love, childhood, patriotism or religion have in fact, immortalized his name. In his poems starting from his earliest collection of odes and ballads to those published posthumously, he gives us a wide variety of themes expressed poignantly, sometimes with unsurpassable charm and beauty.[16]

We are here strictly concerned with his views on the concept of God and His relation to the world and man. There is, in fact, a constant reference to God in his 'Les Contemplations' and many other poems some of which came out posthumously. But according to some critics Hugo makes no attempt to maintain a coherent attitude all through. The concept of a personal God is found when Hugo speaks of God as 'Le bon Dieu' (kind or good God), or as

---

16. In his early writings viz., 'Odes et Ballades' (1828) and 'Les Orientales' (1829) Hugo followed the romantic tradition and was hailed as the leader of the new generation. A series of successful poems followed thereafter, Viz., 'Les Feuilles d' automne' (The Leaves of autumn—1831), 'Les Chants du Crepuscule' (The Song of Twilight—1835)'Les Voix interieures' (The Voice Interior—1837) 'Les Rayons et les ombres; (The Rays and the Shadows —1840).

The supreme achievement of Hugo is generally said to consist in (i) 'Les Chatiments' (The Chastisement—1853), 'Les Contemplations (The Contemplations—1856) and 'Les Legende des Siecles' (The Legends of the Ages—published in three instalments in 1859, 1877 and 1883). 'Les Chatiments' is a collection of political verse directed against the government of Nepoleon III whose arrival in power had been the cause of Hugo's exile in the Channel Islands, for eighteen years. 'Les Contemplations' is based primarily on his personal grief at the loss of his daughter drowned with her husband. 'Les Legende de Siecles' ranks with the great poems of the world literature by virtue of its epic breadth of conception.

Some of his poems on childhood are marked by singular tenderness and depth of feeling, while his patriotic poems ('Annee Terrible'—The terrible year—published in 1872) breathe a spirit of fierce hatred for all that is tyrannical, cowardly and sordid. The poet's breadth of vision and humanitarian sentiments are forcefully revealed in all such poems.

'Dieu pour benir' (one who blesses) or as 'notre amour c'est Dieu' (God as our love). The lines clearly explaining the orthodox Christian view, for example, are :

"C' est Dieu qui remplir tout.

Le monde, c' est son temple" !

(It is God who holds all ; the world is His temple). The earth is the Lord's, but as P. E. Charvet explains it, the poem is entitled "Pan" and the God in question is really no more than the force in Nature. In Charvet's view Hugo's religious attitudes are conflicting. "At times God is a personal God whom men can pray to, at other times God is depersonalized and becomes only the 'divine spirit'.[17] This view is not without foundation. When Hugo contemplates the beauty of Nature or the splendours of the universe he is full of gratitude to God who is supposed to have created this world. But at times when he penetrates the problems of life or looks for a meaning in life and surveys its miseries, agonies and cruelties, the monster of doubt raises its ugly head. And yet, as Charvet himself admits, the sight of a cross in a cemetery produces in the poet a sudden flash of Christian sentiment. The idea of a personal God returns when an agony of personal sorrow demands the comfort of a supernatural being and makes the survival of the soul more than ever desirable. The premature death of the poet's daughter and son-in-law lacerates his heart and yet he seeks consolation from God and does not fail to retain his faith in and devotion to Him. The poet expresses the feelings of his grief stricken heart in the poem 'A Villequier, (At Villequier') which remarkably brings out the religious attitude of the poet.[18] We may quote here some important

17. Vide : P. E. Charvet : A Literary History of France ; Vol. 4. p — 124, 126.

18. 'Les Contemplations'—strikes an eligiac note largely inspired as it was by the death of Hugo's daughter and son—in—law who were drowned near 'Villequier' in Normandy. Hence the name of the poem.

passages which explain distinctly the poet's attitude to God:—

(i) "I come to you Lord!
Confessing that you are good, merciful
indulgent, and gentle.
O living God!

Again the poet even in his heart-rending grief does not lose faith in values, nor in the possibility of the triumph of good over evil. So he says:–

(ii) "The world is dark, O God!
The unchangeable harmony is made of
tears as well as songs;
Man is only an atom in this infinite shadow,
the night where the good ascend
and the wicked fall".

(iii) A devotional attachment to God is noted in these lines again:—

"I implore you, O God! to look upon
my soul, and to consider that I
come to worship you as humbly
as a child and as gently as a woman".[19]

Again in another poem viz., 'The poet's faith' (included in 'The Contemplations') the poet retains his faith in God unimpaired when he says:–

"You say, 'where goest thou?' I can not tell,
And still go on. If but the way be straight,
It can not go amiss! before me lies
Dawn and day; the Night behind me; that
Suffices me; I break the bounds: I 'see'
And nothing more, 'believe' and nothing less.
My future is not one of my concerns".[20]

---

19. English rendering—by Anthony Hartley. Vide: The Penguin Book of French Verse (3), 19th Century. P—60—66.
20. Translated by Edward Dowden.

There is a good number of short improvisations in his books of poems which undoubtedly demonstrate the theistic faith of the poet. In the 'Trust in God', for instance, the poet says :—

'Child even this day trust ! And
to-morrow have faith,
And all tomorrows ! The darkness grows less.
Trust ! And each day when first gleams
the dawn - breath,
Awake thou to pray ; God is wakeful
to bless !'[21]

In an ode 'Thanksgiving' the poet says : –

"My bark thou bringst to port,
safe from the stormy main,
My branches well - nigh dead have budded
forth again,
I bless and thank thee, Lord,
for that life-giving breath
Which kindled up the flame
so nearly quenched in death".[22]

The poet sometimes asks the child to pray for him in the following lines :—

"Then go, go, pray for me !
And as the prayer
Gushes in words, be this the form they bear : —
'Lord, lord, our Father,
God my prayer attend ;
Pardon ! Thou art good !
Pardon ! Thou art great !"[23]

Hugo, in fact, had no fascination for any particular religious dogma or doctrine. His unshrinking faith in God reflects the theistic faith of the Christians. Although sometimes he maintained an attitude of stern criticism and even

21. Taken from 'The Song of Twilight', - translated by N. R. Tyerman.
22. Translated by Charles Matthew.
23. 'Prayer,—taken from 'The Leaves of autumn'.

scepticism towards doctrinal theology, he was essentially a religious and reverent mind. The last special expression of his views before death declared his desire to be carried to the grave in hearse of the poor. He wrote :— "I refuse the prayers of all Churches. I ask a prayer from every human soul. I believe in God".[24]

General observations.

From our foregoing analysis it becomes abundantly clear that none of the French poets mentioned, advocates pantheism in the sense in which it is found in the Upaniṣads. The concept of God which these poets finally arrive at widely differs from the cosmic conception of Brahman as demonstrated in the Upaniṣads. All these French poets, as we have seen, evince a theistic conception and look upon God as a just, benign and merciful person. In Lamartine's poems there is no doubt a pantheistic touch, but his Christian sentiment predominates and very naturally he lays stress on the devotional element in man's attitude to God —an element which is completely absent in the Upaniṣads. Alfred de Vigny follows the same line of thought. Further, in the Upaniṣads there is no touch of pessimism which forms a distinctive mark of Vigny's poems. Vigny, however, finally attempts to dispel the gloom of life by a sort of stoical resignation. When we come to consider Hugo's poems, we find that he does not fundamentally differ from his immediate predecessors in developing the conception of God as related to the finite world. These poets may thus be regarded as sponsors of theism rather than Upaniṣadic pantheism. But as we have indicated earlier, there are evidences which prove beyond doubt that they were acquainted with the ancient Indian thought. It is not, therefore,

24. Vide : 'Select Poems and Tragedies by Victor Hugo'-Translated by Bishop Alexander and many others.—Introduction.

unlikely that there is an indirect influence of the ancient Upaniṣads on them. Our observation is based on the following premises,

From 1800 on France tended to become the centre for oriental study. The preparation of an inventory of the Indian manuscripts which were being accumulated in the 'Bibliothéque Nationale' had begun. The 'Asiatic Researches' published in Calcutta were immediately translated into French as were the works of Charles Wilkins and William Jones.[25] Following the ideal of 'Asiatic Society' founded in 1784 by Jones in Calcutta, a similar institution was established in Paris in 1822.[26]

Further, it is well-known that the complete works of William Jones was published by Jone's wife in 1799. This Volume includes all the annual lectures delivered by Jones. One such lecture delivered in 1785 was on the Gods of Italy, Greece and India.[27]

On the strength of these facts it seems reasonable to infer that the French scholars of the 19th century had adequate opportunity of being acquainted with the cultural thought of ancient India. When Louis Renou, therefore, mentions the names of Lamartine, Vigny and Hugo as poets interested in different aspects of Indian thought, his observation does not appear to be groundless. Regarding Victor Hugo in parti-

25. Vide : 'Influence of Indian thought on French Literature',- by Louis Renou P—5-

26, It may also be noted that following the same example other similar institutions were founded in different parts of the world, e. g., (i) Royal Asiatic Society of Great Britain and Ireland—founded in London in 1823 ; (ii) American oriental Society in 1842 in America, (iii) German Oriental Society ('Deutsche Morgen Landische Gessellschaft') in 1844.—Vide : G, G. Sengupta : 'Videsīya Bhārat Vidyā Pathik',—P—14.

27. Vide : 'Asiatic Researches'—Vol. 1—4. Referred to by G. G. Sengupta in his book, P — 15.

cular Renou says: "He (Hugo) is often full of respect, and even 'panic respect' before the literary monument of India". One of the poems of Hugo—'Suprématie' ('Supremacy' included in the 'Legends of the Ages') that had left the deepest and most permanent imprint on the readers, is a free development of a narrative portion of the 'Kena Upaniṣad' where the strength of Agni and Vāyu is tested and the supreme and mysterious power of Brahman is sought to be established. The passage relating to Agni [28] is given by Hugo a colourful and grandiloquent version in his poem 'Suprématie' with a view to demonstrating the supreme power of Almighty. We, therefore, agree with Louis Renou when he observes: "In all three (i. e., Lamartine, Vigny and Hugo) the aspiration towards an indefinable divinity, the urge to expression sometimes in the form of a hymn, and sometimes in the epic—are all features connecting them 'by instinct' with ancient India. Hence their wonder when they made acquaintance with the great Sanskrit writings in translation".[29] It is, therefore, neither groundless nor unfair for us to infer that the Upaniṣadic concept of Brahman served as one of the causes that stimulated the thoughts of the aforesaid French poets. But their strong theistic bias stood in the way of developing the pantheistic world-view in deference to the Upaniṣads.

Conclusion.

The broad thesis sought to be propounded is that the pantheistic world-view born of the concretisation (mūrta rūpa) of the abstract (amūrta) Brahman as elaborated in the ancient Upaniṣads, produced a tremendous impact—direct or indirect on the philosophical and literary thoughts of

28. Cf. The Kena Upaniṣad ; 3/4 5, 6.

29. Vide : Louis Renou : Influence of Indian thought on French Literature. P - 8—10.

the occident. Our survey has been confined strictly to the nineteenth century western thought and we have indicated that it is in the nineteenth century that this impact has been traceable for the first time following the Latin translation of the Upaniṣads which is undoubtedly a significant achievement of Anquetil Duperron. There is hardly any scope for disputing the fact that this Latin rendering made a splash on the western thought and some of the outstanding figures in the realm of philosophy and literature, as mentioned in our dissertation, were deeply inspired in their creative works by the unique conception of Brahman of the Upaniṣads Without questioning their philosophical or literary acumen or their originality in the thought it can, in view of what has been analysed by us, fairly be said that the writings of these thinkers have to a considerable degree been enriched by the Upaniṣadic conception of pantheism. We may also note here that after the publication of Duperron's Latin translation the thoughts of the Upaniṣads became widely accessible to the European readers through translation into different European languages. There is evidence moreover to show that the pantheistic concept of the ancient seers of our country has continued to shape the thoughts of the western scholars of the twentieth century in the field of literature and science alike. There is hardly any scope for dilating on this point here. But a few illustrations may be given in support of our contention.

Albert Einstein the greatest scientist of all ages did not restrict his deliberations to the field of science only. His speculations overflowed to the fields of philosophy as well. As a matter of fact there is no clear line of demarcation between higher physics and philosophy, as their field of investigation sometimes overlaps. It is no wonder, therefore, that Einstein's thoughts drifted to philosophy also. Scientists in general are usually wedded to the materialistic view of reality. But Einstein along with many other stalwarts like Jeans, Eddington and Schroidinger could not accept materialism. Rather all of them admitted the existence of non-material spiritual factors like thought and life-force.

Einstein has left no scope for any speculation about the nature of his idea of God. He does not accept the theistic conception of God whose major function is to dispense justice. He is quite precise on this point, for he holds that he does not believe in the personal God of theology, but in an impersonal power which is essentially of the nature of intelligence. In other words, to him it appeared to be a creative impersonal force which pervades the universe and works unseen according to a plan and is endowed with supreme intelligence. The relevant observation is : "This firm belief (the intelligibility of the universe) - a belief bound up with a deep feeling in a superior mind that reveals itself in a world of experience represents my conception of God. In common parlance, this may be described as pantheistic".[30] Evidently these observations echo the thoughts of the ancient Upaniṣads. The concept of Brahman which took shape in these treatises bears a close similarity to Einstein's concept of God. To the ancient seers of India, as we have repeatedly indicated, Brahman is a pervasive spirit endowed with superior intelligence which sustains the universe. In Eienstein's observation we find a reaffirmation of this truth.

Furthermore, Einstein's way of life excites our utmost admiration. He loved to lead a simple life dedicated to spiritual pursuits. He had a conviction that the 'good' of a man lies not in pursuing a life of 'pleasure', but in developing his humane qualities and intellectual and artistic powers. "No wealth in the world", he observes, "can help humanity forward, even in the hands of most dedicated worker". ('Ideas and Opinions'). The three guiding principles of his life were truth, beauty and compassion and this is con-

30. "Ideas and Opinions ; Scientific Truth" —P—261.

firmed by the following observation : "The ideals which have lighted my way time after time and given me new courage to face life cheerfully have been Kindness, Beauty and Truth ... ... The triple subjects of human endeavour - possession, outward success and luxury have always seemed to me contemptible".[31] Here again to our agreeable surprise, we find an echo of another word of wisdom of the Upaniṣad which observes that material wealth can not satisfy a man. (Na vittena tarpaṇīyo manuṣyaḥ'-Kaṭha).

In the domain of the twentieth century literature also there are thinkers who are found to have imbibed the Upaniṣadic spirit to a considerable degree. T. S. Eliot, for instance, is one such important figure. Although he is pre-eminently a Christian poet and does not appear to have advocated pantheism, there are evidences which clearly indicate that he has been influenced by the teaching of the Gītā and the Upaniṣads.

Eliot's faith in Christianity seems to have crysta... th after the holocaust of the first world war (around about 1926). He found that 'the Christian scheme seemed the only possible scheme which found a place for values'. He sought to maintain, for instance 'in holy living and holy dying, in sanctity, humility, austerity'. In fact he seems to have always recognized a need for order and discipline which are readily found in the Catholic Christianity. But before Christianity became his principal concern Eliot appears to have shown a considerable interest in other religions. He studied both Buddhism and Hinduism as part of a course of Indology in Harvard. It is true that Eliot does not surrender to Indian religion fully. But he finds at least some aspects of Hindu religion and philosophy easier to reconcile with his Christianity. There are, in fact, important layers of 'The Waste Land' and 'Four Quartets' which are Buddhist or Hindu in inspiration. He pays the highest compliment of

31. "Forum and Century". Vol. 84

Maugham's novel 'The Razor's Edge' which can be regarded as one of his masterpieces. This novel depicts the story of the spiritual journey of a young American in search of God and the Infinite. Maugham here reflects the message of the Kaṭha Upaniṣad : "The sharp edge of a razor is difficult to pass over ; thus the wise say, the path to salvation (i.e., knowledge of the Supreme Self) is hard". ("Kṣurasya dhārā niśitā duratyayā durgaṁ pathastat kavayo' vadanti". - Kaṭha : 1. 3. 14.)

The impact of the Upaniṣads, therefore, in some form or other continues unabated. In regard to the Upaniṣadic concept of pantheism in particular, we entertain the belief that this concept, interpreted properly, will continue to inspire and illumine human life for all times to come.

INDEX

CORRIGENDA

Page	*Line*	*Incorrect*	*Correct*
14	last line (foot note)	menation	mention
16	17	Upniṣads	Upaniṣads
24	13	fiirst	first
45	13	hypotheis	hypothesis
53	6	Hyacin The	Hyacinth
104	17	phllosophy	philosophy
105	last line (foot note)	n	a
137	9	generate	generates
176	29	nothings	nothing

—o—